The Fellowship of Song

CROOM HELM SOCIAL HISTORY SERIES

General Editors

PROFESSOR J.F.C. HARRISON and STEPHEN YEO

University of Sussex

CLASS AND RELIGION IN THE LATE VICTORIAN CITY
Hugh McLeod

THE INDUSTRIAL MUSE
Martha Vicinus

CHRISTIAN SOCIALISM AND CO-OPERATION IN VICTORIAN ENGLAND
Philip N. Backstrom

CONQUEST OF MIND
David de Giustino

THE ORIGINS OF BRITISH INDUSTRIAL RELATIONS
Keith Burgess

THE VOLUNTEER FORCE
Hugh Cunningham

RELIGION AND VOLUNTARY ORGANISATIONS IN CRISIS
Stephen Yeo

CHOLERA 1832
R.J. Morris

WORKING-CLASS RADICALISM IN MID-VICTORIAN ENGLAND
Trygve Tholfsen

THE COLLIERS' RANT
Robert Colls

PATERNALISM IN EARLY VICTORIAN ENGLAND
David Roberts

YOUTH, EMPIRE AND SOCIETY
John Springhall

THE ORIGINS OF BRITISH BOLSHEVISM
Raymond Challinor

THE MERTHYR RISING
Gwyn A. Williams

KEIR HARDIE: THE MAKING OF A SOCIALIST
Fred Reid

SEPARATE SPHERES: THE OPPOSITION TO WOMEN'S SUFFRAGE IN BRITAIN
Brian Harrison

THE RISE OF THE VICTORIAN ACTOR
Michael Baker

AN ARTISAN ELITE IN VICTORIAN SOCIETY
Geoffrey Crossick

THE PEOPLE'S HEALTH, 1830-1910
F.B. Smith

INDUSTRIAL CONFLICT IN MODERN BRITAIN
James E. Cronin

RICHARD BAXTER AND THE MILLENNIUM
William M. Lamont

PROSTITUTION AND VICTORIAN SOCIAL REFORM
Paul McHugh

The Fellowship of Song

Popular Singing Traditions in East Suffolk

Ginette Dunn

CROOM HELM LONDON

Croom Helm Ltd, 2-10 St John's Road, London SW11

British Library Cataloguing in Publication Date

Dunn, Ginette
The fellowship of song – (Croom Helm social history series).
1. Folk-songs, English – England – Blaxhall – Social aspects 2. Folk-songs, English – England – Snape – Social aspects
I. Title
301.5'7 ML 3652

ISBN 0-7099-0044-9

Printed and bound in Great Britain by
Redwood Burn Limited
Trowbridge & Esher

CONTENTS

ILLUSTRATIONS

Dedicated to

the memories of Bob Hart
Priscilla Savage and
Percy Webb

ACKNOWLEDGEMENTS

I have many people to thank for making this study possible, and those that I thank most deeply are the ones who made this an exercise in affection and friendship as well as a discovery of another way of life.

In Suffolk, I am most indebted to Dorrie Hart who has, through her continued hospitality during my numerous visits, made my field-work a very warm and enjoyable experience, and to her father-in-law, Bob Hart, who spent hours of his time talking and singing to me, and who greatly helped me in my field-work by taking me into local pubs with him and introducing me to other singers. I am only sorry that he did not live to see the completion of this book.

I am also extremely grateful for the kindness and help of the Bennett family, George Bennett, Stanley Day, Arthur Drewery, Lil Durrant, Bessie Hammond, David Hart, Reg Jay, Reuben Kerridge, James Knights, Abraham Ling, Mr and Mrs Ben Ling, Bessie Ling, Geoff Ling, Percy Ling, Ruby and William Ling, Alice and Christopher Messenger, Ethel Pearce, Mr and Mrs Cyril Poacher, Mr and Mrs Frank Reeve, Wickets Richardson, Mr and Mrs Lenny Savage, Mrs James Smith, Clive Woolnough and Mr and Mrs Frank Woolnough. Several singers have died since I began my research and I wish to acknowledge my debt to them: Basil Bennett, Priscilla Savage, James Smith, Percy Webb and Dick Woolnough, and also the melodeon player Fred Pearce.

I am grateful to the landlord and landlady of the Ship Inn, Blaxhall, Mr and Mrs Jack Saunders, to the landlady at the Butley Oyster, Mrs Vera Noble, and to the landlords of the Snape Key and Snape Crown for welcoming me into their pubs and allowing me to record there on numerous occasions.

George Ewart Evans, who lived in Blaxhall when his wife was schoolmistress there, has been kind enough to spend time talking to me about the area, and to suggest bibliographical sources and hypotheses to account for local social traits. I am very grateful for his help.

I wish also to acknowledge the support of Tony Green and Stewart Sanderson of the Institute of Dialect and Folk Life Studies at the University of Leeds, where I undertook this research for my doctorate degree, and the untiring help of the technician, Reg Ross, in supplying me with equipment for my field trips. My gratitude also to the Association of Commonwealth Universities and the British Council for the financial support that made this study possible.

I am indebted to my husband Keith Sullivan for his love and help during the final preparations for this book, completed so near the birth of our first child, and to our friends Simon Lichman and Rivanna Miller for their involvement in our many long conversations about singers, songs and traditions. And to the people of Snape and Blaxhall we send our gratitude and love.

PREFACE

My first field-trip to Snape was on 16 April, 1974. I saw the village spread out as I passed the church at the crossroads and followed the village street down the hill as far as the Maltings on the Alde River. Blaxhall lay beyond, clustering around its centres of pub, church and common.

In these two villages, and probably in many others throughout England, a kind of subversive activity has been going on which is innate in the communities, unconsciously honoured and carried on against many odds, both environmental and temporal. This activity is singing, most notably in the local pubs and at local gatherings; it is subversive because its practice and continuance is an affirmation of community (and the necessary ties of community with past and thus with tradition), and a denial of modern society and its spatial fragmentation and temporal disjointedness. The singers are not rebels: their vote is strongly Liberal, given *ambience* by Toryism and socialism. But it is the nature of their very conservatism that makes their activity subversive, since it denies innovative transitory modernity and supports the values and consciousness of a past, whether real or ideal, with which they identify.

The songs sung, those remembered, the singers now dead whose lives are recalled each time an old favourite is performed, all connect the present with the past. The primary aesthetic concern within these singing traditions is that a man should sing, whatever the objective quality of his performance; and a song should tell a good story. It is clear that the words of the songs and the old familiar tunes are first valued existentially, as a way of evoking a state of timelessness, as a disguise for the chronological, the personal, the specific. Also, the words of songs remembered and performed give a virtual exegesis, if not of the singer's actual life, then of his values; and these are, as always, the values of the past, the learnt opinions and knowledge of a community-based man. Thus, the songs in performance affirm past and the ties of present with past, and the individual singer assumes a special role in performance since he becomes spokesman for a group and gives voice not only to personal but also to social concerns, dynamics and emotions.

The songs are the lifeblood of the tradition. They are not static texts that exist in print, but changeable transient entities that exist actually during delivery and potentially as part of local knowledge. Thus they have a realised as well as an intellectual existence, and it is the nature of the tradition that insists upon scrutiny of the songs in performance and context rather than in textual suspension. The aesthetics of the tradition therefore are not lodged in an external critical edifice but in the tradition itself, which creates its own metafolklore and oral literary criticism by its very nature. That which is, is aesthetically pleasing since the performance of songs *per se* is the prime aesthetic. Aesthetics thus, in the traditional context, have a social as well as artistic dimension, and man's expression of his own humanity is clearly shown to be a major motive of the fine arts. Song is an expression of self, but since self has no meaning outside society, song expresses man's understanding of his humanity, his contact with others, his view of the world, and his realisation that the world has a view of him. Therefore it is the sung song and not the textual song that is crucial here.

Previous research on traditional singing has followed four main strategies. Early scholars studied the textual ballad and did not often cast their eye on contemporary traditional phenomena, but preferred to erect hypotheses about a past traditional society in which ballad singing flourished.[1] The concept of a homogeneous popular culture in which professional and itinerant minstrels as well as home-based singers performed long narrative songs with definitive texts arose from this scholarship. Secondly, the Folksong School arose around the turn of the century, peopled by members of the English upper middle classes and American academies, who were intent on collecting the songs of the dying peasantry of Britain.[2] Cecil Sharp's crusade for the gathering of these songs was motivated by nationalism and a romantic understanding that the songs of the rural classes were pure, since they existed in a non-literate environment. Consequently, concepts of typological purity arose about the songs, that they were the true heritage of the British peoples, that they were transmitted solely by oral means, that they were prized by their singers above any popular or textually based songs that might be known; and the singers were viewed as simple, non-literate rustics in whom education and a varied repertoire of popular as well as traditional songs were indications of tainting. Thirdly, oral poetics turned the field-work methods of the Folksong Society and similar bodies away from prescriptive collection and analysis to descriptive collection and analysis in terms of context. The work of Milman Parry and Albert Lord on Serbo-Croatian epic[3] tried to establish why the songs contained the features that they did, not whether these features were correct or signs of cross-cultural influence or the influence of literacy. Their work supported the autonomy of the songs as oral traditional compositions, and in exploring so deeply the nature of oral art forms suggested that the textually-biased, romantic, literary concepts about traditional singing might well be inaccurate and distorted. Fourthly, more recent scholarship, particularly in the United States, has insisted on contextual studies of song, in performance,with singers identified, talked to, and respected.[4] Certainly, the singer has passed through a number of transformations in the hands of his annotators, and it is difficult to tell how much he himself has changed. The singer has been anonymous, mainly rural, the repository of the traditions of an age of minstrelsy, or alternatively of domestic traditions. He has also been pure of heart, uncontaminated by print and modern life; he has been a spokesman with no voice of his own; only more recently has he become a man with a face, with likes and dislikes, living in a real environment.

This study follows a different strategy from those of the ballad, Folksong, epic and contextual schools, although it is informed by them all and related to the latter. It is an exercise in what might be called the anthropology of community situations, in that it tries to describe a small community through its singing, principally by using oral testimony, and thus the field methods and theoretical background are different from those of other accounts.

My main concerns have been to present a synchronic account which is contextual and descriptive, rather than a time-worn account which would be textual and prescriptive; to describe the historical background and social setting of the communities in order to give them their context, temporal as well as spatial; to regard performance in this context, informed also by recordings of singers and audience talking about songs, singing and their lives, and by recordings of the complete repertoires of each singer. The theoretical bias is therefore one of synchronicity, contextuality and oral literary criticism, in which the singing events and practices, and the singers and their audience, provide a model for local life and values, and live out these values in their singing activities. Central to the tradition is the pub, where most of the singing occurs, and surrounding this in the village environment are alternative places for and types of performance. Within this network, the dynamics of the tradition exist.

I began field-work in April 1974, and continued until late in 1976. During this time, I was based at the Institute of Dialect and Folk Life Studies at the University of Leeds, and travelled to Suffolk as often as

I could to stay for a week or two weeks at a time, recording people who quickly became friends and going with them to their pubs, socials and clubs. I recorded 200 hours of tape on a Uher Report 2000 L reel-to-reel machine, and took photographs with a Pentax Spotmatic camera. In all, I recorded twenty major singing evenings and a total of 350 different songs, and the bulk of the other tapes was made in people's homes. My field-work method was mainly participant observation, with camera and tape-recorder, non-directive questioning supplemented by directive questioning, and song recording both freely given and requested.

This method and my theoretical interests emerged from the material recorded, and developed conceptually in order to satisfy the demands of the information I was being given. Principally, I had intended to record complete repertoires of singers so that a more accurate idea of individual aesthetics could be gained than from selective and prescriptive recording of traditional song. The presence of active and passive areas of repertoire necessitated recording not only in performance situations but also at home, and time was spent with tradition-bearers talking about songs learned or not learned and not often performed, since such songs are a negative indication of aesthetics, just as deliberately learned and favourite songs are positive indications of aesthetics. What the singers say about their tradition is given priority in all cases, since it is this oral literary criticism that is integral to the tradition, rather than objective assessments made by the field-worker. The singers' lives are also of crucial importance since here are the contexts of the songs. And observation of the performance situation itself gives life to the concept of tradition as a whole. As singers and audience spoke and performed, the tradition began to show itself, and I had then only to gather the strands together and continue to participate and to watch and listen.

Informants were chosen mostly as one singer referred me to another, as I got to know non-singing members of pub audiences, and as I became friendly with the families of singers. Interviews were informal and generally conversations rather than question and answer situations, and I found that the tape-recorder only rarely acted as a deterrent to speech. People were not self-conscious in front of it, and mostly seemed oblivious of its presence. Occasionally a conversation occurred when I did not have the tape-recorder handy, in which case I took notes later. In any event, I made field-notes each day to supplement recordings made.

There are, of course, difficulties with any field-work-based study, and in one such as this there are always the dangers of incorrect implications, stresses and interpretations. Although I was warmly accepted into these communities, I did not live there and, as one informant told me, you would have to live there ninety-nine years before you would truly belong. There is a danger that the people come to be seen only in terms of the singing tradition rather than the singing tradition in terms of the community of people, but I hope I have avoided this pitfall to a reasonable extent. There is also a danger that the singing function may seem of greater importance than it is, although I think it is true to say that it is of great importance; the difference is that there is little self-conscious awareness of it in the community, little assessment of its quiddity, and therefore a study must by nature destroy to some extent this state of affairs simply by turning an eye to the singing.

The aim of this study is to describe the singing traditions of Snape and Blaxhall as paradigms of the life of Snape and Blaxhall through the words of the singers and other villagers.[5] The account begins with the historical background of the villages, their physical setting, housing and population, transport and communications. Family life is dealt with, and the employment patterns of the area, followed by a study of poverty and the domestic economy, and lastly by an account of entertainment and leisure. Thus a context is given for the singing and for modern life by the words of the villagers themselves, since this introductory chapter is based on oral accounts almost entirely, occasionally supported by documentary evidence from parish records and works on agriculture, economy and local history. In Part I, I deal with the people and their songs. Chapter 1 describes where the men sing, and how they sing, principally by presenting an evening of songs in the Blaxhall Ship Inn. Chapter 2 describes the place of women in the local society, especially in relation to the singing tradition, and it is found that women generally do not sing in the pubs because of social sanctions, but sing at home or at local social events. Chapter 3 shows the young people to be potential tradition-bearers rather than active tradition-bearers, and suggests by implication that a feature of the tradition may be that there is a chronological development from potential or latent tradition-bearers to active ones.

In Part II, I deal with some of the characteristics of the tradition. Chapter 4 discusses in greater detail the processes of learning to which a youngster in the villages may be subject, and some of the causes that make him become either an active or a latent singer, or change from a latent to an active singer. Chapter 5 discusses song ownership, a set of rules whereby a certain song is thought to belong to a certain singer, and which allows transmission of songs by acceptable means. Chapter 6 deals with local aesthetics, and suggests that the primary critical concept is that performance is good in itself, and that there are secondary detailed concepts which praise, condone or censure performances or singers. Finally, the Epilogue offers a summation of this study and an indication of further work to be done.

Notes

1. See, for example, Bishop Thomas Percy, *Reliques of Ancient English Poetry* (Dover, New York, n.d.) (first published 1858); Joseph Ritson, *Ancient Songs and Ballads* (Payne and Foss, London, 1829) (especially 'Observations of the Ancient English Minstrels'). Sir Walter Scott, in his *Minstrelsy of the Scottish Border* (Longman, Hurst, Rees and Orme, Edinburgh, 1810), comes nearer to a presentation of the songs in their social and historical context, but it is clear that he compounds some of his versions from various sources and is not concerned with individual informants: he writes of 'Annan Water' (Vol. III, p. 73) that it is 'given from tradition'. A more recent and more successful attempt at such scholarship is David Buchan's *The Ballad and the Folk* (Routledge and Kegan Paul, London, 1972). For an excellent critique of folk-song scholarship, see D.K. Wilgus, *Anglo-American Folksong Scholarship since 1898* (Rutgers University Press, New Jersey, 1959).

2. In this category, notably, are the volumes of Francis James Child (*English and Scottish Popular Ballads* (Dover, New York, 1965)), as well as the works of Cecil Sharp (for example, see *English Folksong: Some Conclusions* (EP Publishing, Wakefield, 1972) (first published 1907), and numerous song collections), and essays and collections by other members of the Folk Song Society: a broad cross-section of these can be found in the volumes of the *Journal of the Folk Song Society*.

3. See Adam Parry (ed.), *The Making of Homeric Verse. The Collected Papers of Milman Parry* (Oxford University Press, Oxford, 1971); Milman Parry with Albert B. Lord, *Serbocroation Heroic Song* (2 vols., Harvard University Press and the Serbian Academy of Arts, Cambridge, Mass., and Belgrade, 1954); Albert B. Lord, *The Singer of Tales* (Harvard University Press, Cambridge, Mass., 1960).

4. Notable examples are the works of Roger D. Abrahams: 'Creativity, Individuality and the Traditional Singer', *Studies in the Literary Imagination*, vol. 3 (1970), pp. 5-34; *Deep Down in the Jungle. Negro Narrative Folklore from the Streets of Philadelphia* (Aldine Publishers, Chicago, 1970); *A Singer and her Songs. Almeda Riddle's Book of Ballads* (Louisiana State University Press, Baton Rouge, 1970); also Edward D. Ives, *Larry Gorman. The Man who Made the Songs* (University of Indiana Press, Bloomington, Indiana, 1964); Henry Glassie, Edward D. Ives and John F. Szwed, *Folksongs and their Makers* (Bowling Green University Popular Press, Bowling Green, Ohio, 1971). Allied to this is the broader anthropological work of John Blacking, *How Musical is Man?* (Faber and Faber, London, 1976), and Alan Dundes, 'From Etic to Emic Units in the Structural Study of Folklore', *Journal of American Folklore*, no. 75 (1962), pp. 95-105, and 'Metafolklore and Oral Literary Criticism', *Monist*, no. 50 (1966), pp. 505-16.

5. This study has its original form in my doctoral thesis, 'Popular Singing

Traditions in and around Snape and Blaxhall', completed in the Institute of Dialect and Folk Life Studies, University of Leeds, 1977, 804 pp.

Ordnance Survey Map of Snape and Blaxhall

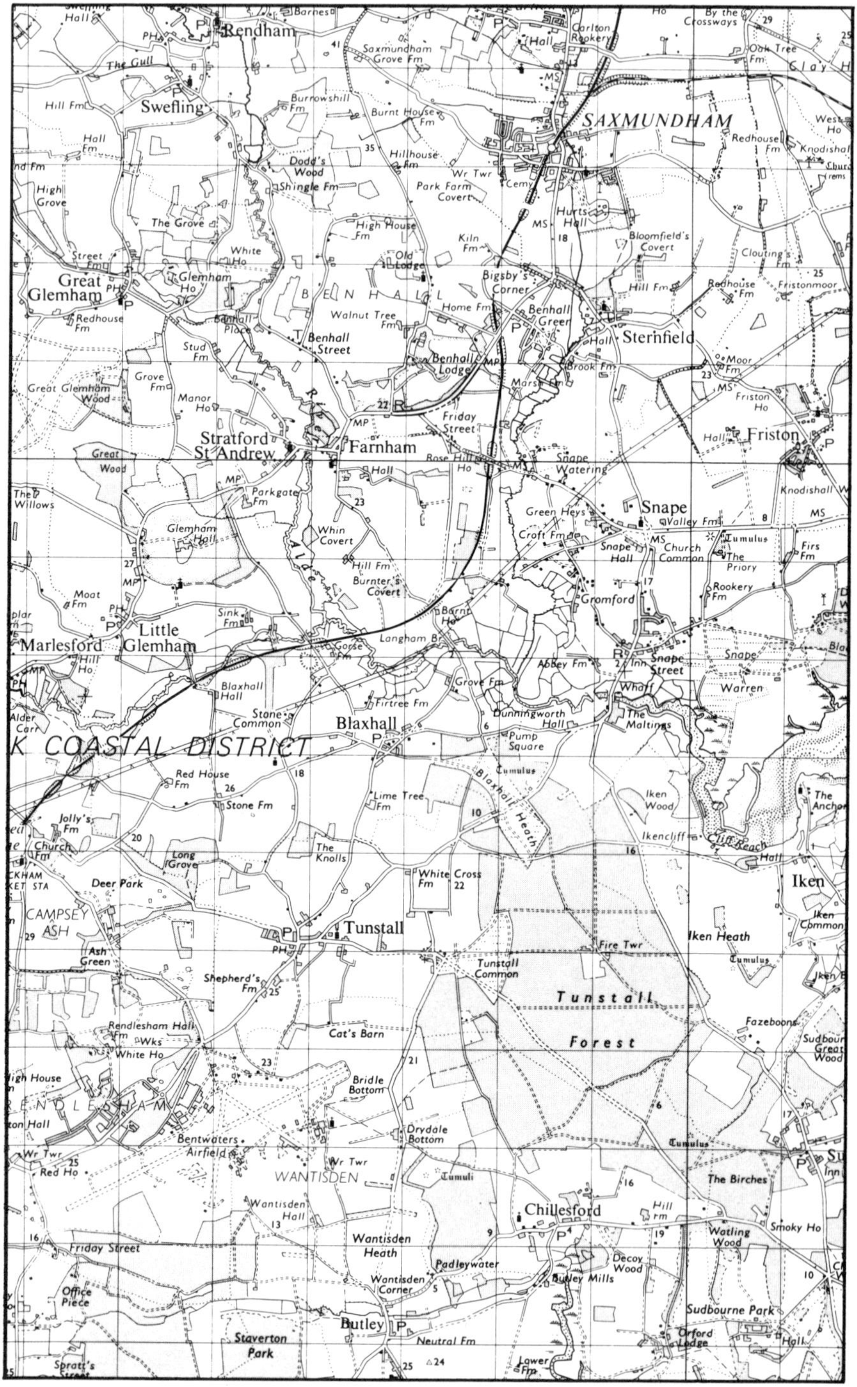

INTRODUCTION: VILLAGE LIFE AND WORK, 1880-1975

The Villages

Amid the heathland, farmland and forests between Ipswich and Lowestoft lie Snape and Blaxhall, scattered flint and brick-built villages that stretch from their churches to their pubs amidst narrow leafy lanes that follow ancient grinds of human settlement and agriculture. Several of the cottages, particularly in Blaxhall, are tied to farms, although with the division of estates many have become freehold, and through hard seasonal work some villagers have been able to buy their cottages at fair prices. Squatters' rights were claimed by some who built their own homes on the common lands of both Snape and Blaxhall, and the rest of the local population occupies council housing, for few can afford homes at the inflated prices which wealthier outsiders are able to pay.

The population of Snape is approximately 600, of Blaxhall approximately 300. In 1851, Blaxhall had 577 inhabitants in 121 houses; its population has been declining ever since, whereas Snape has had a more stable population.[1] The people of Blaxhall have always depended heavily upon agricultural work, employment which is poorly paid with no pension, which seldom protects its workers against job loss and eviction, and which is subject, on a local scale, to the fluctuations of economics and the effects of mechanisation. The old men of Snape worked in the Maltings for most of their lives and received pensions when they left. Closure (in 1964) came near the retiring age of many of them, and younger men had to look to the East Suffolk County Council, the Catchment Board,[2] the nearby air-force bases and agriculture for work. The long-term stability of the Maltings (which began operating in 1854 and at its peak employed one hundred men), however, may have encouraged population stability, and now Snape is mainly settled by the retired and pensioned Maltings workers and their wives: other people are moving away and strangers are moving in.

East Anglia is removed from the north-south communication axis of England, and within this vast peninsula, the road network is sparse, major roads bypass most small places of settlement, and villages are commonly reached by access roads rather than by through-roads. Blaxhall is usually bypassed because of its central position amidst a rectangle of small roads, but non-local residents, including American servicemen, come to its pub now whereas in former decades pub customers were generally village people or their relatives and acquaintances from neighbouring villages. Traffic through Snape is now much more common because the Snape road is a quick route to the American air base at Bentwaters and because of concerts at the Maltings, and increased numbers of strangers now stop at the pubs in the village.

Situated where they are, however, Snape and Blaxhall had long been isolated, eking out their existence in local trades and services and agriculture, depending on the world at large for some tools and machinery, cloth and leather, and basic foodstuffs, but making most of the products necessary for life. Transport has always been scarce and it was common for people to walk the three miles from Snape and five miles from Blaxhall to the market town of Saxmundham on Wednesdays or Saturdays. Walking was the most common form of transport. The service of a pony and trap was provided around the turn of the century by John Hewitt, landlord of the Ship Inn, and by Tom Jay in Blaxhall. Some men equipped themselves with bicycles in order to get to work and to the local pubs, and one local man, Basil Bennett,[3] cycled to London in the early 1920s when he decided to try for work there. Now there is a bus on market day from Blaxhall and Snape to Saxmundham, and also on Saturday, and Saxmundham has a railway station and a National bus station. Those local people with cars are generally willing to ferry people about, especially the sick and elderly, and to take friends and neighbours on trips when they have to travel away on business.

Nowadays, there is much greater facility for travel, by bus, train and private car, than there was in the younger days of most of the native inhabitants. The two world wars took men and women from the villages and transported them all over the world; economic decline and the incursions of Londoners into local life have forced many villagers away to new settlements where work is more readily available and houses are cheaper; and greater ease of communication through modern transportation, telephones and mass media has led to an opening of the villages and a consequent breakdown of old village life. Consumerism has replaced near self-sufficiency within the villages and transport and broadcasting have improved communications and reduced isolation, insularity and parochialism. Some of the advantages were lost along with the disadvantages. Helpfulness was in many cases replaced by commercial enterprise, and co-operation by material competition.

The Family and the Community

Most Blaxhall people are related to each other, and the Lings and the Smiths are the most prolific families, having intermarried and dominated the kinship network of the surrounding area. The communities are close-knit, taking care of their own infirm, their subnormal and their illegitimate wherever possible. Marriages have generally depended on parental approval and thus on the availability of work and the possibility of accommodation, and the high number of bachelors now is probably a reflection of the economic condition of England's rural working population early this century, when girls had to move from home into service and boys had to stay on the land. Most migratory movement of the female population was to urban areas and many women stayed to marry men in their places of employment. The few men who left Snape and Blaxhall to seek work usually returned with wives, and thus fresh blood found its way into the villages.

Babies were born to women who returned from work in service, and often these children, sometimes as many as four by different fathers, were incorporated in new families when the mother married a man from her own village. It was especially common, and is now less so, for couples to marry after the conception of a child, as is clear from examination of the Snape and Blaxhall Parish Registers, and for men, married as well as unmarried, to father babies out of wedlock. Because marriage was an economic as well as an emotional relationship (and is so to a lesser extent today), it was feasible that a couple's fertility should be proved before marriage,[4] and that after marriage the partnership should be maintained even if husband and wife were incompatible. If one person died, remarriage ensued whenever possible, even if this meant a wide discrepancy of ages.[5] People who had missed out on marriage in their younger years sometimes had the opportunity of marrying later: the housekeeper commonly became the wife, and the bachelors or widowers and their housekeepers were and are often suspected of having a sexual relationship.

It is possible that the fluidity of sexual relationships and the tolerant candour with which they are treated within the villages is an indication of concern about survival, both as a community and an economic unit. The forming of partnerships or family groups is of great importance. George Ewart Evans writes of Blaxhall:

> Illegitimacy . . . had no great stigma attached to it, and the child was normally well cared for. Therefore, a bare statistical account would tell very little, and would even be misleading. At the school [in the mid-1940s], about a third of the children were formally illegitimate; that is, born out of legal wedlock. But none of them seemed to suffer from either the stigma or the deprivations normally associated with

illegitimacy.[6]

Accounts of premarital and extramarital sex are generally free from censure, and the bravado of tales of unreproductive liaisons does not colour the accounts of illegitimate and near-illegitimate births. The primary concern is with fertility, the child and its successful absorption into a family unit of some description, and other sexual contact is generally treated as pleasurable, humorous or inescapably human.

However, there are humourless stories of painful sexual relationships, most commonly adulterous, which tell of the violent suicide of a betrayed spouse. Whereas adultery is generally treated tolerantly, the cases of the conjunction of suicide and adultery in local legend are too numerous to be coincidental, and it is possible to view such tales and their subject-matter as a sign of social distress, as a possible result of deprivation and general dissatisfaction. The erstwhile insularity of the villages and the relationships of the villagers meant inbreeding, a scarcity of marriage partners, and a certain propensity for rivalry and, therefore, for violence; the rigours of mechanisation and mass communications have further undermined the local constraints and concessions aimed at alleviating socio-sexual problems.

Violence of any kind may be viewed as a release of tensions: suicide by hanging or shooting is self-annihilatory, drunken fighting is temporarily socially annihilating. Violence associated with alcohol may give release to tensions caused by poor conditions of work or by an unhappy home life where the wife has irreparable grudges in her struggle to supply food and clothing for a family beset by poverty and overcrowding. In these villages, violence was as likely to occur amongst friends and relatives as it was to flare in confrontations between groups of men from neighbouring villages. Chris and Alice Messenger of Blaxhall:

A.M. They got a drop of beer and then the balloon would burst. That's when fights would happen on a Saturday night . . .

C.M. They didn't like Snape people.

A.M. Didn't like Snape people at all when I was a child. I don't now, something about Snape. They seemed a different sort of people. They seemed foreigners, somehow, if you can make out what I mean.

C.M. We don't know 'em, do we, there's no way of knowing 'em.

A.M. See, you just got in your own little village. They were foreigners when they came.

C.M. No, they came to the Ship, they told them to go back where they belonged, didn't they? Especially if they kicked up a row.

G.D. How long ago did they start to be friendly?

A.M. I think it was the war, weren't it, the First World War really. That was the start of a lot, that really was, weren't it?

C.M. Well, you see, going back to the First World War, there was young chaps on the land who had never been out of the village, had they?[7]

Local chauvinism, suspicion and sometimes even fear can probably be attributed to geographical isolation and the competition for jobs and wives.

Gypsies were thought to instigate some fights. They, as seasonal invaders, were regarded by some villagers as trouble-makers and by others as foreign but legitimate inhabitants for the time they were present. They habitually camped on the commons, held small fairs, traded, took casual work, and sang and danced in the pubs. Eventually they were rounded off the commons, although enough had settled through marriage in the villages or had fathered children there to ensure a definite trace of gypsy blood in Blaxhall and Snape today. Wickets Richardson recalls their eviction from Blaxhall:

> They used to be on the common every year, and in Snape, and in Tunstall, and the farmer got so many [local men] to go and pull them off one Sunday morning, and then he give 'em a pint of mild. They went and pulled their rights away, and pulled them off, look. We still got a common, but when they pulled them off we lost our common yards and allotments. The gypsies never done no harm. They used to come to the Ship and dance and fiddle and spend money. I couldn't see what harm they were doing up there. I never went and helped. I was down there at the Ship the Sunday morning they went and pulled them off the common – the old farmer went and treated them to a pint of beer each, they pulled their old rights away.[8]

The use of common land by gypsies annoyed the farmer, perhaps because it encouraged independence in the villagers by suggesting to them the possibility of becoming squatters and thus releasing them from ill-paid and dependent farm labouring; gypsies were also accomplished poachers.[9] Workmen were eager to help the farmer because of his bribe and because they could be persuaded that their jobs were jeopardised by the presence of itinerant workers who were, what is more, strangers to the area.

Most of the workers of this area were obliged to leave school at an early age to supplement the family's income. Even while at school, they had to do numerous jobs such as berry- and acorn-gathering, medicine-fetching, stone-picking and weeding, and attendance at school was irregular. Bob Hart left at Michaelmas 1905,[10] the time of year when jobs became open on farms, as his father did not consider it worthwhile waiting until he was fourteen the following January and thus wasting an opportunity for employment. Margaret Howell was taken from school by the age of ten so that she could look after her younger brothers and sisters.

Illiteracy was high in the villages before the turn of the century, and the customary urge to contribute to a family's income rather than to advance in education continues to prevail. The old people were not generally trained to read for pleasure, let alone for learning, and politically their opinions tended to be handed down rather than revised. At work, they were bound to their employers to such an extent that many could not vote for whom they liked if they had an opinion, and the conformists and those who tried to conceal their vote wore the blue rosette of the Conservatives. Bob Hart relates the following account:

> I was a Liberal, been a Liberal all my life. My father was a Liberal . . . The steward on the farm where father worked, he say, 'You'll soon be old enough to vote boy.' I said, 'I've got a long way to go yet.' 'No,' he said, 'that won't seem long to you. And,' he said, 'what do you vote for?' I said, 'Liberal,' 'cause me father was a Liberal, but he always used to wear a blue rose, that's where he worked, see, the boss was Conservative.[11]

The Labour Party was not an alternative to many of the older people primarily for chronological reasons, and the rebels voted Liberal and passed their Liberalism on to their children as an anti-Establishment protest. As young men, these villagers knew hard times, but they still had the satisfaction, albeit vicarious, of belonging to a Britannia that ruled the waves; throughout their lifetimes, they have seen the loss of all that, correlated with the rise of the Labour Party, and without, until recently, the compensation of much improvement in wages and living standards for farm workers and other rural labourers. Hence, few of them vote Labour and most cling to the Liberal vote of their parents and grandparents.

Farms, Farmers and Labourers

The farms of most areas of Suffolk were commonly run by tenants of large estates, and worked by labourers who lived in tied cottages. Today, most of the estates have been divided and bought by managers, and these still exist as farms and smallholdings.

For most of the farm workers both employment and accommodation were dependent upon the goodwill of their bosses. Respect for and fear of one's betters were fostered by the ceremony surrounding the estate lords, as Stanley Day recollects:

> Every Sunday, you'd see Lord Oldswater ride around here on a white horse and beat the bounds, and he lived up at the High House, Campsea Ashe, and when he died they pulled his place down and that was a beautiful place too. He had deers. Campsea Ashe Park, hundreds of deers.[12]

Self-deprecation, respect and fear flourished:

> And you had to look up to them people that time of day, you dursn't go in the covey or on their land, or shoot or go after grouse or anything, you weren't allowed to do that, that was a sin.[13]

> Oh, they used to be very strict, farmers in those days. I met me father's boss, he was on horseback, and, I didn't take a lot of notice of him, and he went to my father, and he said, 'I met your boy this morning, and he didn't make his obedience to me,' he said. 'See it don't occur again.' Supposed to touch your hat, you see, yes.[14]

There was a strong likelihood that if the labourer answered his master back, he would be discharged from work and thus lose his tied cottage as well. Disagreement between employer and employee seldom gave the employee any recourse but to find alternative work and this could be difficult as one farmer could refuse to take on a man who had left the hire of another. Ruby Ling says:

> You see, years ago, people were all on the move – if you done just one little thing, you see, you had to go. Farm labourers and people – worse than it is today – I mean, if you just said one thing to the farmer and he didn't like you, see, he'd give you the sack, them days, you see. Yes, that's how it was years ago. They didn't care anything

about you then, not like they do now, because people don't care whether they work or whether they don't, 'cos they get the money, don't they?[15]

When Bob Hart, at the age of thirteen, had a disagreement with his boss, he ran away to sea:

I was in the right and knew it. I wasn't very old, I suppose, but the boss was sorta interfering. He came up to me that day and said I'd left the gates open. I'd got a load of maize – I can picture it now, this here corn with the big heads, they give them to the cows. Well, I went through and I shut all the gates behind me. He come out and said that I hadn't – I'd let the cows out – so what happened I don't know. Father said, 'Well,' he said, 'the boy shut the gates,' he said, 'I saw him come across on to the fields, on to the meadows,' and I just walked out of the field. Well, he kep' on and on and on and I walked away, and I was afraid to go home so I carried on right through to Lowestoft and got a job. . . . Nothing at all [with me], just as I stood.[16]

Naturally, eviction followed a man's dismissal, but a new job almost always offered new accommodation; however, on the death of the worker, his family was often made homeless and it was their plight to find somewhere to live.

The family of a labourer badly injured or killed at work received no compensation from the farmer: Wickets Richardson's mother had to keep pigs in order to support her family and the parish allowance supplemented the income:

We lost our father, which was on Christmas Eve, he was athrashing and he slipped off the stack and broke his back and he was brought home in a cart and I think there were six of us at school then, two was out in service, and he died the Boxing Day. I'll never forget it, that was in 1908, and I was nine and I shall never forget it. . . My mother kept a little shop, she sold pork, she sold two pigs a week, I've turned a sausage machine when she was grinding by night for sausages. . . [She got] nothing. They got so much off the parish, eighteen pence and a half stone of flour a week – we used to have to scrape some food up, had to work herself to the bone, more or less, but there you are, she brought us all up and lived to be eighty herself, but they weren't the same as there is today. If you'd lost somebody like that, you'd had it, and that's all there was about it, which was hard. Times were very hard then to what they are today.[17]

Priscilla Savage's parents also received the parish allowance because her father was crippled in a mining accident near Durham; relief of a sort was paid not by the employer but by parish charity. Mr Garthwaite, a rector in Blaxhall in the mid-nineteenth century, bequeathed £28 10s 0d annually, and other amounts from local gentry were used as well.

Once a man was hired, if he pleased and was pleased, he was likely to stay at the same farm for many years: Cyril Poacher was the cowman at Grove Farm for 30 years until his recent retirement. Robert Savage was shepherd at Grove Farm 29 years, Percy Webb's father was shepherd for John Goddard for 35 years. There are many other examples of such long service. Men also moved from job to job, in search of higher pay and better conditions: Percy Ling worked at the Old Barn on the land, then at the Maltings, and then as a stoker at Bentwaters. He became a ditcher and rabbit- and vermin-killer for Iken Hall before returning to Bentwaters as a general labourer. Many people relied on seasonal work, whether by habit or by choice is not always clear. Safe in a tied cottage, a labourer could vary his job depending on the farmer's needs or, independently housed, he could find whatever seasonal work was available as his need arose. Frank Woolnough and George Bennett still live by this means, but in times of hardship and job shortages, such labourers were in great difficulties as those who had been regularly employed lost work and entered the competition for seasonal jobs; men were sometimes laid off at the Maltings as well, and they too needed work.

Most lads began full-time farm work at the age of twelve or thirteen, and because they were still in effect children, most of them stayed to work on the same farm as their fathers, often doing their father's jobs with them.

Percy Webb. I was a boy, see, when I left school, I went there and went with my father with the sheep, and that was seven day a week – setting the folds for sheep, . . . and nets, and grinding the food up for them.[18]

Lenny Savage. I was bred and born in Blaxhall, me father [Robert] was a shepherd and backhus' boy, he was on the Grove Farm where I started. In fact, I used to go there before I left school, I used to go there Saturdays working the gardens, then I went backhus' boy for about a year, I suppose. That was when I first left school.[19]

Robert Savage took each of his sons into shepherding with him for a while, but only one, Robert Russell, kept to shepherding. Many other men began to learn farming under their fathers' guidance, for example Bob Hart, Basil Bennett, Reg Jay, James Knights and Abraham Ling, but turned away from farming altogether, or took farm work only casually. Harvest work was sometimes the first job a boy ever did, and his father offered his services to the farmer while he asked for a job himself. Percy Webb's father, a full-time shepherd, took extra work during the harvest period:

> My father lived here, he used to go and mow for that farm, and I used to go with him,and when he got his job he used to say, 'I got a son can do a job.' 'All right,' he say, 'he can have a job.' I went. First job I got was six bob a week. I was thirteen. I left school when I was thirteen, that's the first job I went and done.[20]

Those years of the farm worker between leaving school and marriage were, to the farmer, years of cheap and almost certain labour. The usual necessity for the boy to stay at home, unless he went as backhus' boy elsewhere or took up an entirely different life (as Bob Hart did when he turned his back on the fields and ran away to sea), meant that he received tutelage from his father in an informal apprenticeship or could be used by the farmer in many jobs about the farm. There was sometimes little flexibility of movement for these lads since their father's employer often interpreted the fact that the children, too, were living in his property as giving him a right to their labour. Basil Bennett:

> There were eight boys and three girls . . . We all had to work on the farm, you see, as we left school. Me father was shepherd and the oldest one went with him, and when the other one left school, this one went on the farm, and we had to carry on all through us lot. We lived in a tied house. I left and went to Chillesford, I had to walk about four miles . . . and I went and got a job down at Church Farm, sixpence more a week. I got only half a crown . . . I'd only been there a fortnight, and the steward said to me father, he said, 'The boy'll have to come back,' he said – wouldn't let you work anywhere else, you see, and 'Oh,' he said, 'you're in our house,' he said. Had to come back you see, so me father, he said to me, 'You'll have to come back, boy,' he say, 'otherwise we'll have to get out,' so I had to go and tell the man I wanted to leave, so I had to go back to work there.[21]

Most village children, especially those living in tied cottages with their parents, did work on farms while they were at school to supplement the family income; women also took such work. Stone-picking was necessary both to the farmer because it improved his land and to the casual workers because they needed the money, however small the pay. Ruby Ling:

> They had a lot of children and when she had seven children, all my father earnt was seven and six a week [*c*. 1900], you see, and we used to when we were children, we used to have to go stone-picking, picking all the stones off the land, and you see, the money wasn't anything then.[22]

Other farm jobs were given to children by parents: animals could be fed, the cows led out, the crops weeded and picked. Fruit- and acorn-picking also added to the family's income and food supply, and farmers as well as parents encouraged children to go rabbit-running:

> We used to go in the harvest field and run the rabbits, yes we did. My father was on the farm, you see, and we used to go there as children, my sister and I, and we used to go and take his dinner . . . you see, when they were cutting . . . we used to ride on the horses, . . . and then we had to run the rabbits, and perhaps we'd take four or five home on a stick, you know, two of us, on our shoulder. . . Just run them and hit them with a stick, you see. That's how we got 'em really. Well, that was our main meals, them days.[23]

Basil Bennett describes another method of rabbit-catching:

> When father had his sheep on the meadows and he saw a rabbit sit – they set in seats, you see, in the summertime, they get a clust of grass, and a rabbit will sit in there, look – and he used to go and lay his coat in front of that and that rabbit'd . . . watch that, and he'd go round the back of it and strike it on the head with a stick, see, and the rabbit wouldn't see him go round the back, and yes – we catched lots on the seats, and we used to go in the harvest fields, you know, and run the rabbits when they are cutting the corn.[24]

Once a child had left school, as Alice Messenger says, 'Girls had to go into service, boys had to go on the land, that's all there was, they didn't see no further.'[25] A common first job for a boy was backhus' boy:

Robert Savage began as backhus' boy at Grove Farm when he was twelve, and his son Lenny took the same job at the same farm many years later. James Smith began as backhus' boy at Dunningworth Hall and stayed there twelve months; Dick Woolnough did as well:

> I got a rum memory, you know, and I done twelve months on the farm at two and six a week [*c*. 1909], seven days a week, so when it comes to the end of the year, I told the master I thought I was worth a little more money. He said, 'Well, I don't know,' he said, 'I'll give you another sixpence,' and it would be rude for me to tell you what I told him to do with it. And I left, off I went. The Redhouse Farm, at Campsea Ashe, they call it. I worked there twelve months and he thought I was worth another sixpence! I didn't think so, no. I got more money when I come down to the Maltings, pony boy. You see I wouldna been only thirteen year old when I come out of school . . . I learnt to milk and I was what they call backhus' boy, kitchen boy. I had to do odd jobs what they wanted me indoors. I used to clean the master's shoes and the mistress's shoes, and go out round with milk and eggs and butter with the pony and cart, and I used to have to hold the pony while he done his business. That was my job.[26]

Another job for new labourers was crow-scaring.

> *Percy Webb.* I used to go scaring crows on the field, and the foreman came round one day, and there weren't no crows so I got in the ditch and read a book . . . He say, 'This won't do,' I say, 'That'll do for me – ain't no crows about.' He laughed.[27]

Odd jobs were given to these young lads, and they were sent all over the farm as need for them arose, and consequently, the job that a man eventually did was not always the one he began with.

Farmland in the Snape and Blaxhall area is mainly arable; the large flocks of sheep[28] that used to graze the heaths have disappeared because of the changes in farming methods, and because of their disposal during the First World War.[29] The replacement of horses by machines[30] has led to a change in the use of arable land since horse fodder crops have been replaced by money crops, and dairying has largely occupied the land formerly used by sheep and fodder crops. Some of the old labourers, such as Percy Webb, decry these changes; the effects of machine ploughing, he believes, will be evident in the future, although the apparent savings and profits in the present disguise the inefficiency of modern techniques:

> Where we had twenty men, the modern farmer hadn't got three or four, you see, and they hurry over the work. That in't done, they never plough, they just crome it up, but in years to come they'll find that'll pay. They'll want to plough it.[31]

The immediate benefits of reduced numbers of workers, larger monetary crops and speed are thought to attract the farmers, and efficiency has cut the number of men per farm so much that village life has been radically altered through job shortages. Geoff Ling comments:

> There used to be sixteen at Lime Tree Farm here before World War Two, used to be eight down at the Firtree Farm, and up at the Redhouse Farm there used to be another twelve, and then down at Mr Rope's, there used to be another ten, and now there's hardly any, is there? There used to be four cowmen up here and four horsemen, and that was eight, and then there used to be what was called labourers.[32]

Whereas today the few workers on each farm share most jobs except for certain aspects of husbandry, before mechanisation there was much specialisation alongside general labouring, as Geoff Ling indicates. Besides the horsemen, cowmen or shepherds, there were cartage men and drainage contractors; harvest work, some crop work and vermin-catching were done mostly by casual labourers, and by specialised workers in off seasons and during harvest.

The crucial summer harvest called for many hands, and Percy Webb describes one way by which the farmer assured himself of workers:

> We worked on the farm and we knew when harvest was due. The foreman used to come and tell us, 'Harvest tomorrow', . . . used to call it 'taking the harvest' when you paid your shilling, and that bound you there for that time . . . Mustn't leave there in that month, whatever that took . . . He'd buy two big bottles of beer and put the bottles agin' you, so when we paid a shilling to sign on for the harvest, he'd give us a night of drinking this here same night . . . Got drunk I did – I only a boy, and they give me too much, gin and beer that was. All the people on the farm . . . and from houses round about the estate . . . pay a shilling and you do a full man's harvest or three-quarters or half a man. He said to me, 'Do you want

to be a harvester?' I said, 'Yer.' 'Well,' he say, 'we'll give you half man.' I say, 'No,' 'cos you gotta work just as hard as a full man, so I went and told him full man. I was about seventeen, sixteen or seventeen when I done a harvest . . . We used to get about £5 for the harvest.[33]

And jobs were taken by seasonal migratory workers.

James Knights. If you worked on a farm, you went in the harvest, the same as me. I used to be away, I used to come home for the harvest, and I used to do the harvest, you see, just for the months. We used to start a harvest, you see, late in July and then carry on to August and through that up to September. How did I get it? By seeing the farmer and getting the job. Say, 'Do you want a harvest man?' 'Yes.' Well, of course, you got it. He'd employ you, see, for the harvest. I went to Burton when I was younger and come home and then do a harvest and then come back again, come back to Burton-on-Trent, and do the winter season as a maltster and do your harvest and then go back again.[34]

After the harvest was the harvest frolic or supper, at which the farmer might appear and sit at the head of the table, a reminder to all of his rank. However, the image of the benevolent farmer or lord of the manor treating his workers to a joyful meal is far from the truth, and is the exception rather than the rule.

Percy Webb. After the harvest, after we'd gathered it all in, the men off the farms, they all used to have what we called a farm feast . . . You go to some pub and they boil the meat, and boil the potatoes in a copper, 'cos there's a lot of us. We had a rare old spree up in the top room of the pub up at Bawdsey, where I had harvest frolics. No [the bosses didn't go]. The foremen did . . . We got it up between ourselves. We used to auction the rabbits off, you see, and then with that money we put towards that, and we paid about half a crown each and we had all the beer we wanted. And of course, in there, if you didn't sing a song, you had to buy a gallon of beer, so they went round from one right round, to sing. Bawdsey Star, the pub was called . . . People stand up to sing, foreman sing too . . . he only had a better job than us, he used to give us orders and we done the work. Just one of us, the same as we when we go there. No, the farmer never went, well, he was a real gentleman. We had it between ourselves, you know.[35]

Priscilla Savage. They used to hire the big room, and then, you see, the harvest supper, the mothers of the men what were doing the harvest, they used to cook the meat and vegetables and then they used to hire that and have a supper there, you see . . . The man at the Ship, he used to heat a frying pan, he'd save the ha'pennies up for a year, and he put them into a frying pan and make them hot and then he used to throw them out of his bedroom window and we used to scramble for them. There used to be some happy made-up times in years gone back, but of course there isn't that now, dear . . . the supper was at the big room, at the Ship, you see . . . the men's wives used to pay, have a meal, you see, them used to get the piece of beef and one'd boil it, and one'd boil the carrots and have beef and carrots and then you used to have the batter puddings with it, see, and nice gravy. That used to be an old fashioned way of having harvest supper, but that isn't the same now . . . Blaxhall Grove Farm, they'd hire that and have that on their own, and then Blaxhall Hall, they'd have their own, if they had one, but they didn't used to hardly ever have one . . . the farmer used to sit down and have his supper with you. No, the lord of the manor never come . . . farmer sat down at the head of the table . . . The farmer's wife'd come, but she used to always have a maid at home to see after the children, see. Women used to go and have supper with the men . . . They have one now, nearly always once a year . . . they hire the village hall, and then they have it catered for.[36]

James Knights. When I was harvesting, we always did go to harvest frolic. I had two at Clopton, I had three or four at Debbidge . . . The farmers put them on. When they finished harvest, they used to have what they called the harvest frolic, used to have a big feed and a real carry on, eat and drink, all you could eat and drink and everything up . . . Each farm had their own frolic . . . In the farmhouse. Damn good feed, you see, and then a singsong afterwards.[37]

One of the benefits of the harvest on which these people relied was gleaning, which was necessary for household economy, with farm labourers' wages being so low.

Priscilla Savage. He used to toll the bell and then we could all go agleaning, you see. 'Course, they don't go pick the corn up now,

> they drag it all up and let the cattle have it, you see. There's no gleaning now, you don't see anybody pick a bit of corn up now, in fact, I don't think the farmers let them . . . but we used to go gleaning . . . When [the farmer] used to thrash his wheat, he'd thrash what you'd picked up with that, and then he'd take it down to the miller, and he'd grind it up for us into flour and then he'd bring it to us – flour as we wanted it. So that's how we used to live them times . . . And you weren't allowed to go and pick up a bit of corn, not until – the farmer used to leave a sheaf of corn in the field where you were going to glean, and before he took that away, he'd go to church and toll the bell and so you could go gleaning.[38]

Now, of course, efficiency of mowing means that women can no longer go gleaning in the fields after harvest.

General Employment: Dissension and Variety

The people of these villages have relied mainly upon agriculture for employment, but there have been other important sources of jobs. At the Maltings in Snape, jobs were varied, and many men stayed there all of their lives: William Ling for 54 years, Bob Hart for 40 years, and James Smith worked there all of his life as his father had before him. Some men worked there when they were young, and moved to other jobs (Percy Ling, Dick Woolnough, Reuben Kerridge), or worked there in the months when farm work was hard to come by (Wickets Richardson). James Knights was one of many who travelled each season to the Maltings at Burton-on-Trent; most of the women went into service, and, after their children had grown, took housework locally as independent cleaners or as home helps; several men worked in forestry, others went to sea, and Bentwaters air base has provided work for many of them. There are other jobs in the area that are less frequently taken, and several men, not only those who have retired, survive by doing odd jobs such as concrete-laying, fence-building and gardening.

Earlier this century, most villages had their own service tradesmen, such as bricklayers, cobblers, knife-grinders, millers, salesmen, smokehouse operators, thatchers and wheelwrights. Now, the smokehouse at Snape, the mills, the cobblers' shops are all closed, and the local service trades ended. Matthes Bakery vans travel the area; shops supply ready-made foods; shoes, clothes and other goods are bought in Saxmundham or Woodbridge on market days. Odd-job men now replace local tradesmen where possible, but skilled tradesmen have to be summoned by telephone from the surrounding market towns. The closeness of the villages had the advantages of co-operation, help and friendliness, as well as the disadvantages of lack of privacy and rivalry. With the opening up of the area through communications and the media, the old trades have disappeared.

Although the Maltings employed many men at its peak, and farm work employed the majority of the adult male population and some of the female and juvenile, other jobs were done for the sake of variety, or more often for better pay and brighter prospects. Those who went to sea as fishermen often came back to land jobs in later life, those in farm work sometimes moved to forestry and labouring. Seasonal work, although insecure, was popular. There are not many old fishermen left in these villages, although many are remembered and their songs are there as witness in the repertoires of younger men. Bob Hart's career as a fisherman came about as a reaction against the injustice he received as a farm worker; Dick Woolnough was also inspired to go to sea, on cargo boats, in the hope of better treatment and adventure. Life on board ship gave the worker a small world which, if he was lucky, could be comradely; the presence of a kindly skipper could create a family atmosphere; in place of the usual hat-doffing servant-master relationship of the farm worker to his boss.

> *Dick Woolnough.* He was a Christian and he used to look after me like a father. He never paid me no money to go sporting about. If I wanted some to go ashore, he'd give me some, he'd buy me clothes, so he looked after me just like a father . . . I went to sea with him, and I was at sea with him until the war broke out in 1914.[39]

> *Bob Hart.* I've seen [the trawlers] when we've had the sails up and . . . it's been snowing . . . and freezing, and you couldn't get your sails down, everything was all frozen, but otherwise, when it was nice weather, it was nice to be on them. . . My actual job was to haul with the men. . . I was walking along the quay at Lowestoft and there was various offices . . . because, I mean, these firms had boats in those days . . . and I saw this notice in the window, 'Boy Wanted', and I went in, and the old boy behind the desk said, 'What do you want?' I said, 'I come after this job in the window.' And he looked across to a little old man asetting on a seat, he say, 'Will you take him?', and he stood up – he was the shortest little old man I think I ever see, and he looked up at me, he say, 'Yes, if he promise he won't knock me about.' Comical old chap he was, but he was a real nice man because when we come in from sea, he always used to take

> me home and give me a cup of tea or something to eat. He was a skipper, his brother-in-law was mate, and then there was a third hand, deckhand, and I was the boy – there was five of us on this boat.[40]

It is possible that other jobs taken by local men, especially those jobs away from the villages, were attractive because they too were beyond the bounds of the social system which prevailed on the estate farms. Bob Hart has often said that he enjoyed jobs for which he was effectively his own boss, Dick Woolnough was continually fighting authority throughout his life, Basil Bennett left the farm where his father was shepherd because he 'got so fed up with that' and 'disappeared and . . . travelled all over the country on different jobs, all sorts of jobs'.[41] Variety was sought and found by change of job, sometimes by change of place: James Knights travelled a lot in his work as stud-horse keeper, as lorry driver's mate, and as seasonal maltster (and he says a thousand men went from Suffolk to Burton-on-Trent each season); Ben Ling, who also shows a flair for independence in his employment record, having farmed a small self-owned plot of land with his uncle, built a work camp, felled trees and worked for the Catchment Board, emigrated to Canada for some years after the First World War. As Geoff Ling says, 'you had to work on the land',[42] and women had to go into service; otherwise, besides the Maltings, jobs had to be found out of the area or on a more casual and less secure basis.

Poverty

The search for higher wages caused many changes of master and job; as James Knights says, and economic historians support both his observation and his analysis,

> Suffolk is the worst paid county there is round for miles . . . there in't really the industry here, you see, that's where it is . . . They get more money in Norfolk than what they do about here on these farms, you know. Get more a week. Suffolk is a very poor place. Always was.[43]

Agricultural wages in Suffolk were, as will be shown, lower than in most of England,[44] and it seems likely that a state of poverty existed in most labourers' households. A very low standard of living was the norm, and the area remained depressed, suffering from underemployment and unemployment as well as from low wages.

Bowley, in *Wages in the United Kingdom in the Nineteenth Century*, gives the Suffolk agricultural labourers' average weekly earnings as eight shillings and sixpence between 1850 and 1852, and thirteen shillings in 1854; nominal weekly wages for Suffolk farm labourers were as follows:

1851	7s 0d
1869-70	10s 10d
1892-3	12s 0d [45]

A farmer informant of Rider Haggard's from Clare, Suffolk, put labourers' average wages at thirteen to fourteen shillings a week for the years 1901 and 1902.[46] Bob Hart's grandfather, a young married man in the 1860s, was earning ten shillings a week as farm manager for the Earl of Stradbrook, and he was thus earning less than the Suffolk average wage but approximately the nominal wage; Ruby Ling's father earned only seven and sixpence a week as horseman around 1900 when he had a wife and seven children to support; Robert Savage was earning eleven shillings a week as shepherd in about 1903. They were both receiving less than the Suffolk nominal or average wage, which was, in any case, less than the national average. In turn, the national agricultural average was less than the wage average for most other forms of employment; for example, the average annual money wage-earnings (including agricultural) for the United Kingdom in 1900 are given as £57 7s 0d, or approximately 26s 2d a week.[47] Even in the 1930s, Suffolk labourers were earning only about 32s 6d, still 13s 6d below the 1920-1 Suffolk average.[48]

Vast increases in the cost of living between 1914 and 1918[49] are not reflected in wage increases for most of the British population, and it is true to say that in Blaxhall and Snape, where wages were lower than the Suffolk agricultural wage average, and this Suffolk average was lower than the national agricultural wage average (and lower again than the national general employment average), poverty was bound to be rife. Poverty was reflected in housing, life-style, clothes and food. Wickets Richardson says:

> There was eight of us born in that house. Now they want a mansion to bring up eight children . . . Only two bedrooms. Mother and father slep' in one and we all must be in there together in the next one. Slep' across sometimes, you know, instead of head to toe, you sleep out that other way.[50]

Poverty meant deprivation of luxury goods, and even necessities were not available; some people considered frequent visits to the pub as extremely wasteful, and restricted cigarette-smoking; Ruby Ling tells how the evenings were short because oil lamps and candles were used with extreme economy:

> They were all old oil lamps – there was no electricity in them days, you see . . . We used to have to go to bed about half past six, you see, and we used to have to go upstairs to bed, and my father used to go to bed at about seven, and he said, 'It's best you be in bed when I come up,' he said, 'I'll take the candle,' so he used to take the candle away off us, you see. That's the sort of ways we used to live.[51]

Clothes were carefully used and re-used, mended and altered as children grew and more were born. Those born around 1900, and even later (Lenny Savage was born 1913), tell the same story.

> *Ruby Ling.* We didn't do very much in the evenings, you see . . . We used to have to learn to sew, and if we had holes in our stockings or anything like that, we had to mend them. 'Course, a pair of stockings in them days cost sixpence, you see, and that's what we used to have to do . . . we had to mend all our own things.[52]

> *Alice Messenger.* When my little girl was born, when she was a babe, we used to have to take her dress off at night, and she went to bed, wash and iron her dress ready for next morning. That's all she had. They were times, weren't they! My neighbour was a bit better off than I was, gave me a shirt, a silk shirt of her husband's, and I made her another little dress. That's how we got on. I wouldn't like to see that again, not those times.[53]

Clothes were budgeted for very carefully, as replacements, particularly of shoes, were necessary from time to time, and Lenny Savage's mother had a clothing fund in which she put the shilling a week he earned pushing an old woman in a basket chair, and other small amounts of money. In Blaxhall, clothes early this century were bought mainly from a fortnightly traveller called Watson.

The woman's work was to make as much food for as little money as she could, to supply adequate clothing and comfort for her family, to clean the house, and to earn money when possible. It was her duty to use her husband's hard-earned pay with extreme care. She supplied her family with protein in the form of rabbit meat and pork, and those who were able to kept a pig, butchered it and preserved as much meat as they could afford to keep; the rest was sold. It was usually the woman's job to brew beer and wine for the home, and the yeast used was passed from family to family for bread-making as well.

Food was often in short supply, and of limited variety.

> *Ruby Ling.* We used to have half an egg each when we were young. No, we never had very much really. Used to be so hungry, we could eat anything. . . I always remember that on Friday nights we used to like it because my mother used to make the bread, and she used to bake a potato pie . . . all potatoes, you see, and a little bit of gravy, you see, and there was a bit or two of meat, and my father had all the meat and we had the gravy and the potatoes and a bit of the crust.[54]

> *Basil Bennett.* Oh, when we were small, we had bread and milk, skim milk, that used to be about a halfpenny a pint. Bread and milk and bread and jam. I never eat no jam now, we had so much when we were small. And mother used to bake them big old marrow pies, she had a pie dish about as big as this table, and that last all week for us children.[55]

Priscilla Savage always gave most meat to her husband, and to her children if there was enough, and left herself the least wholesome part of the meal. Poverty meant that there was often not enough to go around, and it was usually the mother who went without. Today, the woman's role has changed: she utilises what her husband's pay will buy, whereas before she had herself to create the basic foods and drinks on which she and her family depended.

In the past, before the advent of myxomatosis, poaching allowed the illicit involvement of the men in the fight against poverty. Percy Ling tells his adventures:

> I never used to go out much, because when the children were young, there was about seven or eight of them, and during the War, you know, there wasn't a lot of food about, was there, and plenty of nights my wife used to wake up about two or three o'clock in the morning and find I'd gone out of bed. I'd be taking me old gun and go in the bush and shoot a couple of old pheasants, bring 'em home and put 'em in the pot for her. That was illegal, you can't do that, can you? That's the reason I used to get up at two or three o'clock

> in the morning, you see, when the keepers were asleep . . . that used to be an estate, big woods . . . I got caught only once . . . I was going up a long hedge and I shot an old cock pheasant. There's a bike come down the road, I see'd a light from the bike, and there's somebody come arunning down the hedge. I thought that'd be the old policeman, so I runned. Well, I reckon I runned about a hundred yards, there's a big heap of bushes along that hedge, so I think to myself, well, I'll crawl in here, so I get my gun and I backed right into these bushes and the old policeman runned right by me, and I turned round and runned back the same way as I came.[56]

There was a certain awe in catching a pheasant that the killing of a rabbit did not inspire. Basil Bennett suggests that the labouring people were conditioned to fear the poaching of pheasants:

> No, we mustn't touch or look at a pheasant. No, not even now. I coulda had plenty where I work – I've had 'em penned up in corners and let 'em go. And my wife is the same. She say, 'You bring one home, if you catch it, I wouldn't kill it and I wouldn't get it ready.' That was drummed into us that we mustn't touch 'em, you see, they belong to the estate, and if anybody was caught catching a pheasant, they'd lose their job, get had up, and that weren't worth it, and we never did touch them, and I haven't touched one from that day to this.[57]

It does seem likely, however, that the luxury of the shoot gave some labourers more incentive to poach than their poverty; killing a pheasant was an act of defiance as well as an act of necessity, killing a rabbit was less so because less dangerous and rabbits were vermin anyway. Hobsbawm and Rudé, in *Captain Swing*, write that poaching was, 'of course, not a mere source of income, but also a primitive assertion of social justice and rebellion'.[58] Rabbit-poaching was connived at by some farmers, and dealers set themselves up to buy poached game. In the Crown Inn, Snape, poachers used to come and hide their dogs up on the shelves, the previous landlady, Marjory Blowers, says; these shelves were also the hiding-place of children brought to the pub illegally by parents unwilling to stay at home. The local population recognised necessity, and some of them condoned defiance.

Entertainment and Leisure

Always the old people of these villages will tell that they have relied on themselves for entertainment. The Men's Club, Women's Institute and Old Folks' Clubs are innovations of the twentieth century, but the villages have long provided their entertainment at concerts, fairs, quoits and darts matches, running races and games, and in the pubs, as well as in bell-ringing (handbell and church bell) and carol-singing and other communal festivities. Small fairs moved from village to village and set up on the commons, with roundabouts, coconut shies, stalls selling sticks of rock and competitions; singing matches were held and the winner was given a copper kettle. Gypsies and traders with cheap jack stalls sometimes brought entertainments with them in order to attract customers. Village concerts utilised local talent as they still do, and songs were sung, recitations recited, dances danced. At Christmas time, even in snow and wind, carol-singers walked and sang their way from farm to farm, receiving gin here and whisky there and gradually becoming more and more drunk and noisy as the evening passed and the air grew colder.

The pubs provided the most accessible form of entertainment for most village people, although there have been social and moral restrictions against the presence of women in the pubs. Games such as darts and dominoes were played, competitions held, and men sang and made music, and danced either alone (stepping) or with the women. Not only alcohol was sought there, but also companionship and conversation, and the singing that occurred there so often, especially in the past. Now the singsongs are weekly, if that, but in years gone by some men used to go to the pub and sing almost every night, especially on pay night, and the women were welcome on holidays or at weekends. The singsongs and dancing relieved these hard-working people; sad songs inspired them with feelings of pathos, comic songs made them laugh, and all of the songs, even those heard every week, and perhaps especially those, were enjoyed. The singing of songs by a group of men in a pub increased the feeling of comradeship amongst them and cemented their communal and ancient solidarity, as well as entertaining them.

This is and was more than usually important for the old men, for there is reason to believe that retirement hits them very hard. There is, for example, a discernible pattern of suicides in these villages, which are generally violent in method (hanging or shooting are favoured, rather than the clean and clinical overdose of the city-dweller), and committed by men who have retired or are approaching retirement. George Ewart Evans comments:

> There were, I think, three suicides while we were there, and I have a theory that they were related to the general state of things. I'd observed myself, and had it confirmed in a discussion with a farmer: once a farmworker gave up his work, in many cases his life became empty; and after retirement many went downhill very quickly – died, as it were, through inanition. An isolated community with little to do, and few fresh sights or contacts – and, of course, it was really isolated in that period [pre-1956] just when motor transport was beginning – could be a breeding ground of depression. And of course there was also great hopelessness, especially during farming depressions.[59]

In such a situation, which may be exacerbated by the noticeable fact that suicide is a common topic of conversation (sometimes with the grim humour of the oft-told tale of the man who shot himself through the head in his newly decorated kitchen and should have had the forethought to retire into the garden shed), the leisure institutions take on a crucial role. Blaxhall and Snape people do not walk their roads with stony faces; and it is not suggested that a retired Suffolk labourer must choose between suicide and singing, but a life of hard work and poor wages, of often concomitant poor conditions and an unhappy home life (because the wife did not have enough money for her family's food, let alone their clothing), followed by an empty retirement, was likely to lead a man to depression, to drink, or to suicide, or on the other hand to an occupying and consoling pastime which, in the case of singing, offers a change of role from labourer to singer. Bob Hart says, 'I don't know how I shoulda got through these last years if I hadn't a took up singing. You seem so far away from everybody, but if you do something to amuse them, that's all right.'[60]

This is not to say that there are not or never have been young men acclaimed as singers, but an empty retirement may be an incentive to one who has been passive in his knowledge of songs. The songs in the pub throughout a local man's life provide brotherhood and entertainment; as he grows older, the songs that lay dormant in his mind come forward into his repertoire along with those songs which he inherits or takes from other singers; he is recognised as a singer, and this almost becomes his job, at least his *raison d'être*. If the old men do not sing, as they often do not now with so many more strangers in the pubs, and the fruit machines and juke-boxes, they sit and drink, and are often silent and morose together around the tables, not speaking. Bob Hart, for example, is morose in the pub although he often knows the customers, and it is only as a singer that he truly becomes 'alive'.

Notes

1. These figures were supplied by the Suffolk Record Office, Ipswich. In 1971, the population of Blaxhall was 290 (compared with 536 in 1901), and of Snape 585 (1901 – 529). From *Census of Great Britain. East Suffolk County Report* (HMSO, London, 1971).

2. The Catchment Board is a similar source of employment to the local county council. It engages men in the care of waterways, drainage and irrigation systems, and estuary areas. It undertakes to maintain the ecological balance of a catchment area – many of its workers are skilled, more are general labourers.

3. Brief biographies of all of my informants appear in Appendix I.

4. See Peter Laslett, *The World we Have Lost* (Methuen, London, 1973), Chapter 6, 'Personal Discipline and Social Survival', pp. 135-6, 149-50. Also, Ronald Pearsall in *The Worm in the Bud. The World of Victorian Sexuality* (Allen Lane, London, 1971) describes 'bundling', sanctioned 'courting in bed', which was presumably allowed by rural society since it confirmed fertility or revealed infertility, pp. 341-2.

5. An example is one couple who married late in life, a widow to a bachelor, and she fifteen years his senior.

6. George Ewart Evans, personal communication, 9 Nov. 1976.

7. Chris and Alice Messenger, Blaxhall, 31 Oct. 1974.

8. Wickets Richardson, Blaxhall, 27 June 1975.

9. See, for example, George Ewart Evans, *Ask the Fellows who Cut the Hay* (Faber and Faber, London, 1966), p. 209.

10. Bob Hart says Michaelmas, which is 29 September. Martinmas, 11 November, is often encountered as the beginning of the farming year (see Stephen Caunce, 'East Riding Hiring Fairs', *Oral History*, vol. 3, no. ii (1975), pp. 45-52). Michaelmas is roughly the same season, as it is between harvesting and ploughing. And in *The Horse in the Furrow*, (Faber and Faber, London, 1960) George Ewart Evans suggests that Michaelmas was the end of the agricultural year, since some farmers made up their accounts then: pp. 100, 164.

11. Bob Hart, Snape, 15 July 1974.

12. Stanley Day, Blaxhall, 24 June 1975.

13. Ibid.

14. Bob Hart, 22 June 1975.

15. Ruby Ling, Snape, 9 Sept. 1974.

16. Bob Hart, 5 Oct. 1974.

17. Wickets Richardson, ibid.

18. Percy Webb, Tunstall, 19 July 1974.

19. Lenny Savage, Snape, 18 July 1974. Robert Savage, Lenny's father, as backhus' boy, or backhouse boy, is described in George Ewart Evans' *Ask the Fellows who Cut the Hay*, pp. 23-7. The job involved general duties around the kitchen area of the big house, and often on the farm as well, for example, gardening, milking, looking after horses. Indeed, the backhus' boy did virtually any job that required an extra hand.

20. Percy Webb, 27 July 1975.

21. Basil Bennett, Snape, 2 Oct. 1974.

22. Ruby Ling, ibid.

23. Ibid.
24. Basil Bennett, ibid.
25. Alice Messenger, ibid.
26. Dick Woolnough, Snape, 31 Oct. 1974.
27. Percy Webb, 10 Sept. 1974.
28. Percy Webb's father's flock at nearby Tunstall numbered 500.
29. Evans, *Ask the Fellows who Cut the Hay*, pp. 33-4.
30. See P.J.O. Trist, *A Survey of the Agriculture of Suffolk* (County Agricultural Surveys No. 7, Royal Agricultural Society of England, London, 1971) p. 247: the total horse population in Suffolk in 1939 was 26,308; in 1958 it was 3,952.
31. Percy Webb, 19 July 1974.
32. Geoff Ling, Blaxhall, 2 Oct. 1974.
33. Percy Webb, 15 Nov. 1974.
34. James Knights, Little Glemham, 15 Nov. 1974. He had a regular round of work in the early years of his working life, going to the Maltings at Burton-on-Trent for the season there, and then returning to do harvesting in Suffolk.
35. Percy Webb, ibid.
36. Priscilla Savage, Blaxhall, 15 Nov. 1974.
37. James Knights, ibid.
38. Priscilla Savage, 11 Sept. 1974.
39. Dick Woolnough, ibid.
40. Bob Hart, 25 June 1974 and 5 Oct. 1974.
41. Basil Bennett, ibid.
42. Geofff Ling, ibid.
43. James Knights, 11 Sept. 1974.
44. See Christabel S. Orwin and Edith H. Whetham, *History of British Agriculture 1846-1914* (Longmans, London, 1964), p. 323.
45. Arthur L. Bowley, *Wages in the United Kingdom in the Nineteenth Century* (Cambridge University Press, Cambridge, 1900), p. 33.
46. H. Rider Haggard, *Rural England. Being an Account of Agricultural and Social Researches Carried Out in the Years 1901-1902* (Longmans, London, 1906), Vol. II, p. 401.
47. E.H. Phelps Brown with Margaret H. Browne, *A Century of Pay. The Course of Pay and Production in France, Germany, Sweden, the United Kingdom, and the United States of America, 1860-1960* (Macmillan, London, 1968), Appendix 3, UK, 1860-1913.
48. Bowley *Wages in the United Kingdom*, pp. 170-1.
49. See Bowley, pp. 64-6. An example of a typical price rise is from 1s 8d for a pair of women's stockings in 1914 to 3s 8d in 1918 (p. 64).
50. Wickets Richardson, ibid.
51. Ruby Ling, 11 Sept. 1974.
52. Ibid.
53. Alice Messenger, ibid.
54. Ruby Ling, ibid.
55. Basil Bennett, ibid.
56. Percy Ling, Snape, 16 Oct. 1974.
57. Basil Bennett, ibid.
58. E.J. Hobsbawm and George Rudé, *Captain Swing* (Lawrence and Wishart, London, 1969) p. 73 (see also pp. 82-3).
59. George Ewart Evans, personal communication, 9 Nov. 1976.
60. Bob Hart, 13 July 1974.

PART ONE

1 MEN'S SINGING INSTITUTIONS: AN EVENING IN THE BLAXHALL SHIP

Introduction: the Men and their Singing

The performance environment is created by each village community, its blood and marital ties, its common employment sources, and its shared activities. Within this context, the singer and his audience reside. His role momentarily established and declared, the singer stands to deliver his song. For the time being his audience, also his work and drinking companions, acknowledge his separation from them, and his performance is approved by the part they play as audience, and his song is similarly approved over a period of time as he claims it as his.

The singer and audience construct emphasises the fluidity and mutuality of the roles, and the environmental, historical, situational and social forces at play upon the construct. The singer is always singer, that is socially accepted, but he actualises the role only in performance. The comparison is analogous to the difference between the Song and the sung song: actualisation of the Song occurs only in performance and it is the sung song which is the Song. Anything else is scholarly hypothesis.

The pub is the most common place for song. It has, in fact, become an institution for those who sing, and a place where hundreds of songs have been passed from one singer to another, where roles have been defined, and aesthetic sanctions made. In the past, different types of singing occurred in different rooms in the pub. The kitchen, taproom or bar was used by the local labouring population, and the best room or lounge (if there was one) was patronised by some husbands with their wives, the farmers, clergy and local tradesmen. Popular and traditional singing took place in the kitchen, whereas in the best room Victorian and Edwardian ballads might be sung by trained or semi-trained singers.

Singing in the Ship and in most local pubs now occurs in the kitchen. The rule used to be that those present must sing a song, recite a poem or pay for a gallon of beer ('sing, say or pay'), and in practice the performance of instrumental music also fulfilled the demand. Thus the people entertained themselves. Cyril Poacher says:

At that time of day when there weren't nothing, no television or not,

> there used to be sing, recite or pay for a gallon, and I don't pay for any gallons, I always used to sing, that's how it used to be . . . They had the option sing or pay for a gallon, but there weren't many pay for a gallon. They'd get up and if they could only say it, they'd get up. Nearly every night of the week . . . and you'd get them right the way round and they sing, sing something or say something to the best of their ability rather than pay.[1]
>
> *Ben Ling.* There weren't many paid for it . . . they didn't wait to pay . . . they used to sing and try and do their best. Used to do it all right, too. They all got to know some old song.[2]

A singsong was common almost every night in these pubs before the Second World War, and without fail on pay nights, weekends and holidays. The sing, say, or pay for a gallon system assured the pub-goers of entertainment, and encouraged conformity to the performance requirements of the song tradition. It is difficult to know whether anyone ever did pay for a gallon, and given the poverty in which most of these men spent most of their lives, it seems likely that the 'sing, say or pay' formula was rhetorical, and chiefly a means of coercing the diffident or bloody-minded into making their contribution to the gathering:

> If you get an old boy, he got a family of children, he was getting about thirty bob a week, in them days which I'm talking about [early 1930s], that wasn't a lot of money, although beer was cheap, I'd agree, that wasn't a lot of money, so he boned up a song and he sung it.[3]

In the Ship, Wickets Richardson acted as chairman and used a pegging board to call 'order'. In the Snape pubs and elsewhere, those involved in the singing took turns to perform, and called on each other with requests, encouragement and challenges. Most local pub-going men had a functional repertoire which prevented excess expenditure on beer, and some amongst them held more definitely the role of singer. Nowadays, it is mainly the latter who perform.

These specialists sometimes took part in singing competitions, some of which they arranged themselves in response to challenges, sometimes for reward, or for entertainment. Stories are told about the Ling brothers in Blaxhall (including the fathers of Geoff and Percy Ling) who sat in the Ship and sang against one another, one winning by a process of elimination. Percy Ling describes this informally organised type of competition which, like that between his father and uncles, was judged on the number and recall of songs performed by each participant:

> I remember one Saturday dinnertime I was in the Ship, me and Cyril, we was singing down there from twelve o'clock till half past two, we was singing against one another, see who know the most songs. I used to sing and used to sit down and have a drink of beer. 'Ooh', Cyril used to say, 'I can beat that one.' He used to jump up and used to break out.[4]

Some pubs ran their own competitions and presented prizes:

> I was singing at the Woodbridge Wagon [and Horses] . . . I was singing in a singing competition . . . Bloody small I was, and the blokes stood me on a table. I aren't very big now but I was only very small then . . . Do you know what song I sung, and I won the prize, a bottle of whisky, that was 'Sweet Genevieve'.[5]

Outside the pub, other institutions provided opportunities for performance, and for men the most common of these was the quoits team gathering:

> One village played another . . . on a meadow, . . . and they'd have a nine gallon cask of beer, and they'd play quoits, you see, and when that was over, they'd all get together and they had the beer and they had a singsong then, one against the other, and sang all the old songs till the beer runned out, you see then when they come to Iken, they'd do the same – have a cask of beer and play there and sing again, you see. That's how . . . they made their own enjoyment, you see.[6]

The Men's Club, British Legion, darts matches and concert parties also provided social opportunities for song performance. Singing is now restricted to informal gatherings in the pub, and occasional performances at meetings of the Legion and Old Folks' Clubs, and at harvest suppers.

The first of the 26 singers whom I was to get to know in the Snape and Blaxhall area was Bob Hart. He is a tall well-built man who does not often glow with happiness, but who has a surprising wit under his apparent reserve. He is a careful and patient informant, and a willing singer of songs. The second singer with whom I came into contact is Percy Ling, born in Blaxhall, who now lives in the same street as Bob and is his friend and drinking companion. I met him at the Golden Key, Snape, when I was with Bob, and he soon became friendly. A week later on a Sunday evening, I took Bob and Percy Ling to the Butley Oyster, where there was another local singer, Percy Webb from Tunstall. He warmly invited me to visit him and promised to talk to me about all of his songs, if I would take him to the Blaxhall Ship on the following Friday night, 19 July 1974. It was there in the Ship, on my first visit, that I got to know Cyril Poacher.

During early conversations with Bob Hart, I asked if there were other singers living locally, and at first he said that there were not. A month later, he said that they were 'not what you would call singers';[7] and yet another month later, he said they were all 'just country people singing songs'.[8] My first impression of the singing tradition, then, was that it had almost ceased and that Bob was the only local singer of any standing. I do not think that he meant to mislead me, as at first he confused my interest in the tradition with an interest in art music, and preferred to name Benjamin Britten and Peter Pears as local musicians[9] rather than the singers of whom I was eventually to hear.

For Bob, traditional singing has been a spontaneous and unself-conscious activity, not immediately identifiable as a feature of local life. On 25 June 1974, he recited to me a poem he had composed 46 years earlier:

Our life at Snape perhaps is dull
Compared with life in town,
Yet in a way we have a busy time.
Just give me your attention
If you have the time to spare,
And village life I'll tell to you in rhyme.
First, our Association we ask each one to join,
Providing they have reached the age sixteen.
This with its winter programme, its host of summer games,
A great asset to village life it means.
We have the Women's Institute
With meetings held each month
From which the ladies get a lot of fun,
And at their Christmas party
When the menfolk they invite,

None of us can help but say 'Well done'.
We have the British Legion,
For ex-servicemen to join,
Old pals who fought together o'er the foam,
Still clinging to that comradeship
They formed in days of war –
Somehow it's not so real
Now we're at home.
We run a dance quite often,
Whist drives and concerts too,
Old folk and children's parties once a year.
We have a football club, a tennis club,
A swimming club as well
As pubs from which we can obtain our beer.
But the chief attraction for the men
Is at the village club,
With membership just turned three score and ten,
And every evening you will find
A gathering of us there
And games that are too numerous for my pen.
On this I hope you'll gather
When you come to think it out
That life at Snape is not exactly tame,
If there's people in the village
Who think the life is dull
I think they've only got themselves to blame.

Here, he stresses the homogeneity of the village but does not give mention to singing, perhaps because this list of organisations and clubs seems more directly indicative of vitality and progress than mention of the ordinary, the self-made and the spontaneous. There is a suggestion that the singing was an integral, very enjoyable, but not necessarily remarkable aspect of local life, and not recognised as an activity as such because of its sheer absorption into the most familiar fabric of village society. Singers, too, like the singing itself, were also not consciously identified by him at first, since they existed primarily as acquaintances, in whom singing was one thread of the multistranded relationships in which local men found themselves.

His notion of local singing habits is a historical and flexible one. He remembers the old days of segregation in the Golden Key when the men stayed in the bar and the women came out of the back kitchen only for dances, he remembers step-dancing on the stone floor, and total participation in singing. He recognises the breakdown in village life brought about by the opening of the society during the wars, and he recognises the growth of the folk clubs. His own singing has had to find new audiences in Old Folks' Clubs, and the Saxmundham Home for the Blind, because the regularity with which he could once sing at the pub is altered now by the restrictions of his age and by the different needs of the pub patrons and their no longer local make-up.

As my field-work continued, and my absorption into the local community commenced, I began to understand Bob's place in a local tradition, a place that is certainly unique because of the size of his repertoire, but that is bonded and intertwined with the tradition. I had now to explore his social role, which I had not yet witnessed outside his home or the Folk Club, and to explore the complementary roles of the other singers in this tradition. In a sense, tradition holds sway over the individuals, and the singers are held in common because of their singing. But it is clear that a continuous give and take is going on, in that there is no tradition without those who comprise it and who are given status and function by it. They dictate what the tradition is by their being, and the tradition is an abstract generalisation of their singing behaviour, but their singing behaviour is likewise influenced and in some way moulded by the singing behaviour of their now-dead singing ancestors. And transmission not only of songs but also of dramatic delivery, stance, style, and so on, is evidence of tradition.

Bob has centred his life on his daily visits to the pub. Until his illness in the winter of 1975-6, he went, in the summer, to the Golden Key, Snape, almost every lunch-time except Saturdays, when he went to the Crown Inn, Snape. Every second Friday night he went to the Leiston Folk Club, other week nights he sometimes went to the Key, and on Saturday nights to the Crown. In winter, the lunchtime visits were maintained, but the early darkness and cold discouraged him from the evening walk down the hill to the pub and the hard walk back up after closing time.

His visit to Blaxhall on 19 July is not unusual since only old age prevents the mobility that used to allow regular pub circuiting, and the ties with regular customers at the Ship have obviously never been broken. In any case, he is able to go there several times a year when rides are offered. Percy Ling's sons play in a country and western band, and Percy often goes with them to local pubs when they play, but his youngest son will take him in any case to the Blaxhall Ship on Friday nights and Sunday lunch-times, or to the George and Dragon in

Farnham. Percy and Bob are good friends, and it is probably because of Bob that he has gone to the Leiston Folk Club a few times, but he prefers a night in the Ship and is a regular customer at the Golden Key, Snape. Percy Webb has a regular pub routine. He goes to the Butley Oyster every Sunday night,[10] to Leiston and Blaxhall on alternate Fridays, to the Gardener's Arms Folk Club in Ipswich on Thursdays, and sometimes to Snape on Saturdays. He has many young friends with cars and he is popular and in demand, so he has maintained a large degree of mobility. Of these three singers, therefore, the oldest is not able to travel as easily or as often as the others who have family or friends in the area with cars; Bob is also a less comic character than Percy or Webby and his more serious attitudes may discourage many invitations. He is prone to illness and tiredness more than the two younger singers, and although he is valued and respected by the Leiston Folk Club, he is a man who does not invite such open affection and camaraderie as Percy with his incisive and bawdy humour, and Webby with his appealing and comical friendliness. In all cases, though, the situation at the Blaxhall Ship is a familiar and enjoyable one, and one in which Bob wishes to be involved more often.

The Evening Begins

During this week of July, I am staying with Bob's daughter-in-law, with whom he lives, and after tea and after Bob has watched 'Crossroads',[11] he lifts himself out of his chair and goes whistling into his bedroom to get ready, although he is already wearing his customary dark suit. We drive two hundred yards down The Glebes and stop at Percy Ling's semi-detached house. He emerges in sports coat, tie, white shirt, and flared blue jeans, smoking a Woodbine. These clothes are certainly different from his work clothes, for he wears cast-off American khaki at other times, and does not bother to shave or comb his hair when he is staying at home. When Webby gets into the car at Tunstall, he radiates the aroma of after-shave lotion, and wears purple socks, a coloured cravat and shirt, sports coat and trousers, and his inevitable cap. The two-mile journey from Percy Webb's old cottage is by farm roads, and the three men talk together about their health, their singing experiences and outings, as well as the treachery of the road we are following to the Ship. Cyril Poacher, whom we are to meet inside, is dressed in his work clothes, except that his cowman's gumboots have been replaced by shoes. I have never seen him in any other attire; it is as customary to him as Bob's suit is to Bob.

The saloon bar at the Ship is oblong, painted a creamy white and unevenly yellowed by nicotine, with heavy ceiling beams and a large open fireplace.

Figure 1: Plan of the Blaxhall Ship Saloon Bar

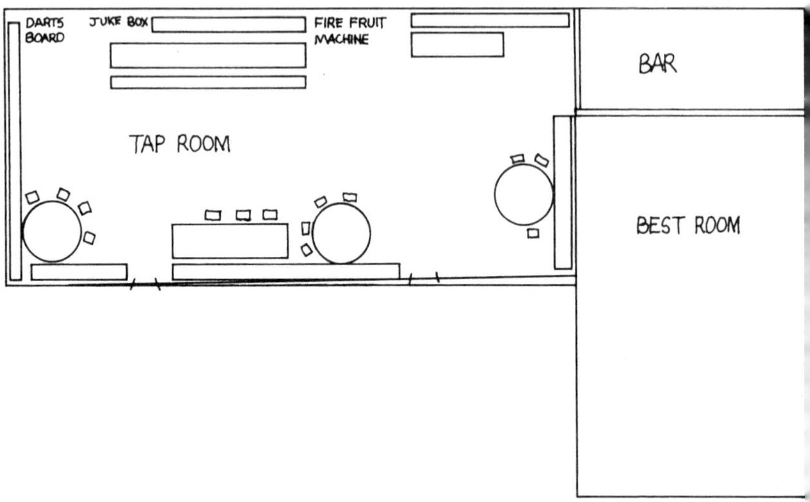

On this summer's evening, there is no fire, but the lights are bright although the dusk has not yet settled. At 7.30 p.m., the room is not full, but there are probably twenty people present, most of them men. I ask Bob which one is Cyril Poacher, and approach him and ask him if I may record his singing during the evening. He is shy, nodding his head in confirmation of what he says, serious about obliging me. We soon sit down, and Cyril has a place of his own against the wall running to the door from the bar, but he also sits with us for a time. During this half-hour, the four men talk about how much they each get paid for songs. Their conversation expresses a need to feel wanted, sought after and valued, and to be equal in the eyes of each other. There is a certain one-upmanship going on that is natural to any situation where people recount their successes. Percy Ling, who is not as involved in clubs or in recording, has a smaller number of experiences to relate, but he maintains his participation and equality in the situation by expressing disbelief or horror at the sums of money quoted, and by joking with Bob,

Cyril and Webby. His use of dramatic irony is taunting and he hooks them without their recognising his ploy. Asides to me like, 'Oooh, you want to watch him, he's a rum bugger' serve to give him the upper hand temporarily, if not completely. The blow comes when Cyril, sitting with us, quietly declares he has been offered fifty pounds to make a record.[12] All three can now express disbelief, but he looks contented and confident, buys his round of drinks, and goes back to his seat.

Figure 2: Seating Arrangements at the Blaxhall Ship, Friday 19 July 1974

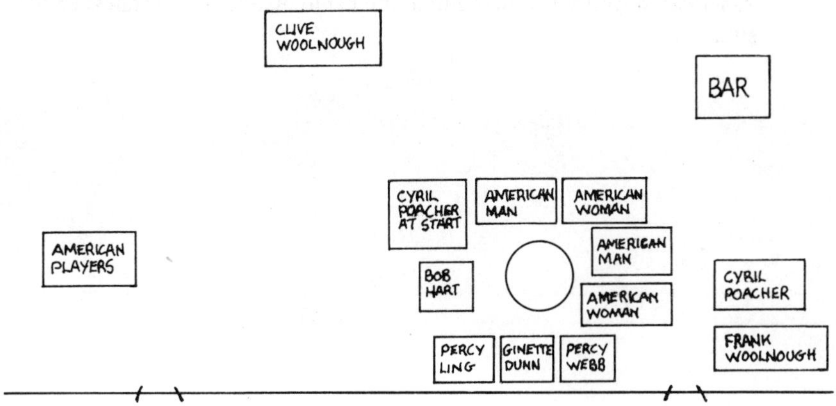

By now, most of the people who are to be audience on this occasion have arrived. We have been joined at our table by two American couples who are from the base at Bentwaters. They are all aged about thirty, and are friendly, appreciative and quiet people. Seated next to Cyril are two local men, one about 55, and the other Frank Woolnough, a farm labourer, aged about 71. By the fruit machine and the fireplace are a dozen more, two with their wives. Lenny Savage comes at about 8.30 p.m. for an hour and a half. The bench alongside us is occupied by two middle-aged couples, local, with whom Bob talks a little. At the bench near the juke-box are six local young men, one of them Frank Woolnough's son, who is to play an important part later on. Near the darts board is a group of eight American servicemen.

Throughout the evening, the younger men play darts intermittently, and Cyril and others play the fruit machine. The American servicemen include two musicians who play guitar and banjo, and would like to play them almost continuously. They appear to be entirely insensitive to public feeling against their attempted monopolisation. Naturally, they are supported by their table companions, and if they would allow the singers a fair amount of time, probably they would be enjoyed each time they play. Instead, they strike up a tune as soon as they or a singer has finished, do not take turns, and have to be quietened. The audience as a whole seems to regard a rotation of performers as the norm, and there are signs of hostility until some order is established, but the American singers with their guitar and banjo maintain a blindness to the situation.

THE SONGS

Singing in the Ship Inn, Blaxhall, 19 July 1974

Cyril Poacher	Nutting Girl
Bob Hart	Comrades
Percy Webb	Old Farmer's Servant
Percy Ling	Boy with No Shoes
Cyril Poacher	Joe Moggins
Bob Hart	What a Funny Little Place to Have One
Percy Webb	Oak and the Ash (incomplete)
	Wheel Your P'rambulator
Cyril Poacher	Flash Company
Bob Hart	On a Summer's Night
	Banks of Sweet Primroses
Cyril Poacher	Black Velvet Band
Percy Ling	Flanagan's Band
Percy Webb	Old Shep
Bob Hart	Female Cabin Boy
Percy Webb	Sailor Boy
Percy Ling	Cobbler
Frank Woolnough	London Apprentice Boy
Percy Ling	Don't Do It Tonight
Percy Webb	Wild Colonial Boy
Bob Hart	Underneath the Apron

NUTTING GIRL

as sung by Cyril Poacher, Blaxhall Ship, 19 July 1974

1. Come all you jovial fellers
Come listen to my song,
It is a little ditty
And it won't contain you long.
It's of a fair young damsel
She lived down in Kent
Arose one summer's morning
She a-nutting went.

With my fal-lal to me ral-tal-lal
Wack for the dear old day
And what few nuts that poor girl had
She threw them all away.

2. It's of a brisk young farmer
Was ploughing of his land
He called unto his horses
To bid them gently stand.
As he sit down upon his plough
All for a song to sing
His voice was so melodious
Made the valleys ring.

3. It's of a fair young damsel
She was nutting in the wood
His voice was so melodious
Charmed her as she stood.
She could no longer stay
And what few nuts she had poor girl
She threw them all away.

4. She then came to young Johnny
He sit on his plough
She said young man I really feel
I cannot tell you how.
He took her to some shady broom
And there he laid her down
Said she 'Young man I think I feel
The world go round and round.'

5. Now come all you young women
   This warning by me take –
   If you should a-nutting go
   Please get home in time,
   For if you should stay too late
   To hear the plougboy sing
   You might have a young farmer
   To nurse up in the Spring.

COMRADES

as sung by Bob Hart, Blaxhall Ship, 19 July 1974

1. We in childhood played together
   My dear comrade, Jack and I,
   We would fight each other's battles,
   To each other's aid we'd fly,
   And in boyish scrapes and troubles
   You would find us everywhere,
   Where one went the other followed,
   None could part us for we were

Comrades, comrades,
Ever since we were boys,
Sharing each other's sorrows
Sharing each other's joys,
Comrades when manhood was (near us)
(dawning)
Faithful whate'er may betide,
When I was in danger me darling old comrade
Was there by my side.

2. When just budding into manhood,
I yearned for a soldier's life,
Day and night I'd dream of glory,
Longing for the battle strife.
I said 'Jack, I'll be a soldier,
'Neath the red the white the blue,
Goodbye Jack,' said he, 'No never,
If you go well I go too.'

3. I enlisted, Jack came with me,
And our ups and downs we shared,
For a time our life was easy
But at last war was declared.
England's flag had been insulted,
We were ordered to the front,
And the regiment we served in
Had to . . . the battle front.

4. In the night the foe came over
And we went for them like hell, [twice]
It was rifle-butt, and bayonet,
And we drove them back pell mell.

There was one chap had me cornered,
I was helpless, wounded sore,
But 'twas Jack that came between us
And my pal was mine no more.

OLD FARMER'S SERVANT

as sung by Percy Webb, Blaxhall Ship, 19 July 1974

1. When I was a master's servant
   I used to have some fun
   In minding my master's business
   When my master was not at home,
   And when my master did go out
   To view the fields so gay
   I was up to the door
   With my rap-a-tat-tat,
   Yes either by night or day,
   Yes either by night or day.

2. It happened on a Thursday
   My master to market did go
   He asked me to mind his business
   As if he was at home.
   As soon as my master's back was turned
   I blundered out of the barn
   For I's up to the door
   With my rap-a-tat-tat
   And sure I thought no harm,
   And sure I thought no harm.

3. Now who should come to the door but my misteress
She bade me to come in.
I complained of the bellyache
She gave to me some gin.
She bade me drink it up, my boys,
With never a word to say
That I'd been there
With my rap-a-tat-tat
And to bed we went straight way
And to bed we went straight way.

4. So there we laid a-sporting
For three half hours or more,
The missus enjoyed the sport so well
I thought she'd never give o'er.
'You've won my heart forever,' she cried,
'My husband no more for me,
For he can't come with his
Rap-a-tat-tat
Not half so well as thee,
Not half so well as thee.'

5. Now my master returned from market
He asked me how I got on.
I said I minded his business
As if he was at home.
He ordered me O ale, my boys,
But little did he know
That I'd been there
With my rap-a-tat-tat –
If he had of he'd never done so,
If he had of he'd never done so.

BOY WITH NO SHOES
as sung by Percy Ling, Blaxhall Ship, 19 July 1974

1. Now as I was a-walking
   Up fair London Street
   I met a poor boy
   Who'd no shoes for his feet.
   Being's I had money
   And plenty to spare,
   I popped in a fruit shop
   And I bought him a pear
   Toodle ooo, toodle aye
   You ought to have seen him eat it.

2. Now I once knew a man
   He was tattered and torn,
   He was mowing the grass
   On a gentleman's lawn.
   When the door opened wide
   And a lady so fair
   Said, 'Come round the back
   O it's much longer there.'
   Toodle ooo Toodle aye
   You ought to have seen him run round.

3. Now I once had a dream
   And to heaven did go
   Where did you come from?
   They wanted to know.

'I came from Blaxhall.'
Old Peter did stare,
Said, 'Come round the back,
You're the first bugger from there.'
Toodle ooo toodle aye
You ought to have seen me run round.

'This is one I like' –

4. Now I called on my sweetheart,
Her name was Miss Brown,
She was having a bath
And she could not come down.
I said 'Slip on something
Come down half a tick.'
She slipped on the soap
And she did come down quick.
Toodle ooo toodle aye
You ought to have seen her come down.

5. Now a nasty black eye
Had my Uncle Jim,
He said someone threw a tomata
At him.
'Tomatas don't hurt,'
I said with a grin,
'O yes they do when they
Come in a tin.'
Toodle ooo toodle aye
And a nasty black eye had he got.

6. Now put four young ladies
Round four cups of tea,
They'll talk of more scandal than
Ever you'll see,
But put four young men
Round a barrel of beer,
They'll talk of more work
They can do in a year.
Toodle ooo toodle aye
I've proved it so I ought to know.

JOE MOGGINS

as sung by Cyril Poacher, Blaxhall Ship, 19 July 1974

1. My name is Joe Moggins,
A farmer am I,
I once courted a pretty girl,
Who felt rather shy.
I fell in the water tank,
Got nearly wet through,
Then she said, 'Joe, my love,
Won't you come in and dry yourself?'
I'm a careless young lad,
I don't care if I do.
Fal-a-ral lad-i-ty
Fal-a-ral lad-i-ty
Fal-a-ral laddy ri
Fal-a ral day.

2. I went down to the kitchen
I made things all right
Ten pound of fat tiger
I popped out of sight.
Then she said, 'Joe,
Have a dumpling or two,'
I'm a careless young lad
I don't care if I do,
etc.

3. I hugged her, I squeezed her
Till lover's delight,
She wanted for to get married
All on that same night.
Then in came the parson,
Book in his hand,
And from the book these very words said,
'Better or worse, take her and go,'
I'm a careless young lad,
I don't care if I do.
etc.

4. And now we are married
And happy live we,
We've got two little children

To hop round our knee.
Then she said 'Joe,
We'll have a dozen or two,'
I'm a careless young lad,
I don't care if I do.

etc.

5. And now my song's over
I hope I've pleased all,
I couldn't sing another
If you were for to call.
You've heard one before
And this one makes two,
I'm a careless young lad,
I don't care where I go.

etc.

FUNNY LITTLE PLACE TO HAVE ONE
as sung by Bob Hart, Blaxhall Ship, 19 July 1974

1. Now I know a fella who has just got wed,
Only this morning unto him I said,
'Where are you going to spend, old man,
Your honeymoon along with Mary Anne?'
He whispered in my ear,
'We shall spend our honeymoon
In a railway tunnel, we can save a bit of rent,
But I couldn't
What a funny little place to have one,
What a funny little place, I say.
You can't see each other for it must be dark,
You can't have a cuddle or a nice old lark.
I've heard of people going to a hotel or a flat,
Somewhere on the quiet to spend their honeymoon,
But never in a place like that.

2. Poor ma lost 'er nose the other day,
Seeking a bad escape of gas, they say,
She went to the 'orspital along with pa,
They stuck an artificial nose on ma,
But it would not stick on
Where a boko ought to be,
So the doctor made a hole just a little lower down,
And he stuck it on her chin, you see.
What a funny little place to have one,
What a funny little place, I say,
O baby clutches it and grabs it O
Think it is a little feeding bottle, it's true,
It's like some big tomata
O it is so red and fat,
I've seen a lot of funny noses in my time,
But I've never seen a nose like that.

3. Now my brother, Tom, he joined the volunteers,
When he went away we gave three cheers,
In his uniform he did look grand,
Till he came home on his furloe and
He had his Scotch kilt on
And his Scots cap on his head,
But the way that he wore that little fillet bag

All the neighbours looked at him and said,
What a funny little place to have one,
What a funny little place, I say,
O there it was hanging round his neck, O dear,
Like a bunch of whiskers only not round here,
Our servant, she said, 'Tommy, I'll get your pussy cat,
No girl'll want to stroke your little fillet bag
If you wear it in a place like that.'

4. Now I shan't forget the day when I took Mother Brown
Into the country and we both sat down,
In a field where it was full of hay,
Don't I recollect that summer's day,
She said a mosquito had got down her back you see,
And she wanted me to try and get it out,
But I shouted, 'Goodness gracious me,
What a funny little place to have one,
What a funny little place,' I say,
She said, 'It's now down the middle of me back,
O do put your finger down and try and get it Jack,'
I shouted, 'Holy Moses, you are a saucy cat,
I'd do it in a minute were it anywhere else,
But I couldn't in a place like that.'

WHEEL YOUR P'RAMBULATOR
as sung by Percy Webb, Blaxhall Ship, 19 July 1974

1. Wheel your p'rambulator, John,
Be careful how you go,
Don't get riled,
Mind the child,
Wheel it nice and slow,
When you turn the corner, John,
When you cross the road,
Cock the front wheels up a bit
And over goes your load.

2. Now first time I took the baby out
I took it in the pram,
I turned the bloody thing upside down,
I don't know where I am.
I cracked the baby's head
And I took a bit off its nose,
And now I daren't go home again
For fright of my wife's full blows,
So wheel your p'rambulator
etc.

3. Now if you have a tooth ache
You're suffering with pain,
Never go to the dentist
For that's a silly game,
Just fill your mouth with water, lads,
Been mixed with castor oil,
And sit upon the fire awhile,
Until it begins to boil
etc.

4. Now if you have a jawing wife
Get her in the brook,
Take her out and throw her in
To see if she can float,
If she go down and up three times
Then you sit and think,
You take your oars and row away
And leave the old bugger to sink
etc.

FLASH COMPANY

as sung by Cyril Poacher, Blaxhall Ship, 19 July 1974

1. Once I loved a young girl as I loved my life
   And to keep her in flash company has ruined my life,
   Flash company, my boys, like a great many more,
   If it hadn't been for flash company I should never a been so poor.

   So it's take the yellow handkerchief
   In rememberance of me
   And tie it round your neck love
   In flash company.
   Flash company, my boys,
   Like a great many more,
   If it hadn't a been for flash company
   I should never a been so poor.

2. Once I had a colour as red as a rose,
   And now it's as pale as the lily that grows,
   Like the rose in the garden with all my colour gone,
   You can see what I am coming to through loving that one.

3. So it's fiddling and it's dancing have been my delight
   To keep her in flash company has ruined my life,
   Flash company, my boys, like a great many more,
   If it hadn'ta been for flash company I should never a been so poor.

ON A SUMMER'S NIGHT

as sung by Bob Hart, Blaxhall Ship, 19 July 1974

On a summer's night while out astrolling,
Met a pretty maid with her eyes a-rolling,
First she looked at me, then I looked at she,
Wasn't it delightful bliss?
Very soon refreshments she suggested,
Little drops of port we very soon tested,
Fella big and strong, quickly came along,
Kindly gave me this.
What for? Can't guess?
Come a-listen and I'll tell you,
I was out last night with that man's wife,
He came along and caused some strife,
He hit me, he punched me,
Right on my bloomin' jaw.
He gave me, don't you see,
What what what what for.

BANKS OF SWEET PRIMROSES

as sung by Bob Hart, Blaxhall Ship, 19 July 1974

1. As I strolled out one summer's morning
   To view the fields and to take the air,
   Down by the banks of sweet primroses
   There I beheld a most loverly maid.

2. Three long steps O I took up to her,
   Not knowing me O she passed me by,
   I stepped up to her thinking to view her,
   She appeared to be like some virtuous bride.

3. I said, 'Fair maiden, where are you going?
   On what occasion all this thy grief?
   I'll make you as happy as any lady
   If you will grant me some small relief.'

4. 'Stand back, stand back, O you are deceitful,
   You are a false deceitful man, 'tis plain,
   It's you that caused my poor heart to wander
   To give me comfort would be all in vain.

5. I'll go away to some lonesome valley
   And there no man knows you'll e'er me find,
   Until the pretty birds change their voices,
   And every moment shall blow boistrious winds.'

6. Now all ye fair maids who go acourting,
   Just pay attention to what I say,
   There's many a dark and a cloudy morning
   Turns out to be a bright and sunny day.

FLANAGAN'S BAND

as sung by Percy Ling, Blaxhall Ship, 19 July 1974

1. Now of all the bands that ever I've heard,
   And I think I've heard a few,
   But with your kind permission
   I'll describe one unto you,
   But before I do I'll let you all know
   And I'll give you to understand
   The credit is due to old Ireland
   And the boys in old Flanagan's band.

   And the drums went bang
   And the cymbals clanged
   And the cornet played the way,
   Upon the floor a dear old 'ore
   Whenever the pipes began

There was Ali and Cushy, Cushy Kilarney
And Micky could hardly stand.
The credit is due to old Ireland
And the boys in old Flanagan's band.

2. Now the Prince of Wales to Dubilin came
To have a jolly spree,
And as the prince walked in the ring
To have a waltz with me,
And as we were waltzing round and round
The music, it was grand,
He swear he'll never leave us
Till he's one of old Flanagan's band

etc.

3. And, and now my song is ended
And I have no more to say,
But with your kind permission I
Will call some other day,
But before I do I'll let you all know
And I'll give you to understand
The credit is due to old Ireland
And the boys of old Flanagan's band

etc.

OLD SHEP

as sung by Percy Webb, Blaxhall Ship, 19 July 1974

When I was a boy and Old Shep was a pup
Over fields and meadows we'd go,
Just a boy and his dog, we were so full of fun,
We grew up together that way.

I remember the time by the old swimming pool
When I would have drowned beyond doubt,
But Old Shep was right there, to my rescue he came,
He jumped in and then pulled me out.

Now the years quickly go and Old Shep has grown old
And his eyesight is fast growing dim,
And the doctor looked at him and then said,
'I can't do no more for him, Jim.'

With trembling hands I picked up my gun
And aimed it at Shep's faithful head,
But I just couldn't do it, I wanted to run,
And wished they would shoot me instead.

He came to my side and looked up at me
And laid his soft head on my knee
And I saw the best friend that a man ever had
And I cried till I scarcely could see.

Now Old Shep has gone where the good doggies go,
And no more with Old Shep will I roam,
But if dogs have a heaven there's one thing I know,
Old Shep has a wonderful home.

FEMALE CABIN BOY

as sung by Bob Hart, Blaxhall Ship, 19 July 1974

1. O it's of a fair young maiden as you will understand,
   Who had a mind for roving into a foreign land,
   So dressed in man's apparel she boldly did appear,
   She engaged with a captain to serve him for a year.

2. She engaged with a captain his cabin boy to be,
   The wind was in his favour and he put out to sea,
   The captain's lady being on board, O it was to her joy
   That her husband had engaged with this female cabin boy.

3. Her cheeks were red like roses and with her sidelock curl,
   The sailors often laughed and said she looked just like a girl,
   But eating captain's biscuits her colour did destroy
   And the waist did swell on pretty Nell, the female cabin boy.

4. Was in the Bay of Biscay our gallant ship did plough,
   One night aboard the vessel there was an awful row,
   They tumbled from their hammocks 'cos their rest it did destroy,
   It was all about the moaning of that female cabin boy.

5. 'O doctor, O doctor', the cabin boy did cry,
   The sailors swore by all the gods the cabin boy would die,
   The doctor came a-running and a-laughing at the fun
   That a cabin boy should either have a daughter or a son.

6. Now when the sailors heard of this they all began to swear
   It did belong to none of them they solemnly declared.
   The captain's lady standing near to her husband said so coy
   'It's either you or I betrayed that female cabin boy.'

SAILOR BOY

as sung by Percy Webb, Blaxhall Ship, 19 July 1974

1. Was on one stormy winter's night
   The snow laid on the ground,
   A sailor boy stood on the quay,
   His ship was outward bound.
   His sweetheart standing by his side
   Shed many a silent tear,
   And as he pressed her to his breast
   He whispered in her ear.

   'Farewell, farewell my own true love,
   This parting gives me pain,
   I'll be your own true guiding star
   When I return again,
   My thoughts shall be of you, of you,
   When the storm is raging high
   Farewell my love, remember me,
   Your faithfull sailor boy.'

2. And with the gale the ship set sail,
   He kissed his love goodbye,
   She watched the craft till out of sight
   Till the tears keeped in her eyes,
   She prayed to him in heaven above

To guide him on his way
And the loving words he spoke to her
Re-echoed o'er the bay

etc.

3. And with that gale the ship returned
With her loved sailor boy,
He died whilst on the voyage home,
The flag was half-mast high.
And when his comrades came on shore,
Told her that he was dead
A letter he had wrote to her
The last one sadly read,

'Farewell, farewell my own true love
You'll not see me no more
I soon will be o'er storm and sea
On that eternal shore
I hope to meet you in this land
That land beyond the sky
Where you will never be parted from
Your faithful sailor boy.'

COBBLER
as sung by Percy Ling, Blaxhall Ship, 19 July 1974

1. Now my name it is Fagin the cobbler,
I've been cobbling all of my life,
I've been trying to earn a shilling
To take home to my darling young wife.

While I keep twine, twine twine twiddle twine
Twine twine twiddle all day
With my a wack for the riddle all addy
With my wack for the riddle all day, pom pom.

2. Now my wife she is spending my money,
As fast as I'm bringing it in,
She's spending it mopping up beer
Down at the old Sheep Inn, and I'll keep etc.

3. Now my wife, she has turned a teetotaller
She swears she won't mop any more
So both of us started our savings
Our money by galore, while I keep etc.

LONDON APPRENTICE BOY
as sung by Frank Woolnough, Ship Inn, 19 July 1974

When I to my master's . . . [inaudible]
To rob and to murder him it was my full intent.
I took three hundred sovereigns, the knife I threw away,
For he was a master good and kind to a London 'prentice boy.

Fourteen days after, my trial it come on,
Brought before those magistrates to right a bit of wrong,
And she was dressed in silks and satins and so did me appoint,
For she tried to swear the life away of a London 'prentice boy.

My sister came and spoke to me, the only friend I had,
My parents were both dead and gone and in the grave laid low,
But I was sentenced then for life with scorn,
. . . [inaudible] to a London 'prentice boy.

Now all you young apprentices
. . . [inaudible] rue the day
They leave you as they left me
To blow the candle out.

as sung by Dick Woolnough, 12 The Glebes, Snape,
30 October 1974

'Twas at the hour of twelve at night I to my master went,
All for to rob and murder him, it was my full intent.
I took five hundred sovereigns, the knife I threw away,
He was a master good and kind to a London 'prentice boy.

Twas on the fourteenth of July my trial did come on,
I was brought before the bench to prove a bit of wrong.
He was dressed in silks and satins and did me so annoy,
He tried to swear the life away of a London 'prentice boy.

And I was sent across the sea, likewise five hundred more,
Some did weep and some did moan, my heart was bitter sore.
The governor he then noticed me, and he gave me slight employ,
Twas then I thought of that happy day when a London 'prentice boy.

DON'T DO IT TONIGHT

as sung by Percy Ling, Blaxhall Ship, 19 July 1974

1. Don't do it tonight, the moon is shining bright,
   The little stars are twinkeling in the sky, O my,
   Somebody's watching you, watching you on high,
   Let's go round the corner and have a bit on the sly.

2. I went a-gathering water cress, water cress, water cress,
   Down by the old mill stream.
   Instead of gathering water cress I got her in a hell of a mess
   Down by the old mill stream.
   Don't do it tonight etc.

3. We went a-gathering roses, roses, roses,
   Down by the old mill stream,
   Instead of gathering roses I lifted up her clotheses
   Down by the old mill stream. etc.

4. We went a-gathering barley, barley, barley,
   Down by the old mill stream.
   Instead of gathering barley I introduced old Charlie
   Down by the old mill stream. etc.

WILD COLONIAL BOY

as sung by Percy Webb, Blaxhall Ship, 19 July 1974

1. There was a wild colonial boy, Jack Duggan was his name;
   He's bred and born in Ireland in a place called Castlemain;
   He was his father's only son, his mother's pride and joy,
   And he set out from his parents from that wild colonial boy.

2. At the early age of sixteen years he then the navy joined,
   And to Australia's sunny shore he was inclined to roam,
   He robbed the rich to help the poor,
   A terror to Australia was the wild colonial boy.

3. One morning on the prairie as Jackie was riding along,
   He was listening to the mocking bird, singing his little song,
   Out sprang three mounted soldiers, Kelly, Davis, and Fitzroy
   And they all set out to capture him, that wild colonial boy.

4. 'Surrender now, Jack Duggan, you see it's three to one,
   Surrender now Jack Duggan, you daring highwayman,'
   He drew two pistols from his belt and proudly aimed them high,
   'I'll fight but never surrender,' cried that wild colonial boy.

5. He fired a shot to Kelly which brought him to the ground,
   And turning round to Davis he received his fatal wound,
   A bullet pierced his proud young heart from the pistol of Fitzroy,
   And that was how they captured him, the wild colonial boy.

UNDERNEATH THE APRON
as sung by Bob Hart, Blaxhall Ship, 19 July 1974

1. Pretty Little Sarah, a-sweeping up the home,
   Had to loose her apron strings to make a bit of room.
   Her master, he came to her and unto her did say,
   'What is that you have got underneath your apron?'

2. 'O nothing sir, O nothing, nothing sir,' cried she,
   'Nothing but a musilin gown me mother made for me,
   I'd nowhere to put it to keep it nice and clean
   So I tucked it snuggily underneath me apron.'

3. A few months after a baby boy was born,
   Born without a father, without a home at all,
   Her master he came to her and unto her did say,
   'I see now what you had underneath your apron.

4. Was it by a tinker, was it by a clown?
   Was it by a soldier lad who fights for England's crown?'
   'No, it was by a sailor who ride the angry sea
   And he tucked it snuggily underneath me apron.'

5. 'Was it in the kitchen, was it in the hall?
   Was it in the parlour or in the house at all?'
   'No it was in the garden up against the wall
   Where he tucked it snuggily underneath me apron.'

6. Now all you single ladies wherever you may be,
   Never trust a sailor lad an inch above the knee;
   If you do you'll rue the day he'll leave you in the lurch
   After he has tucked it underneath your apron.

THE SINGING

At about 8.30 p.m. the singing begins with Cyril Poacher being asked by a few of the men to sing 'The Nutting Girl'. His reaction is to stand immediately, his beer on the table in front of him, facing his audience, hands in pockets. His face becomes very lively and bright and, not looking anyone in the eye but turning his head upwards, he begins. His first note is prolonged, a way of drawing attention, and it is also the introduction to the lines which refer directly to the audience present, and to the song situation. Cyril's energetic and pronounced tremolo on the syllables he accents invites close listening, and the rhythm is emphatic.

It is important that the song is the first requested since it is one of the few of the entire evening which addresses the audience so directly. Cyril is the most regular customer of the Ship of all the singers present, and it is therefore fitting that he should sing first, invited to do so by some male members of his regular audience, and that he should oblige so willingly, perhaps in recognition of his own special position in the company. It is likely too, that if he is usually a willing singer, then he is more likely to be first called upon. He is associated with 'The Nutting Girl' and, in my experience, is usually asked to sing it whenever singing is taking place in that particular pub.

At the end of his introduction, still sung with energy, he prolongs the last note and then moves into the narrative. The feeling of the sixth line of the verse is that he is making a factual statement, that the cessation of the singing rhythm established in the introduction is deliberately made to bring the song into the realm of truth. Under the guise of reality, the song's sexual fantasy can continue. A few, including Percy Webb, join in with the chorus, which Cyril repeats, with a flourish that is like a short descant to the singing, and which is exclamatory, attention-drawing, and highly rhythmic. This repetition of the first chorus seems to be another way of catching the ear of the audience. In the second verse, the declamatory rhythm of 'His voice was so melodious' is an indication of the power of the ploughboy's singing, and is oral expression of his youth and virility rather than a classical interpretation of his melodious performance. Cyril seems, in his singing, to be able to reproduce the sounds which he describes. The chorus is sung once, and he moves into the third verse. Very clearly the words are enunciated, and there is a line less in this verse so that the sexual suggestion of the last two lines is rapidly reached. Melodic variation from verse to verse is great but established, since Cyril follows almost the identical patterns in his performance of this song on the record, 'Songs of Seduction',[13] recorded before 1961. The variation is therefore comparative rather than formal, and an indication therefore that verse structure may be fairly irrelevant to the singer. He may not know that, when transcribed, this verse has seven lines whereas the others have eight, although he may know that there is a dramatic effect involved in the sound of this verse. The truncation of 'She could no longer stay' suggests that something unusual is about to happen; it stops short and allows a moment of suspense, and the slightly quickened speed of the verse's final two lines is by way of emotional and narrative answer to this. The chorus this time is sung by far more people in the audience, and there is laughter as well. Momentum increases as the seduction draws nearer, a fact now fairly clear to the audience, whose increased participation is heard in the chorus singing and in their vocal reaction to the story. 'He took her to some shady broom' is sung with preliminary and final pauses, the first of which adds suspense, since so far in this verse the ploughboy has been the attracting still centre and she has been the active character, and the last of which allows the audience to express its reaction to his sudden and unmistakable move. Percy Webb gives a hoot of mock prudery, whistles come at the end of the sixth line from men sitting nearby, and Cyril maintains the declamatory pitch and utilises a sexually suggestive euphoric running together of words in the line, 'She said, "Young man I think I feel the world go round and round." ' In Cyril's final verse, the emphases he uses again suggest direct appeal to the audience, from him, and not from any hypothetical creator of the song, and the rhythm he chooses is peculiar to the verse and therefore suggests that it has a special purpose here. Cyril uses some of the stylistic rhetoric of the sermon, suggesting that he is delivering a personal warning, but his rendition of the last two lines is not ponderous and inverts the earlier solemnity in its comedy. This resolution does not appear to take the girl's fate very seriously, but rather to enjoy the sexuality and virility implied. It is in contrast to the mood Cyril sets at the beginning of the verse that the outcome gains humour, and it is the declamatory style which decides favourable reception of the events here presaged. There is loud and prolonged laughter and there are cries of 'Good old boy' amid the applause.

Besides being a good opening song, which involves its audience in its preliminary address and in its declaration that a story is to follow, 'The

Nutting Girl' is a sexual song. What could be more attractive to an audience than a song allowing such varied levels of audience participation: cat-calling, chorus-singing and whistling, and short-lived but jointly experienced sexual fantasy? In the fellowship of the songs, the more that the community of audience and singers experiences together, the better. Since the tradition is by nature tied to the past through the styles of delivery and performance and the ways of learning and transmission, each singsong that occurs is an affirmation of village activities, village beliefs and village knowledge. And each occurrence of the singing thus cocks a snoot at social alienation, change and disintegration.[14] By performing old songs in old ways, the community entertains itself and gives itself a local focus; as each man stands to sing, the spotlight turns on him, and he is dominant for the moment, a receptacle for and expression of traditional practices and values. And it is not only the manner of delivery and audience participation that is of great significance here, but also the reiteration of song content. Since songs are traditionally selected and sung, content is important, and familiarity of content in particular since it invites an ultimate conjunction of singer, song and audience in that the individual takes on the role that is expected of him when his turn comes, and gives to his audience a song which they know in a manner which they honour, and social obligations are thus fulfilled.

Cyril Poacher is in some ways a sober man, but a gleam comes into his eye as he stands to sing this one. He is nobody's idea of the sexually promiscuous, nature-loving, fancy-free, bucolic seducer, and he is shocked on another occasion when I laugh at two of Percy Ling's often-told dirty jokes. He is serious about his singing and how people regard it, since for him the singing role is endowed with value and he takes the spotlight with gravity. But once he has crossed the threshold from audience to performer, he changes. Perhaps he expresses his fantasy life as he sings. His manner would suggest this: in song, there is a quickening of his face, and a more forthright way of confronting the eyes of his audience. The unfixed gaze at the beginning soon becomes animated and moves over its audience, his head moves, his body sways, his eyes are bright, and his face holds back a wide grin.

Bob is asked to sing some five minutes later, after the Americans have been requested to give 'lovely order' by Frank Woolnough's son, Clive.[15] Although Bob sometimes sits to sing in the folk clubs, in pubs the tradition has established a precedent, and he stands with his hands on his hips, facing diagonally across the room towards the bar, with his back half turned towards the Americans. He does not dally when asked to sing, but is prepared to start straight away. However, a few banjo chords are struck, and he becomes disturbed. Clive Woolnough takes the initiative and calls loudly for order, and Bob begins 'Comrades', sung with sustained notes and gentle tone. His style is unobtrusive, lilting, the words and melody always clear, the speed slow and suitable to the content. With each chorus, more people join in. The values of comradeship, faithfulness, patriotism and the willingness to die for others are treated with respect by Bob's quiet singing. The slow clear rhythm of the song touches Percy Ling so that he stops joking and pulling faces at people, and joins in the choruses. He is the first to shout 'Good old Bob' at the end, followed by Webby, before the clapping, quieter this time, begins. Bob's eyes do not waver from the corner above the bar during the song, until he falters, and he is still and utterly undramatic in his delivery: the words are untouched by gesture, facial appeals to the audience, or vocal effects like the staccato, glissando grace notes, and sforzando that Cyril uses. The words are allowed to carry themselves.

The contrast with the previous song is as marked as it could be. 'Comrades' is perhaps chosen for that reason, because it expands the range of emotions being shared, although it is at the time one of Bob's favourites. He seems to revive a group of four or five songs every few weeks, to perform them whenever he sings publicly, and then to assemble another group. There is a fantasy element in the song, which idealises friendship and romanticises it, waylaying tragedy by the noble act of sacrifice. Bob's own gruelling experiences in the First World War probably have much to do with his inclusion of this song in his repertoire. It is an easier expression of the pain of war than a description of the sheer waste and butchery which he hesitatingly recalls in conversation:

> 'Course, they couldn't see you to take aim but they very often used to shoot over your trench, yes. And rats, rats as big as cats. I never want to see anything like it any more. You see, this last war, well they had their misery I know, but they never knew what it was to march from one spot to another, miles and miles you'd march, if they wanted you in another position . . . No wars are worth anything. That's something I don't – well, of course, I talk about it more *now*, but that's more when us old ones get together, and something'll bring the old memory up, but, ah, for years, I never used to mention the war, no . . . Cheap labour, that was.[16]

As he sings calmly, the war becomes bearable, and in this social context there is a jointly experienced resolution. Percy Ling, among others, joins in the chorus, seeming to support Bob all the way, leading the applause at the end. Bob sits quietly and takes the applause due to him.

The next singer to stand is Percy Webb, who rises shakily but willingly to his feet, sustained by a few pints of stout and mild and cajoled and encouraged by many of those present. It is about nine o'clock, and he winks at the two American women at our table and warns them that this is a naughty one, digging me in the ribs with his elbow and laughing. It is at about this time that two more middle-aged couples arrive and sit near the bar. Webby puts his hands in his pockets, tilts his head on one side, and grinning, commences to sing. His voice is light, rhythmic and lilting, and he does not always clearly enunciate his words. He and his audience are familiar, and he is silent for one bar while they bang the tables with bottles, glasses, and fists to provide the 'rap-a-tat-tat'. He has succeeded in winning audience participation, and thus the fantasy he is telling has been accepted. The taps and his slightly faster speed indicate the audience's acceptance, and his ability to bring the song to fullness. Rhythmically, his song is rapid and exciting, and the high notes on which Webby sings 'misteress' in verse three have an air of confidence; he sounds triumphant and the high pitch suggests that he can take liberties with the master's wife as well as with her name. It is the greatest melodic variation, verse by verse, in the performance, and it is also the prelude to seduction; it therefore seems to function like emotional onomatopoeia. Glissandos and grace notes carry the mood of triumph and exhilaration, and these vocal devices are used most frequently in the parts of the song which tell of the forthcoming seduction, or which most suggest it. They are therefore anticipatory and also celebratory. As well as occurring in the choruses, they occur most during lines 5 and 6 in verses 1, 2 and 3, and during lines 4 and 5 in verse 3. These passages deal with the consequences of the master's absence (verses 1 and 2), the mistress's pleasure in her lover (verse 4), and the preliminary sign of her approval (verse 3).

Webby's vocal techniques are supplemented by his obvious enjoyment of what he sings, and the song takes life from his face as well as from his voice. He is a genius at holding an audience, with his bright eyes, his glances at individuals, and his ever-present sense of humour, and whereas he exercises his control over audience and song primarily by his mood and his dramatic appeals, Cyril manipulates response mostly by his brilliant singing with its apt choice of vocal expression. Emotion in 'The Nutting Girl' is therefore communicated musically and by the tension of Cyril's personality as the fantasy is played out into the room, whereas Percy Webb's warmth comes from him as he sings, and his delight with the words is shown by his smiles as much as by his manipulation of the words. He does allow the words to work for themselves, but he also casts the die of his own personality on them so that they gain dramatic joy. His role in the pub is not only that of singer, but also that of playboy, as any woman who has sat near him will know. He is not simply an old man using his age to take licence, but a man whose life story attests his love of women. The fantasy element is still there in the song, just as it may be in his life story, but the sexual adventure seems to be more attainable in his rendition than it does in Cyril's performance of 'The Nutting Girl', where he turns from an emotionally sober man to a teller of licentious tales. Cyril's is a supremely musical rendition, just as Bob's is, and it is perhaps in this variety of performance styles that the tradition has its strengths, since a wide range of responses is demanded of the audience not only by the emotional content of the songs but also by the differing relationships of the singers to their material.

Percy Ling is called on by many people, they bang upon the tables, he feigns deafness, he laughs, concedes defeat, and stands up to sing. This is his usual prelude to performance, and one that is indulged by the audience, and probably expected and enjoyed by them. His first reactions are to look around in a puzzled way after his name is called, as if he cannot understand why anybody should be calling him, then gradually to show comprehension, to act as if they are ridiculous to ask him, and finally to give in as if what he is about to do will be punishment enough for them. His most effective ploy is his feigned deafness; at other times he disappears to the toilet or to another room when it seems likely to be his turn again. For his first song of this night, he is less coquettish than usual, perhaps because of the competition from the Americans who may threaten to interrupt his habitual dalliance. He may simply feel less need to prevaricate amongst friends and before his first song of the evening. In any case, he reaches the pose of 'giving in' very rapidly, and begins to sing his own choice, 'The Boy with No Shoes'.

There is a definite style which Percy uses to deliver these stanzaic jokes: three lines with note lengthenings, pauses and syncopation, and a fourth line of comparatively regular rhythm which gives the impression of a faster beat. The rhythms are like those of speech, and in fact Percy's comic technique in song is very similar to his method of telling jokes, which is to go slowly, even fitfully, elaborating and excusing, and then to deliver a rapid punch line. Of course, the words of the song are themselves successfully humorous, depending as they do on pun and word-play, and it is natural for a man like Percy, who is recognised as a 'rum bugger' and a 'comic' by his companions, to choose to perform such a song. He himself has adopted and been confirmed in a comic role, and the inclusion of such songs in his repertoire is evidence of his own establishment of role and his audience's approval of it. With a bland performer, 'The Boy with No Shoes' would be funny, but with a comic singing it, it is hilarious. Percy does not only rely on the words and his melodic use of them, but he also give a dramatic performance. His movements are bird-like dartings of his head, to and fro, his eyes gleaming at person after person. He also smiles a toothless grin, and holds his arms bent in front of himself, turning his hands outwards in gestures of innocence and bewilderment, singing one line with one hand outstretched to a group on whom he fixes his gaze, and then turning to another group on the following line with his other hand outstretched. His face alters all the time, from wide-eyed innocence to sinister smirking. He seems to gather his audience to him until there is accord between them, although his singing itself, when heard on tape, can be flat, sharp or unmelodic. In performance, however, his vivacious comedy is infectious and nobody winces at a change of pitch or key; they laugh at him for his comedy, and approve of him as singer; they do not find fault with his musicality.

His dependence here is on the virtuosity of dramatic performance, since he suspects that his musicality alone is not sufficient to carry him to the heights of approval that he desires, and his reliance on extra-musical devices clearly pays off. In any case, his singing would be greeted with joy because it adds a familiar song of familiar style to the evening and he thus fulfils his obligation to perform, but he has cannily assessed that the role of comedian is a special one which endows him with an alternative appeal to his audience besides songmanship, and he thus uses gestures to the extreme.

The personal recounting of the jokes in 'The Boy with No Shoes' gives credibility and immediacy to the song, just as the localisation does. Thus Percy himself is given credibility and immediacy, and he and song are one. There is no sense of distance, of adopted fantasy, as there could be. The singers seem to have devices to prevent this; so do the songs: for example, the personal 'I'm going to tell you a story' beginning of 'The Nutting Girl', a song which otherwise might seem as separate from Cyril as the North Pole from the South; the quiet sincerity of Bob's performance of the potentially melodramatic 'Comrades';

the personal words of 'Old Farmer's Servant' that are never overstated by Percy Webb. Role and song collude in successful performance to present a cohesive if momentary art work.

The four men have now sung, and although a majority of people present will have heard all of these songs many times, knowledge of the events does not seem to detract from enjoyment of the narrative. Suspense and interest come from performance rather than from newness of material or originality of interpretation. The known is the heart and soul of the singing tradition, and interest lies not in the words as they would appear starkly in a text, but in their living rendition. It is in the telling and the singing that words are given colour and events are set in motion. Thus the singer, as he takes the spotlight, fulfils expectations because he delivers up to his audience some known part of their shared experience in a time-honoured way. Community is regaled as life's emotions and experiences are uplifted in song, and the adoption of the singing role by individual after individual also attests the importance of personality and variety which exists within the fellowship and unity of the tradition.

Somebody starts to call once more for CP and the circle starts again. The Americans have played in the meantime, complete tunes and interrupting snatches, so that their silence as Cyril is invited to sing seems to encourage him to oblige straight away. His song is prefaced by three bangs on the table with a beer mug, to call order. His face carries a mischievous expression, but he does not actually smile or laugh, and he stands with his hands in his pockets looking up above the heads of his audience. The sexual implications and innuendo of the first two verses he allows to carry themselves, by his suggestive rather than comical manner, and as the sexual fantasy of the song becomes more explicit in the third verse, where the protagonist's prowess and attractiveness are laid bare, the reaction from the audience suggests that the titillation of the previous verses has succeeded, and that the expected and the desired have occurred.

'Joe Moggins' is hardly a song of sexual fantasy in the same sense as 'The Nutting Girl' because it involves the conventional sequel to seduction, marriage and children. But the responsibility is offset by Joe's character, which is free and easy, like that of the hypothetical and possibly mythical bucolic lover. Again it is of note that Joe is unlike Cyril, but that Cyril has chosen to sing this song. During the enthusiastic applause, Cyril, still standing, picks up his beer mug and raises it with a broad grin.

Bob is the next to sing and, as always, he is willing and happy to oblige. He says 'I'll sing you a little easy one, then,' and begins 'What a Funny Little Place to Have One', one of his favourites which never seems to budge from currency in his immediate repertoire. When Percy has called for order, Bob begins his clear rhythmic performance, standing with his weight on one leg, his hands on his hips. Throughout the song, he does not look at anyone but keeps his eyes on the ceiling beams, nor does his face register much emotion. This is the one song, however, where he uses gestures, probably because he learned them when he learned the song.

It is in the third verse that the audience responds to the sexual innuendo of the words, and they roar at the sudden explicitness of the chorus. This verse is also the one in which Bob does his actions: his movements are slow and done in almost a dreamlike way; they are not demonstrative and do not directly seek the audience's attention. They reflect the nature of Bob's performance, which scarcely utilises any dramatic gesturing or facially expressive devices, but relies on his singing the song in a highly melodic, rhythmic and straightforward manner. It is also in this verse, especially during lines 5 and 6, that Bob's musicianship is demonstrated: he has perfect breath control, vivacious rhythm and a fluent handling of the narrative. The audience is enthusiastic and it is clear that, because of his formal control over and identification with the song, he does not need extra-vocal devices.

Bob's seeming innocence in the delivery of such a song as this, comical and also in the first person, may well be a device which he finds as effective as the more extrovert styles that Percy Webb and Percy Ling use. The clapping, and cries of 'Good old Bob' at the end indicate that he has endeared himself to his audience, he has won affection by the unstriven-for humour of the song and his own unforced manner which borders on *naïveté*. Perhaps as a younger man, he would not have been received so warmly as he is here, because youth would reduce his guilelessness. He is very much supported in his singing by his friend Percy Ling, who calls for order at the beginning and again during the song, and is the first to say 'Good old Bob' at the close. Percy often becomes the protector of other performances, and an encouragement to other singers. He is also at this stage becoming angry with the two American servicemen, and has jumped up to call for order, looking directly at them. He knows that Bob becomes hurt and angry if people do not listen carefully to him and thus he sometimes tries to control the audience so that Bob gets good order and can enjoy his singing. Percy Webb cries out after the song is over, 'He sing some funny songs don't he,' and somebody answers, 'In funny places'. There is more laughter.

Percy Webb is the next to sing, eager, slightly tipsy, swaying as he stands. Clive Woolnough calls for 'lovely order', and Webby begins 'The Oak and the Ash'. He completes one verse, with a giggle, and is enjoying it, but he has pitched it too high, has difficulty with the words, and is upset by the lack of chorus singing. Clive Woolnough tries to help, but it is perhaps significant that the experienced singers do not. Webby calls, 'Come on', and then says, 'I don't think you know that one, so I'll sing another one.' He is accused by Percy Ling of simply forgetting the words and of using this ploy as an excuse to change songs, and after protesting he begins 'Wheel Your P'rambulator, John', which somebody requests.

He is very much a man who sings to his audience and who needs their support. For over a year he refused to sing for me unless we were in a pub or folk club,[17] and the fact that the audience does not join in the chorus of 'The Oak and the Ash' may make him feel it is best to turn to another song, one which he often sings and which he knows to be popular. His change of songs is an indication of his dependence on audience, and also a hint at his conception of audience role. He does not expect an audience to be passive, and he likes people to sing choruses with him; familiarity of songs could therefore be a criterion of his aesthetics.

'Wheel Your P'rambulator, John', is another comic song in which not only the words but also the delivery add to the humour. Webby smiles in a cock-eyed way as he sings, his head on one side, a laugh coming from his lips every now and then. Although not all of his words are audible, the comedy and the lightheartedness of the narrative, reflected in his carefree performance of the song and in his own euphoria and jollity, carry the audience to a peak of excitement during the boisterous choruses. Percy Ling meanwhile, has said that Webby's voice is going with the beer, and pulls faces of disapproval. At the finish, however, he says, 'Very nice' and claps as loudly as anyone; he has also joined in the chorus singing.

These songs both reinforce those performed earlier and stand in contrast to them. The sexuality of 'The Nutting Girl', 'Old Farmer's Servant' and, to a lesser extent, 'The Boy with No Shoes' is reiterated in this round of songs but is not the central concern of any of them. Slapstick comedy and the war of the sexes is more evident here, and there is none of the gravity and sentimentality of 'Comrades'. Bob Hart thus shows another side of his personality and repertoire, and Cyril and Webby vary their presentations to deliver songs of differing sexual nuance. Percy Ling, on the other hand, has no intention of singing now, and he escapes the calls for him by buying drinks, going outside to the lavatory, and calling for others to perform. During a conversation on 16 November, I asked why he sometimes does not sing when asked to:

> That's a funny job, isn't it? Well, in one place . . . you hear another bloke sing, you concentrating on his song, you think to yourself, well he's a better singer'n I am, then they jump on you and say – you thinking about him a-singing, you know what I mean. That's the reason, you know, I'm hung up sometimes [laughs].

He is aware that he is regarded as a singer, and that if he goes into a pub where he is known, he is likely to be asked to sing, but it seems that at times he feels that he does not want to oblige. The role he has adopted of rallying other singers is very important to him, and his calling for order for others is part of this. He sometimes acts like a protector, particularly to Bob since Bob, out of the four, is likely to be most offended at an inattentive reception, but Percy is also a catalyst and one who guards the situation and makes it suitable for performance.

Cyril now stands to sing 'Flash Company' amid shouts for order, and Webby whispers to the people at our table that it is his song, not Cyril's. By this time, most of us have been drinking for about two hours and accompanying and chorus singing is sporadic and out of tune. Cyril uses more grace notes than in his earlier songs, possibly because of the amount he has drunk.[18] However, he sings in such a way that sympathies are directed. He is once more narrating a first-person experience, and the tragedy of the events is suggested in his emphasis of the low dominant, which runs through the song like a ground bass. The rests after 'fiddling', 'dancing' and 'delight' are evocative of the downfall that has resulted from this love affair; legato singing of these lines may suggest happiness in these apparently pleasurable pastimes, but the breaks make sure there is no such ambiguity. The tale of treachery is also emphasised by the staccato end of 'delight', and the triplet on 'my' is sung like a cry of despair; similarly, the two passages or ritardando draw out the despair and give it voice. The *a tempo* recoveries serve to highlight what has gone before and to make the mood more explicit by contrast. Cyril sings each verse flexibly, turning the melody he knows to the best medium for each set of words; there is variation from verse to verse, which is best seen as a local suitability to words. Rhythms are altered, rests, pauses and grace notes added as the feeling aroused by the words and the melody which carries them surfaces. It is a fittingly sober tone and speed that Cyril uses, with a slightly faster rendition of the symbolic chorus. But the speed and tone do not prevent the performance from being energetic, and vocal ornamentation helps make every phrase alive. The significance of the yellow handkerchief seems to be lost, but the words 'in rememberance of me' must call up echoes in most people present. A fatalistic mood which ennobles the story of the verses emerges from Cyril's singing of the chorus.

It is true that this song is most often sung by Percy Webb, and that it is often requested from him. This brings up the problem of song ownership,[19] which exists among these singers, but is like sexual morality in that it invites double standards. There is a local repertoire, and several singers may know or perform the same song, but they will not give credit to the idea that they could each have learned the songs from the same or different sources, and not necessarily from each other. The usual process by which a song becomes someone's is interwoven with performance and audience acceptance: the more a singer sings a song, the more it seems likely that each audience will request it from him. Thus the process of identification of singer with song is perpetuated, and particular local audiences may attribute to one singer a song that, in the pub across the road or in the next village, is attributed to someone else. Now if that second singer visits the first pub, there is likely to be a clash of ownership. The more a song is sung, the more easily it can be learned.

Cyril's choice of 'Flash Company' is important since he must know it is associated with Percy Webb, though it is current in the area amongst other singers. Percy Ling and Bob Hart of Snape both recognise its owner to be Dick Woolnough, a man born in Blaxhall, but who has lived in Snape for many years, Frank's brother. Perhaps Cyril uses it on this occasion as a counter to his two earlier fantasy songs, to indicate the realities of life. Perhaps it is innocent liking for it that makes him choose it, or perhaps he is baiting Percy Webb. In any case, as both he and Webby claim to have known it first, the dialectic will continue.

Bob is asked to sing 'The Banks of Sweet Primroses' by Webby and Cyril, and he begins a performance of bare-faced lies and humour that is a technique he has developed when he wants to feel more at ease with his audience. There are people present who are strangers to him, and in conversation, he has often admitted that he likes best to sing amongst friends. Part of the reason for this is that in the First World War, he was wounded by a shell and his jaw blown away. He explains:

> When do I sing it? When the strangers are out – when the strangers come down in the summer-time . . . holiday makers.

Why do you do that?

Well, uh, you know, I – you know, I still get embarrassed about this [fingering his jaw]; but, uh, if I can get them in a good mood . . . they're all right before I start singing, that's how I like it.

Don't you ever tell them what caused it?

I never tell them, no. No, well, they could see, I should think . . . Well, I've got them in good humour then and I can laugh with them then, but I remember the first night I went to the folk club, that was very embarrassing, there was a lot of young girls there and one thing and another, and you know . . . They take no notice of me now as regards the looks. Well, I can always say, well that weren't my fault.[20]

In the interval between Bob's previous song and this one, a large group of young couples has arrived, and it may be their presence that makes him decide to use 'On a Summer's Night'. Perhaps he thinks it will improve his accord with the audience which seemed, in any case, very good during 'What a Funny Little Place to Have One'. He is very mild when, standing, he begins to explain why he will not sing the song asked of him: 'I really ought to tell you a little about meself. Just how I got this. Ah, you'll all be interested, no doubt.' He is so undemonstrative that Clive Woolnough calls for order several times, but the audience around him is attentive. Most of the noise is from the other end of the room. At the close of his song he says, 'Now what was that song you wanted?', and the audience recognises his ploy and laughs. His manner is withdrawn and understated so that his wit is almost lost, but the surprise which comes as his audience responds to his canniness once more makes him the centre of attention.

He begins 'The Banks of Sweet Primroses' which, like 'What a Funny Little Place to Have One', is one of his all-time favourites. His singing is measured and rhythmical, and the words are clear. Once more he stands looking into space, and does not seem to realise that Percy Ling is calling for order, or that he has won one of the quietest audiences so far. The styles of Percy Webb and Percy Ling are more marked by personality than Bob's style, but it would be a mistake to think that because he does not infuse his singing with direct appeals to his audience, Bob's performance is less interesting. It is a beautiful rendition that deserves its applause and Percy's comment, 'Very nice'.

Next, Cyril sings 'Black Velvet Band' with so much audience participation that he cannot cope with the song.[21] Through no fault of his own, his pitch changes and he loses his tune. The problem is that the two American musicians decide to accompany him and they play in a different key and lead chorus singing of a different tune. Cyril struggles to maintain his melody, shouting and accenting some syllables very heavily, almost choking on them as he comes at them from a higher pitch than the one he intends to rest on. He is almost panic-stricken as he tries to control the singing, but he fails and leaves the song after three verses and walks out. The Americans call to him to continue but he shakes his head, and with derision on his face, leaves the pub, over an hour before closing time, which is full indication of his anger.

In the Ship Inn on 6 September, Cyril is able to sing 'Black Velvet Band' in the way that he wishes, according to what he calls 'the old tune', although even on this occasion after he has sung only one line, somebody says it is not the right tune and he has to begin again. His adherence to the 'old tune' is therefore a slight problem even with a mainly local audience, and this is a case where faithfulness to the tradition has caused a singer to suffer since it puts him in direct conflict with a modern popularised version of a song which is more familiar than the traditional version.

Percy Ling is now coerced to sing, and his behaviour until now suggests that his earlier refusals have been leading up to this performance. It is a sort of seduction, in which the repeated refusals and evasions make the final succumbing all the more noteworthy. 'Flanagan's Band' is a song which is very much associated with him, and he performs it often, usually borrowing Bob's cap as a prop. He begins with a flourish on 'Now' which is accented and held over, and in a more conversational way he goes on to place the song, like 'The Nutting Girl', in a story-telling context. The comedy of his vocal style in this performance is based on recapitulation. It depends on altering speeds to give interest to what is being described, and to make moments of the song climactic. His style is indicative of an aesthetic of contrast.

His performance is also a highly dramatic one that always causes much laughter and applause. The way that Percy sings is intimately and inseparably connected with the actions he does, since the long notes before the chorus give suspense to the movements he is clearly about to make; the pause on 'boys', which is a climax note, the highest in the song, usually spurs a great deal of audience participation, and is simultaneous with his lifting his cap in mock reverence to the band. His actions throughout the song are as follows. On 'now of', he opens his arms wide, and as this first line continues he turns first to the left and then to the right, and on 'I think I've heard a few,' he once more opens his arms. His face is very expressive: when he sings, 'But with your kind permission', his eyebrows are raised high and he is looking from one group to another, his hand raised. When he says, 'I'll let you all know,' he gives a quick shake of his head, as if to underline the sincerity of his intention; on 'The credit is due to old Ireland' he lifts off his cap, and replaces it before the chorus begins. The 'and the' introduction is sung with his body not at rest but in such a position that movement is inevitable: his knees are bent, his arms are poised, his neck is taut. As he sings 'the drums went bang', he hits his chest; as he sings 'the cymbals clanged', he raises and lowers his cap; and as he sings 'the cornet played the way', he moves his arms in and out from his chest as if he is playing a trombone. When he sings 'upon the floor', he crouches and sweeps one hand in mid-air about one foot above the ground; when he sings 'There was Ali . . . could hardly stand' he turns from one group to another with alternate arms outstretched, bobbing up and down on bent knees, and once more he raises his cap on 'the credit is due to Old Ireland', and holds it there till 'boys'. Part of the humour of these movements comes not from their fluidity, but from the obvious difficulty that Percy has to do them all in the appropriate place without stopping his singing. The actions are vital to the song, and he learnt them with the words and tune:

> Yer, well my wife's father used to sing 'Flanagan's Band', that's where I learnt that orf. He used to sing it about the pubs, down the Key and down the Plough, Reg Ling, O he's dead now, he's been dead lots of years.
>
> Did he do those same actions that you do?
>
> Yes, that's where I learnt them from, yes.[22]

The inclusion of this song in his repertoire is an indication of the sort of song he likes and the sort of character he likes to become as performer. The comedy suits him since it allows his extra-musical skills to come into play; the other type of song that he favours is very sentimental, and there are no songs between these extremes. Thus both on the extended level of repertoire and on the particular level of delivery, he exhibits an aesthetic of contrast, of dichotomy, of extremes.

Percy Webb is next to oblige, and he invites himself rather than waits to be asked. 'I'll give you another one,' he says, and Clive Woolnough calls for order. Webby has clearly decided what he will sing, for when a request is made, he says, 'No, not that one,' and begins 'Old Shep'. He sings slowly, slurring his words, and ignores or does not hear the whining noises the servicemen make, and the calls for order. He does not use heavy emotionalism, but allows the words to tell themselves in the context of his largely non-stanzaic rendition. Some people sing with him and the quieter clapping may be a sign of the nature of the emotions he has called up.

It is true that quiet songs do not always elicit loud clapping, and that a sentimental song such as this is not likely to be as loudly applauded as 'Flanagan's Band'. The fun made of the song or of Webby by the young Americans may prevent the creation of a sentimental pact between performer and audience, since people do not generally feel free to let emotions flow if another group is making fun of the cause of their emotion. Webby has cited instances when this song has reduced some of the women in the audience to tears, but this does not occur here. On the same afternoon, 19 July, he has said of 'Old Shep':

> I'll tell you a good song and a lot of girls don't like to hear that because that's a sad song, really, but that's a good one. I sing it and I sing it well, too. One young woman, she said, 'It make me cry.' Well, that's how some people are emotional, aren't they, if you sing a song like that.

The truth and emotional appeal of the song are clearly very important to Percy Webb, and it is probable that he decides to sing it on this occasion because he thinks it will be sympathetically accepted and enjoyed. Perhaps it is a song he relies on to induce a certain type of response in his audience. So far he has sung a bawdy song ('Old Farmer's Servant') and a comical song ('Wheel Your P'rambulator, John'), and 'Old Shep' has the potential of crediting him with a vastly different role as singer, and a more varied repertoire. Any man who values his art is likely to want to feel capable of calling forth serious and heartfelt emotions in his audience as well as laughter, and such a pact, if successfully established, would unite singer and audience in a common response to the truth of the song. It is also a fact that Webby likes singing the song, and it is in performance, in communication with his audience, that he finds its meaning. Thus he adheres to the aesthetic of narrative truthfulness, although the usually ensuing bond of feeling between singer and audience is somewhat dissipated by the interference of the outsiders present.

Bob now sings 'The Female Cabin Boy' with the same vital rhythm that characterises all his singing. Drink has not marred his control, whereas Percy Webb is clearly affected when he shakily stands once more and begins 'The Sailor Boy'. He does not make very much effort to attract anybody's attention, and is quite drunk, just swaying and letting it come naturally, but the benign grin on his face makes for some comedy. He stumbles with his words a lot, and Percy Ling once more comments on the deterioration through drink of Webby's singing. But it is Percy Ling who calls for order a number of times and who sings with him towards the end of the song, as if in support. And it is Percy Ling who praises Webby at the close and who leads the applause, for whatever the objective quality of Webby's rendition, he is fulfilling his obligation to perform, and with Cyril gone and the number of singers diminished, this is of great importance. The fellowship of the pub evening is thus enabled to continue.

Percy is next called on to sing, and it is possible that he so takes the limelight in his supporting role to another singer that he makes himself, consciously or not, the next obvious choice. At first when asked, he says 'Aye?', pretends he is confused, and then enigmatically takes my clogs from my feet. He sits with one clog on his knee and the other on the floor, and begins 'The Cobbler'. This is another song which involves actions, and it has a rhythmic chorus during which he bangs the clogs together as if he is mending them. He localises this song, as he does with 'Boy with No Shoes', by naming the Sheep Inn, the old name for the Ship Inn, Blaxhall; and although it is a song about a man who has to work long and hard hours to support his alcoholic wife, Percy makes light of the serious considerations of alcoholism, hard work and poverty by his actions and his ever-changing and basically humorous face. However, real comedy is kept at bay by the narrative line.

During this song Frank Woolnough, in cap, white shirt and jacket, has come and stands in front of Percy, swaying and watching his every action. Percy largely directs his performance towards him, and Frank mouths Percy's words and drunkenly follows his shoe-making actions. It is soon after this that Clive and Percy ask and persuade Frank to sing, and he, looking bemused, suddenly begins 'The London Apprentice Boy'.[23] He sings in the same straightforward manner that Bob does, though he is not clear and does not maintain his melody well. He finishes and says, 'That's all I know,' and Percy lavishes praise on him. All through the faltering performance, Percy has held Frank's eyes, has mouthed words with him, has nodded a rhythm and has generally aided and abetted him in his singing. Percy can again be seen here fulfilling his function of helper, encourager and protector to other singers.

Dick Woolnough, Frank's brother in Snape, also sings this song. He was born in 1898, five years before Frank, and although they had different fathers, they were brought up together, and it seems likely that the two brothers learned the song from the same source. The melodies are not identical, nor are the words, but the two brothers have lived separately for more than fifty years and Frank was drunk and Dick was ill when I recorded them. Frank has obvious memory lapses, and so does Dick, but both performances have an atmospheric completeness of their own that gives cohesion to the sparsity of the storyline. Perhaps the two give an indication of a fuller story, of a narrative potential that neither brother realises individually, but neither performance can be discredited because of this, and thus the reality of a song's completeness in performance can be seen as opposed to any hypothetical textual reality or completeness.

Frank's singing is usually confined to a work situation because in this context it does not function as performance or consequently have to submit itself to audience approval. He does not regard himself as a singer, and he is encouraged to sing in the pub only rarely. He says:

> I never used to sing a lot, only join in the chorus with 'em, but I never sing. Singing's something I could never get the tune right . . . I got no voice for singing at all. She [wife] keep saying, 'Shut up that bloody noise' . . . lately I sung sometimes when I been half boozed, 'London Apprentice Boy'.[24]

There are several people like this in the area, it seems, who know songs but who are not regarded as singers. These people are in a twilight world; they do not hold the same singing status as Bob Hart, Percy Ling, Cyril Poacher and Percy Webb, but are sometimes recognised as performers of particular songs. One who falls between the singing type and the latent singing type is Lenny Savage, who was present for a while on this occasion, but was not asked to sing. He is sometimes asked and is usually more evasive than Percy Ling, but his refusals are seriously spoken and are supported by comments on his ill health. Lenny has had problems with the reduction of his repertoire by other singers' incursions into it, and he has consequently been discouraged from singing often. It is true that his repertoire is small ('Dark Eyed Sailor', 'The Foggy Dew', 'Nancy from Yarmouth', 'Rose of Tralee' and 'The Volunteer Organist'), and because of the common or disputed ownership of some of these songs there is a likelihood that there will be nothing left for him to sing if both Bob and Cyril are present on any occasion. 'Rose of Tralee' and 'The Volunteer Organist' are named by him but cannot be regarded as part of his active repertoire since he does not sing them. The falling off of his singing can therefore be seen as a consequence of the size of his repertoire, and of its commonness with other local singers.

After Frank Woolnough has finished, Percy Ling is asked for 'Don't Do It Tonight', some of the men sing lines from it, and there is a lot of noise. Clive Woolnough begins to sing and shout, and Frank asks for the song as reward for 'The London Apprentice Boy'. Percy tells me to switch off the tape-recorder since I have already recorded it; this is by way of reference to its bawdy nature. Percy says, 'I'll see what I can do,' and stands. He raises his eyebrows very high, and touches the air delicately with his hands, as if he is singing about flowers and rainbows and kisses. He looks from person to person, and moves up and down a little in time to the singing. The chorus line, 'The little stars are twinkling in the sky, O my!', is one that he uses to emphasise the mock innocence of his delivery, by adopting a look of purity and by pointing to the heavens in awe. In general, he sings as if he is describing something sweet and pleasantly surprising, and this could well be a defence against disapproval. On the other hand, he looks people in the eye as if in an attempt to embarrass them, or as an indication of his own innocence. His double-barrelled delivery of course protects him and also emphasises the highly sexual nature of the song; once more he gives a performance of contrast.

Sexual fantasy again becomes tantalisingly obtainable, both because of the ambiguous innocence which becomes bare-faced suggestiveness as he sings, and because of the character he presents throughout the evening. He has set himself up and been accepted as a comic, and this neutralises the crudity of the song and, potentially anyway, makes it more acceptable to those who might be shocked by a straight delivery. However, Percy does not feel entirely comfortable, for all his techniques, and he cuts the song short and protests when some of the men in the audience demand completion. Clive Woolnough shouts out the verse that Percy has censored from his performance, while Percy laughs and says 'No, no,' as Clive advances and tries to make Percy join in.[25] He abuses Percy and accuses him of cowardice. Percy does not complete the song, and he says to me: 'Two or three of them went out, you got to be careful, two or three of them went out.' He interprets this exodus as disapproval, so he cuts out what is not necessarily the most crude verse, but it is at least as explicit as the preceding ones.

Percy Webb begins to sing 'The Wild Colonial Boy', in a slow lilting way, looking to one side and grinning benignly. It is interesting that his songs of the evening group into two sections like this, the comic and the sentimental, and it is probably due to mood and the languor of sentimentality as he becomes drunk, that he refrains from comedy at this stage.

Some people ask Bob to sing 'Barbara Allen', which may again suggest that sentiment has caught on in some of the audience, but he is intimidated by its length and opts for the frivolity of 'Underneath the Apron', standing up and holding on to the table.

It is perhaps significant that at least two songs he sings utilise a similar form of humour, which relies on word-play of a particular kind – the juxtaposition of an ambiguous or colourless phrase with other lines that eventually or sometimes throw sexual and humorous light on the phrase. 'Underneath the Apron' is like 'What a Funny Little Place to Have One' in this respect. Bob appears to feel more comfortable with this type of comedy which does not need to be made explicit by attention-drawing techniques of his own (such as in Percy Ling's funny songs), but which speaks for itself. He has often said he likes a song with a story, and there is something in Bob's unaffected delivery of 'Underneath the Apron' which suggests that the fusion of words and tune is self-sufficient, as the song interpreted, and his performance gives the song being before his audience. Cecil Sharp has stressed[26] that melody and words are inseparable, and this is of course obvious, but it is perhaps in a performance like Bob's where no gestures, facial expressions or asides are used, that the song stands most pure, and can most clearly be apprehended. The tune is a medium for the words and the words are a medium for the tune, and this seems to be the nature of Bob's delivery and an indication too of his idea of his singing role. Although he says he likes a song with a story, he regards himself primarily and with pride as a singer; he is not a story-teller, he does not *use* the song in order to tell a story. Song and story are one and the same thing.

The Evening Ends

On the way home from the Ship, Percy Ling and Percy Webb say that there has been a competition during the evening between songs and music. The next day, Bob said:

> There were two parties in there last night. In opposition of each other. Did you notice it? The music and the singin'. Landlord couldn't do nothing about it. I said to him, I said, 'You've got two companies in here' then – before I come away I had a little talk with him. He say, 'Yes,' he say, 'there's nothing I can do about

> it.' I hear as some of the Blaxhall ones, they don't bother to go so much. But I was brought up in the days when you never used to have a lot of music when you're singin', just an accordion [sic], he'd sit and play tunes, and you'd sing. Now they want so much noise.

What Bob has to say gives an indication of the state of the singing tradition in this part of Suffolk. Because of the American servicemen, and because of the darts club, fruit machine and juke-box, which have been fostered by the landlord to attract young people, there is a possibility that singing in the pub will fall off greatly. The pub is the centre of the tradition, and the Blaxhall Ship is one of the pubs in the area known for its singing. In Snape, singing has been common at the Golden Key, but the pub is now host to young country and western singers and bands on Saturday nights. The landlord of the Crown is interested in tourist and passing traffic rather than in local custom, and although he is kind to Bob Hart, and also to other local singers, it sometimes seems that his prime interests are in business. The Blaxhall Ship is unique, therefore, in these two villages as the one pub which has maintained its singing tradition.

This description of a singing evening at the Blaxhall Ship on 19 July 1974 gives an indication of the nature of the local singing tradition, of the singers' roles, of their values, and of the audience's role. In performance, the day-to-day characterisation of the singers becomes exaggerated or refracted in the fantasy of song narrative: Cyril can for a short time lose his moroseness in pursuit of easy game, and Bob Hart's painful war experiences become subsumed into noble sentiments about comradeship; Percy Webb seeks proximity with his audience, and Percy Ling uses the virtuosity of his dramatic comedies to win approval and response. The type of song a singer chooses can broaden the image people have of him or give emphasis to traits they might scarcely notice. With comedy, the singer can reinforce his role as humorist, and so encourage the extreme reactions of anarchy and hilarity in his audience;[27] in this way, his role is established and given great worth in the society.

Each singer has his own techniques for dealing with song and audience; he knows on some level the nuances of gesture, grimace, mime, rhythm, speed, syncopation and volume, and he uses these in any combination as he sees fit. He has to take into account the particular song, his intentions, his mood, his own behaviour in delivery, and his audience's preconception of himself. Thus Bob stands with his song in a proximity that is like a creative proximity. Percy Webb's approach is generally similar, except that his personality extrudes when he laughs, and it is significant that Bob finds this behaviour disturbing. Cyril Poacher is a singer who uses vocal techniques a great deal, who makes fewer appeals to his audience as conscious deliverer of the song than Percy Ling does, but who, like Bob, sings it out. Percy Ling is seen on this occasion only in his comic role, and he excels in it, by dramatic devices, by his choice of song, by his joke-telling techniques. He has another dimension which is as singer of sentimental songs, and here he once more regards the song as the salvation of the singer: if it touches the heart of the audience, then he succeeds. Just as Bob is in a sense passive as a singer, he is passive as an audience. He does not often sing choruses, nor does he often call praise to other singers. Percy Webb and Cyril Poacher become involved, but the one who is at the centre all of the time, even when he is being his most evasive, is Percy Ling. He helps and guides the other singers, and holds the evening together. Thus the singers form a community with each other and their audience, supporting, cajoling and reinforcing each other's roles, taking their turns and fulfilling their social obligations, and surviving through darts club, fruit machine, juke-box and American servicemen to go on singing the varied emotions of the human creature in ways learnt over and over in the pubs of Snape and Blaxhall.

Notes

1. Cyril Poacher, Blaxhall, 17 Nov. 1974.
2. Ben Ling, Blaxhall, 2 July 1975.
3. Reg Jay, Blaxhall, 2 June 1975.
4. Percy Ling, Snape, 2 Oct. 1974.
5. James Knights, George and Dragon Inn, Farnham, 15 Nov. 1974.
6. Basil Bennett, 2 Oct. 1974.
7. Bob Hart, 23 Apr. 1974.
8. Bob Hart, 25 June 1974.
9. Bob Hart was Benjamin Britten's gardener for a few years before 1937, when Britten and Pears lived at the Mill House, Snape. Britten was not aware that he had a traditional singer at the bottom of his garden. I wrote to ask him in August 1974.
10. This is run like, but not called, a folk club.
11. 'Crossroads' is an ATV television production with a large following in England. It is shown for half an hour on four evenings a week, and is the continuing saga of a motel, its workers and guests, and is set near Birmingham.
12. 'The Broomfield Wager', Topic records 12TS252.
13. 'Songs of Seduction' (Folksongs of Britain series), Topic records 12TS158.
14. For an excellent analysis of the ideas of community and unity in a singing tradition, see Keith F. Sullivan, 'Popular Singing Traditions and Cultural Change in the Old North Riding of Yorkshire' (unpublished PhD thesis, Institute of

Dialect and Folk Life Studies, University of Leeds, 1978), especially Chapters 2-4.

15. Since Wickets Richardson ceased to be chairman at the Ship Inn, Clive Woolnough has sometimes been requested to act as chairman, and his extrovert personality makes this easy for him.

16. Bob Hart, 15 July 1974.

17. He was finally persuaded to sing for me at his home in 1975 when I stressed that I wanted to record his complete repertoire.

18. See Chapter 6, 'Aesthetics'. Alcohol is likely to increase minor improvisations such as this since it reduces control and increases excitability.

19. See Chapter 5, 'Song Ownership', for a further discussion of this.

20. Bob Hart, 25 June 1974.

21. For this reason, I do not think it worth transcribing.

22. Percy Ling, 16 Nov. 1974.

23. Because of his varying rendition, I have not transcribed the music in this case.

24. Frank Woolnough, Blaxhall, 26 June 1975.

25. The words of the verse Clive sings are:

We went agathering snowballs, snowballs, snowballs
Down by the old mill stream.
Instead of gathering snowballs I introduced my own balls
Down by the old mill stream.

26. See Cecil Sharp, *English Folksong: Some Conclusions* (EP Publishing, Wakefield, 1972; first published 1907) p. xxii.

27. For an incisive and much fuller account of the anarchic potential of song performance, see Sullivan, 'Popular Singing Traditions' especially Chapters 3 and 4.

2 THE WOMEN

Introduction: The Singing Women

Whereas the majority of the men in Snape and Blaxhall are pub-centred in their singing, very few of the women singers have relied upon the pub as their place of performance. They have found their audiences variously in their children, in women's club meetings, and with the men at village concerts and socials, at harvest frolics, at charity concerts and old folks' meetings, at wedding parties, and also in the pubs. The men have also sung after their quoits matches, at men's club and British Legion meetings, and occasionally at home. But overall, the singing habits of the women have been far more varied than those of the men, a strange situation to arise from constraint, both moral and physical. Such constraint is exercised not only by the men, but also by some of the women. As a consequence, the pub is and has been out of bounds to certain women, and performance in the pub forbidden by public opinion to most women. Within the limits of their day-to-day lives, those women who accepted the stricter standards of some of their peers created opportunities for performance which may never have arisen in a more relaxed moral environment. Other women, exceptions rather than the rule, performed as the men did, in the pubs, while a lot more acted as audience.

I have never heard a woman sing solo in a Snape or Blaxhall pub. Bessie Ling and Bessie Hammond both used to sing in the Blaxhall Ship: Mrs Ling will no longer do so because she thinks her voice has deteriorated, and Mrs Hammond has chest trouble but still sings occasionally at The Old Folks' Club. Alice Messenger of Blaxhall and Ruby Ling of Snape have always sung at meetings, concerts and local festivals, but Mrs Messenger stopped singing at the end of 1974 because of ill health. Priscilla Savage, who died at the age of 93, sang only to her family, as did Margaret Howell of Snape. Other women, such as Ethel Pearce and Lil Durrant of Blaxhall, still go to the Ship Inn and join in the choruses, as does Blind Bessie Ling when someone takes her there. But there are also women who do not go, and who express disapproval of those who do: Eva Ling, Ben Ling's wife, and Alice Messenger, for example.

To some middle-aged and older women in Snape and Blaxhall, the male singers are objects of gentle fun, 'old boys' who should be tolerated kindly or laughed at; others enjoy the social evenings and any performance is gratefully received. This latter group comprises some of the and mothers of the singers whilst other wives are angered and hurt by the pub-going habits of their husbands.

The local pub-singing traditions have always been male-dominated, but those memories which extend back to the years before the First World War tell of more women singers then than there have been recently. James Knights, born 1880, of Little Glemham, the next village to Blaxhall, recalls, 'They used to sing along with us. Yes, the women'd sing like the blazes, that they would.'[1] In Blaxhall and Snape at this time, it is also likely that several women sang in the pubs, since they could go there with their children and moral restrictions did not commonly bar them from entry. The oldest village inhabitants, born around 1895, remember more women singers than those born in the first decade of the twentieth century, but even these women were more numerous as audience than as soloists. At this time, women were facing religious, moralistic and legal restrictions to pub entry, and in Snape and Blaxhall at least, their presence in the pub was restricted to the back room or back kitchen.[2] The names of those who did perform regularly then are engraved on village memories; others apparently played their parts, perhaps at holidays when a certain licence was introduced into the proceedings, and these performers are not generally remembered except by sons and daughters. John Hewitt, the Blaxhall Ship landlord during these years, disapproved of the presence of women in his pub and only reluctantly allowed their use of his back kitchen, and also in Snape, until some time before the beginning of the Second World War, women kept to their back kitchen.

Of all the Blaxhall women singers, Bessie Ling, related by marriage to Blind Bess, is the most often recollected. She, like Percy Ling's wife in Snape, also a pub singer and a melodeon player, came from a singing family, and it is likely that this partially accounts for her singularity in the tradition. Fred Pearce recalls:

> Bessie Ling was a lovely singer, before she was married she was one of the Smiths. They used to be a big family, the Smiths were – there were four brothers and three sisters. There used to be four brothers sing and step dance in there, and Bessie used to sing and dance, but the other two sisters, I didn't see them sing or dance, but Bessie, she was good, she was . . . I used to go out with her and her husband, we used to go round all the pubs on Saturday night. She used to do the singing and dancing and I'd play the accordion [sic], you see . . . Yes, she'd get up and sing a song like the rest of them.[3]

His description of Bessie Ling's family suggests that she may have broken through convention because of the strong musical tradition within her family; that the possibility of nurturing talent from an early age in the confines of her family gave her sufficient momentum to do publicly what other women ceased to do on maturity or did only in front of their children. The Smith family, along with the Lings, is generally cited as an example of a singing and dancing family. If such recognition was accorded to the Smiths eighty years ago, Bessie may have been cast in a role which would not normally have been allowed. This does not explain why more female members of the Smith and Ling families in Blaxhall did not become regular pub performers – individual character is important as well.

Blind Bess was born in London and eventually married a Suffolk man. She used to sing and dance in the pub along with Bessie Ling, her cousin by marriage and namesake. Stories she tells suggest she was extrovert, fun-loving, liked by men and daring. Her personal characteristics ensured her confidence in her ability to become a pub performer:

> I used to come down for holidays and I used to love to get down to Snape, 'cause my father-in-law used to work at Snape Maltings, down there with old Bob Hart, and we used to go to the Plough, used to have a nice little old singsong on our own, you know, like holiday time, and my father-in-law used to go back to the Maltings. He'd say, 'How long are you stoppin'?' I'd say, 'I don't like going out till they turn out, I suppose,' I say, 'I'll let you know when I'm going back home.' We used to walk from here, you see, to Snape. Off I used to go. When I got back home here, my young man used to say, 'Where you been?' I used to say, 'Down the Maltings along with your father.' 'What you been doing down there?' 'O,' I say, 'I been out with father,' of which I had been helping him I own, 'cos they used to pull at the corn all on the floor to wet it all and that to make the malt. I used to say, 'Let me help you to drag all that,' and I used to go and do it and I used to lose me shoes in it and I used to throw 'em out, and the poor old boy used to say 'Put these 'ere canvas boots on.' I did but I used to lose 'em 'cos they were so big. He said, 'You'll cop that, my girl, being down here all this while.' I said, 'Well,' I said, 'I know what I can do if he gives me the jaw when I go back.' I said, 'I can soon walk to Wickham Market Station and get on the train and go back home.' I was single then. I couldn't do it after I was married though. It's no good me turning round and saying, 'I'm going to get a train and go back home.' Sometimes he used to jaw me, though. I used to think, 'All right, you wait, mate. Get me own back.' He ain't

going to do as he like with me.[4]

She was clearly very popular at the Ship:

> I used to do the candlestick dance, and there was another man there played the accordion [sic], Mr Fred Smith that was, and he used to say to me, 'Come on my little Woopwoop,' and of course once I'd started to do it, that's how he'd keep – 'Come on little Woop, that's right,' and of course I kep' bursting out laughing you see, and he made me laugh one day in there, and I let the clothes go, and I burnt all the lace off the bottom of my petticoat. O dear, I daren't take that back to London though, I aren't going to have my mother say, 'Where's that slip of yours?' 'O,' I said, 'I left it down there, that'll do for one of his sisters.' I didn't tell her I been dancing in the pub and set fire to it.[5]

The fact that Blind Bess was brought up in London may have given her a different set of mores about pubs, although in this instance she is afraid to tell her mother she has been dancing in the pub. Here, her fear may arise from the damage done to her petticoat rather than from her mother's opinion of pub dancing.

There is an element of straightforwardness and fun in the type of behaviour she describes that could account for the fact that she went to the pub when some women would not, and again that she sang there and most did not:

> Blackberrying time, we used to go in that bar there where the men used to go, 'cos after we'd sold our blackberries we used to go right across, leave our pails and baskets outside the pub, inside we used to go. Remember one dinnertime we hadn't had no dinner, me, me mother-in-law, my husband's cousin, my sister-in-law, her sister, there was eight or nine of us all went in there. They used to have a big fire, and old Mr Hewitt, he used to have a big old iron boiler over his fire, all full of little potatoes what he used to cook up for his pigs, you know, with all the skins on, used to wash 'em and boil 'em in their skins, so we sat there this dinnertime. Elsie say, 'Going to have a look in there.' I say, 'Whatever for, Elsie?' She had a look, she say, 'That's full of potatoes,' got one out. She say, 'And they're all cooked too.' She say, 'Want one Bess?' I say, 'Yes, give us one.' There she was digging these here potatoes out. We skinned 'em and she put all the skins back in this here boiler. O, I think we had about half a dozen

> each . . . All of a sudden, way comes poor old Mr Hewitt through. He say, 'I suppose you don't want the salt with them by any chance?' We said, 'No thank you.' I said, 'We just thought we'd see if they were done.'[6]

Bessie Hammond does not have the same jolly character as Blind Bess, nor did she have a local family tradition to propel her into pub singing. But she, too, was introduced to the Ship by exceptional circumstances combined with a well ripened singing ability. But for the exceptional circumstances, it seems likely that she would never have sung in the pub:

> Years and years ago, they, they used to send the poor children down into the country for holidays and I used to have 'em. Well, then it got from the children coming, they were so pleased me having them, the mothers and fathers used to want to come, and I got taking them and all . . . They were nice people, they wanted just a drink, they never got drunk or anything like that . . . They liked to drink and they used to go down to the Ship and I said, when they used to come, I give them their orders, I said, 'Look here, you can go to the Ship – that's none of my business,' I say, 'but you never come in here the worse for drink, you know.' 'O, Bessie,' she say, 'don't worry about that,' she said, 'we only go for a drink now and again.' 'Well,' I said, 'that's all right then,' I said, 'but I'm just telling you' . . . That's how I started going to the Ship. I'd never been to a pub in my life, I wasn't a pub drinker, never been in, and she said, 'Come on,' she said, 'you're working hard all day, come and have a drink with us,' and I said, 'I'm not bothered to go in pubs,' but, 'O you don't have to drink beer,' and that's how I got going in there. Well, then that got so I used to go down Saturday nights then, for a little while then home again, then they used to ask me to sing sometimes and I tell you what I sung down there sometimes, 'Springtime in the Rockies' – that's an old one isn't it? – Can't get down there now, don't ever go down, but I did then. I went down sometime back and as soon as I got in – 'Are you going to give us 'Springtime in the Rockies'?' You see, the menfolk you know, and ah, 'Eh,' I said, 'don't get the wrong idea,' I said, 'I'm not a pub drinker, yet a pub singer.' 'Aah,' they said, 'we know that,' they said, 'you only doing it 'cos you' – you know, liven the place up a bit don't it – yes. That's how it all started and finished.[7]

Clearly, if Bessie Hammond had not begun to like and respect her

London visitors, she would never have followed their example of going to the Ship, or succumbed to their persuasion. The conversation she describes was with the wife: another woman with a responsible attitude towards drinking was necessary to persuade her. On asking her to sing, the Blaxhall men had to acquiesce to her terms, that she was 'not a pub drinker, yet a pub singer', before she would consent to sing. Mrs Hammond is remembered for her pub-singing but is not cited as a pub-singer by those who mention Bessie Ling, perhaps because of her own attitude towards her role as performer.

Restraints and Rebellions

The importance of family, character and encouragement is crucial in the introduction of a woman to the role of pub singer. For some male members of the community, it is also clear that her assumption of such a role, or her participation in pub activities, increased the feeling of unity that existed in the villages. Several men born since 1910 recall a number of women singing along with the men in the past, and it seems likely that these memories are coloured by nostalgia, as they are usually voiced in conjunction with statements about the present dearth and former abundance of village community spirit. Stanley Day:

> The friendliness have gone. We used to all get together in a family, and I will admire one family – that's Abie Ling's. Every Saturday night the brothers and sisters and friends get in the saloon of the Ship and sort of have a reunion every Saturday, and that's nice to see. Now *that's* the friendly atmosphere of Blaxhall . . . I'm afraid those good days are gone, and not only that, as the people pass away, their property goes up for sale and you have people come from away.[8]

If pub-going in his youth was a family event, at least amongst those families which did not hold moral reservations about the public house, then women could be naturally integrated into the social life of the pub. If with social flux and change, increased mobility and the impact of the media the local life-style began to break down, village life in the microcosm of the pub is also likely to have changed. Moral attitudes from outside the villages could enter and join forces with those reactionary ideas present in a few local inhabitants.

In Blaxhall, the period in living memory seems to have been directly influenced by the old landlord, John Hewitt, by traditional male-oriented values hardened by church and chapel, by Victorian and

Edwardian morality, and less directly but more subtly by a widespread acceptance of and conditioning by strong and possibly changing public opinion. Since the First World War at least, the place of women in the pubs has been questioned rather than accepted. There have been far fewer women than men in the pubs, their singing much less frequent. The remembered exceptions – holiday gatherings and suchlike – have merged into a general impression of a past where women sang as often as the men, where the village had a wholeness it clearly has no longer. Some reminiscences I have recorded are based on oral tradition rather than on first-hand experience, on the memories of grandparents of times no longer in the actual experience of any living Blaxhall people. Holiday times were an exception, special periods that may have gathered memories and stories around them, times that are more likely to have been remembered than the run-of-the-mill Saturday night. Blind Bessie:

> Old Mr Hewitt would never have us in that kitchen where the men all were, only holiday time . . . Holiday times we could sing in with the men, but we gotta keep out this other way unless it was holiday time. Come so we could go in there the whole time then.[9]

Alice Messenger remembers the women dancing when she was a child, about seventy years ago:

> There was a three-cornered green there outside the pub, they used to dance over the lighted candle. I have seen them do it, the women, be like a bank holiday, wouldn't it, dinnertime . . . I was only a kiddy then, I weren't supposed to be looking at it. They used to take that serious. I think that was Whit Monday they used to do that . . . It was just that day they did it, that was that. No men, nothing to do with them.[10]

Ben Ling remembers the candlestick dance being performed at Christmas time:

> Used to have a lighted candle on the floor and two of the old girls used to dance, pull their skirts up, you know, they got long skirts – pull their skirts up and do 'Jack be nimble, Jack be quick, Jack be over the candlestick.' Yes, they used to enjoy themselves.[11]

Perhaps acceptance of women in the pubs grew from the establishment of holidays and Saturdays as times for the lifting of restrictions, for enjoyment and for entertainment, and women were eventually allowed into the men's room where they drink at present. As the occurrence of women's activities in the Ship became habitual, the women were given the right to enter the main room of the Ship during the week as well as at weekends and on holidays.

Two problems are suggested by the women's rooms –

(1) did the women keep contact with the men's singing tradition, and if so, how?
(2) were the women aware of the imposition of segregation and how did they respond to it?

It seems that the isolation was not strictly enforced. Just as holidays and some seasonal activities brought the women into the men's room, particular events on any busy evening in the pub could bring the women out of seclusion into the larger room.

> *Geoff Ling*. They used to come out, that's right, yes. Used to come through. Well, the door used to be open – that used to be summertime often, you see, on a Saturday night. They couldn't go down every night . . . they used to have to go according to the money questions, you see.[12]

Ben Ling is also familiar with the singing and songs of the women in the back room, so clearly there was a degree of contact between the men and women in the pub, despite their physical separation:

> Oh, some of the old ladies used to sing, oh yes. They could sing well, too, that they did. Used to be poor old Anne Smith, she used to sing, and there used to be poor old Emma's song,
>
> 'What have you come to my pretty fair maid,
> With your red rosy cheeks and your curly black hair,'
>
> that used to be her song. O damn, old ladies'd get up there in that backhus' and sing like the devil, they would. Could hear them through there, they used to be enjoying themselves . . . Sometimes we would just listen to them. Yer, there used to be some old sports in there but they're all altered now.[13]

In Snape, women emerged from their room in order to dance:

> They used to go in the women's room – they used to have a chin-wag on their own just the same as the men, yes . . . When the dancing started, they all come out and hop around with the men.[14]

> You could hear them in the other room. They used to like a song, they used to get in the back and sing.[15]

I asked Lenny Savage whether the women would have their own songs while the men had theirs: 'Yer, but they wouldn't clash if that was a good 'un.'[16] He remembers that the women in the Ship emerged mainly for the dancing, and it seems that dancing provided a pretext for the women to come into the men's room that singing in itself did not, perhaps because the normal sexual contact suggested by dancing allowed the mixing of men and women, even for non-partner dances and song.

> *Blind Bess.* We used to join in with the men . . . We used to be as bad as them, really. I use to join in with them, 'The Volunteer Organist', 'The Rose of Tralee' and 'Take the Yellow Handkerchief', I learned them up there.[17]

Accounts from both Blaxhall and Snape tell of women like Percy Ling's wife, Violet, Bessie Ling and Blind Bess, singing in turn with the men, after being in their back room. The physical separation of men from women was therefore diminished aurally by open doors, and totally by the exodus of the women into the men's room. Dance tunes invited the women out, so did pleasing or well loved songs; and men sometimes listened to the women singing and asked for another performance. The women apparently kept contact with the men's singing tradition in the pubs, though not always at close range, and sometimes at home as well, hearing husbands and fathers, and possibly on other social occasions.

It is interesting, then, that although men and women in the pubs could hear each other singing, and had plenty of opportunities to hear each other on various social occasions and at home, there are differences in the men's and women's repertoires. In general, the women's repertoires are popular, whereas the men's are a mixture of popular and traditional. Bessie Hammond's repertoire is entirely popular. She learned a few songs in Yorkshire as a girl, notably 'Don't Go Down in the Mine, Dad', which she describes as a true and moving song which she picked up in an area where pit disasters were a constant fear. She learned other songs at work with other girls, and from the radio. She cannot completely remember any of the songs she heard in the pub, and says that this is because she did not go sufficiently often or involve herself completely enough. Blind Bess did learn a lot of songs in the pub because she integrated herself fully into the performances there; most of the songs she names as part of her repertoire are popular songs learned from Blaxhall men. A few are songs she got to know at home in London. It is difficult to know why she learned only popular songs she heard in the pub. Margaret Howell can sing only three songs, one of which is traditional but was learned from Ronnie Ronald's radio success, and two of which are popular: 'If I were a Blackbird', 'Over the Burning Plains of Egypt' and 'The Sailor Boy'; but these are not necessarily representative of her earlier repertoire which she says was more extensive. She learned all her songs within her family. Alice Messenger learned all her songs in her family and from women who organised charity concerts; all of the songs are popular. Ruby Ling knows almost one hundred songs (the largest repertoire in the area now, apart from Bob Hart's) and almost all of these are popular, learned when she was in service in London; the rest of her songs are older popular and traditional songs which she learned at an earlier age at home. Priscilla Savage's songs were all traditional, learned from her father or husband at home.

Women travelled outside Suffolk to go to jobs, and thus had opportunities of hearing popular songs and visiting the music hall. The men on the other hand, generally worked in the villages or around them on the land. The records of marriage in Blaxhall Church suggest that more women than men were literate in the village around the turn of the century, perhaps because most girls were sent into service and learned to read there;[18] women were therefore more equipped to read song sheets and songs printed in the *News of the World* and elsewhere. Because of greater mobility during early adulthood, which exposed them to strangers, literacy, towns and their professional leisure institutions, the women became in the common sense of the word, more sophisticated: less conservative, less satisfied with old pleasures and pastimes, more interested in innovation. When they returned to the village (or went there for the first time) to marry, they had to accept the dominant male and conservative social structure, but kept themselves apart from it where they could, for example by singing songs from the world they had briefly inhabited. Perhaps the older women like Priscilla Savage knew more traditional songs because these areas of Suffolk were more dependent late last century on tradition than on broadsheet and song paper publication. The men relied heavily on the pub for entertainment, and tradition was stronger there, with innovation inevitably occurring as popular songs spread and were taken up. The women developed repertoires of a largely popular nature by virtue of their backgrounds and personal preferences, whereas the men knew traditional songs and also popular songs.

The segregation of men from women in the pubs is not generally acknowledged as an imposition. The men regard it as an option, something the women chose; the women tend to regard it as something they themselves preferred, with the implication that they also brought it about.

> *Ethel Pearce*. The women wouldn't go in any other room, they always liked that old room best. Used to shut the door and nobody know you were in there . . . The men didn't go in that room, not very often. Sometimes they come in to their wife and give them a drink and go back.[19]

> *Percy Ling*. All Snape women used to get in there – Blaxhall women used to get in the backhus' at the Ship. Well, they wasn't forced to. No. They could come along with the men if they want to. That's just . . . their traditional way, I suppose, used to sit along and talk things over, you know.[20]

Ben Ling also stresses the optional nature of the use of the back kitchen: 'Used to go there . . . do their chinwagging and nattering, didn't have to go. Go where you liked.'[21] The story is repeated, however, that John Hewitt kept the women out of the main bar except for special occasions. The similar pattern in Snape, where no religious or dogmatic landlord is used to account for the situation, may suggest that the women themselves chose the backhouse as a place where they could be free, as Ethel Pearce's statement suggests. It is just as likely, though, that the imposition was soon turned by the women to their own advantage, allowing them privacy, the opportunity for conversation, and a place for the consolation of companionship. The regularisation of privileges, in the repetitive relaxing of rules, gave the women the freedom to engage in social events with the men in the pub, and thus they could enjoy their own company and that of the men. Out of living memory, women seem to have used the pubs more freely, but moral and social pressures towards the end of the nineteenth century discouraged women's attendance in pubs. Their very presence involved a relaxation of rules; their mixing with the men may also have resulted from a certain liberation; perhaps full emancipation may have been indicated by greater numbers of women singers.

The mothers of a lot of my informants did go to the pub. They went before marriage and after their children had grown up. Some of their daughters have entered a pub only once or not at all; some enjoy it as much as their mothers did. It is not clear why some daughters of pub-going mothers have not followed in parental footsteps. Suspicion of alcohol is not sufficient reason, because most of these women have brewed and drunk their own beer. It seems that the women who did go to the pub, who had remained unpersuaded by stricter morality, felt that they should stay home when their children were growing. Percy Ling says, 'Yes, I had five boys and five girls, yes, I got five decent pairs, they're all alive and healthy . . . The wife stopped at home when they were young, yes.'[22] Ruby Ling's mother did not go to the pub, but could have been a singer in other social contexts:

> She used to sing a bit then, you know, but of course she had a very hard life, my mother – 'cos if you have all them children, you don't have much time to do that sorta thing, do you, not really.[23]

This seems to be a common picture, of women ceasing to go to the pub during the years when their children were growing up or at least until the older children could baby-sit. Thus Frank Reeve, Lil Durrant's brother, says that their mother 'very rarely went in the Ship',[24] and so the picture is complicated, not only by some women's never going to the pub, but also by some women's not going to the pub (or perhaps only at holiday times) during the first two decades of their marriages. Ruby Ling went to the pub regularly at a very early age, and has not regularly sung in a pub since. The reason she went earlier was because her sister and brother-in-law kept a pub; this gave her the kind of protection and justification she would not normally have had for pub attendance. She now sings at a pub only if the Old Folks' Club stops there on an outing; these exploits were part of her youth. The use of a piano in her case may also have marked the difference between this type of performance (accompanied singing) and the usual pub-singing (solo). Other women, like Lil Durrant, never went to a pub before marriage, but were happy to accompany their husbands before their children were born, and occasionally when they were growing. She belongs to a generation younger than that of Percy Ling's wife: in her lifetime, there has never been a separate room for women, and pub-going with husbands is therefore more likely to occur.

Women who chose to go to the pub generally had to stay at home during the years of child-rearing. During the years of public house segregation, women did not usually go with their husbands, but those women born during the First World War years and the 1920s did go with their husbands. A still earlier time is remembered by some of the oldest villagers, when children were allowed into pubs and were therefore no bar to pub attendance.

> *James Knights*. Years ago, they used to take their children in the pubs and go to the pubs and used to be there; nothing about it, no. Didn't make a bit of difference if they were religious, not a bit, no . . . no . . . Must a ' been after the '14 War when they wasn't allowed children in the pubs . . . Damn, I used to drink when I was ten and eleven, you don't take any notice of that, no.[25]

He accepts that with the changed ruling, women with children should stay at home:

> There's a lot more go now than what there used to be because a woman what had got three or four children never dreamt of going to the pub on Saturday nights, you see, never thought of it . . . I was five when I used to go, walk down to the pub with my mother and father. They'd just go in for a bit of company, you see, that's all.[26]

When James Knights was five, the year was 1885. James Smith, born 1902, says, 'I think when I was born, children were allowed in the pub with their parents. Asquith altered that – children not allowed in the pubs till they're sixteen.'[27] In 1908, the Children's Act was passed, making it illegal for anyone under under 14 to enter a bar, and thus effectively excluding women with infants and young children. James Smith's testimony usefully substantiates that of Mr Knights in pointing to a changed social pattern consequent upon a change in the law. The statements about parents of men and women born early this century going to the pub together probably refer, therefore, to the time when children could go also, when pub-going was a family event and, possibly, less frowned upon.

Alice Messenger's mother and father would go: 'My father used to sing and my mother used to sing nicely, too . . . Father in the Ship. Mother used to go there sometimes.'[28] Alice herself has never gone to the pub, perhaps because in her lifetime there used to be a separate women's room, and the days of freer pub attendance with children were over. Her mother had grown up when families could go to the pub, and only after her social habits were fixed were the women separated from the men in the Ship.

With children no longer allowed in the pubs, some women did not do what was expected of them and stay at home – some continued to go to the pub. It seems possible that this occurred where a family condoned the action, and this was more likely in a family keen on singing, such as the Ling family. It may also account for Bessie Ling's stardom, as she married into the Ling family from the Smith family, another lineage of dancers and songsters. Stanley Day, born in 1913, cousin of Cyril Poacher, son of Sarah Elizabeth Ling, spent holidays in Blaxhall during his childhood, and remembers his mother leaving him to go to the Ship Inn:

> All the family used to sing, Uncle Lou, Uncle John, Uncle Arthur, Grandfather taught two of us songs . . . My first memory of going down to the Ship was, I came down here one year with my parents on holiday and I was put to bed, I was coming from town and gaslights and streetlights and coming down to a village like this, no lights or nothing, candle to go to bed with. Sleeping on my own was a bit nervous to me, which we all were when we were young. And you thought of everything and spiders and all this, and they said, 'We're not going to be long, we're just going out,' and during the conversation I hear them talking and they were going down to the Ship. I was only a youngster, I was only eight, so they put me to bed, and give me a candle, put it in the saucer, and I had a big smock on, nightdress . . . come to your ankles, flannelette, and I was so nervous and cried that I walked from Stone Common to the Ship.[29] And I asked someone, who it was I don't know, for my mother, and she came out and put a coat around me, took me in the saloon of the Ship, and put me behind a chair that night and till they went. When they got home, I got it – hiding. Well, there you are, that's my first recollection of the Ship, and then as time went on I used to go down there with my parents on a Saturday night and used to stand behind a chair.[30]

Sarah Ling was born in 1877 and did not marry John Day, a Harwich master mariner, until 1902. Stanley was born eleven years later, an only child. His mother could have gone to the pub before marriage in the days when children were allowed to go; she had eleven years of marriage without a child and was therefore free to go during that time. She came from a singing family who gathered in the Ship (apparently in the saloon bar sometimes) and thus would be expected there, too. After Stanley's birth, she continued to go to the pub on their holidays, even though he had to be left by himself, but after he had walked to the Ship by himself, she continued to conceal him behind a chair rather than leave him at home or stay at home herself.

Some pub-going women, in the years when their children were growing, sang only at home; some did not even do that because they were too busy or not musically inclined. Percy Ling says both he and his wife used to sing to their children; he also went to the pub at this time and sang, but she did not. Priscilla Savage and her husband both sang to the children, and he sometimes went to the pub and sang, but she never did. Her own father and mother had sung at home as well, and in the Ship. When mothers stayed at home with their children, they sometimes stopped singing; some of them continued it at the hearth. But there is a likelihood that while children were growing, a period of twenty years or more in the days of large families, those women too busy or too tired or not inclined to sing to their children at home may well have forgotten songs they had sung in their own childhood. Margaret Howell remembers fragments of several songs. Hers was a singing tradition centred around the home, and after the children had left and her husband had died, there was little to sing for: 'I sometimes hum 'em to myself when I'm in bed and got nobody to speak to and don't know what to do with myself.'[31] The women who sang at home or at social events had the potential of emerging as pub singers when their children had grown; very few did, perhaps because as mothers they were cut off from the pub and the tradition, and often taken into a woman's society with its own behavioural patterns and morality.

Work and Leisure

Girls worked hard from an early age, often on farms and in home gardens. Alice Messenger gives an impression of how busy they could be:

> Stone-picking, dropping potatoes for my father, picking beans, picking peas, picking up potatoes, picking up peas, picking up blackberries, there's always something to be done. Chopping up the food to give to the horses, always at work, always something to be done. And then going to the farms for milk in the mornings, go down to Dunningworth Hall . . . then I'd go to work to Wickham Market to the doctor's, five miles, that was ten miles . . . for the medicine, got threepence for going there, getting a bottle of medicine

. . . then go to school. Six o'clock up, five o'clock bed.[32]

Most of them went out to service when they left school, some at the age of twelve. This often involved a move away from the area: Ruby Ling went to London, Alice Messenger to Manchester and elsewhere, Bessie Hammond moved from Yorkshire to Blackpool, and Margaret Howell went to London. Many Suffolk women moved about and saw more of the country than the men did, although some local men went north to the mines, west to Burton-on-Trent, and out to sea as fishermen before they returned to the villages. Most of these women's husbands were too young for the First World War and too old for the Second World War, and all of them worked for most of their lives on local farms, in the Snape Maltings, or on the railways. Priscilla Savage went out to service at Little Glemham, two miles from Blaxhall, and Ethel Pearce went to Aldeburgh, six miles away. Work in service was physically hard and often degrading. Some employers treated employees like slaves, others treated them like whores.[33] Ruby Ling found herself pursued by a series of unattractive male employers. Margaret Howell was working for a drunken and ill-tempered woman from whom she eventually ran away. Ethel Pearce was also forced to run away from her work.

After marriage there was as much work to do, or more. Women bore children and worked hard, producing food and drink, earning small amounts of money in farm work and other tasks. Widows, especially, had to find work. After Bessie Hammond's husband died, she started work at a canning factory in Woodbridge. Burdened with an idle husband, Margaret Howell found herself and her child on the road, and she only just managed to avoid the workhouse by taking work in a laundry in Aldeburgh. Priscilla Savage's mother had to take housework in order to support her family because her husband had been crippled in a mining accident in the north of England. Women with idle husbands also worked hard.

> *Blind Bessie*. I used to go on the fields to work, used to go stone-picking, you know, picking the stones off the fields, make great heaps of them and then the horse and cart used to come, you see, and get them what they used to make roads with, and then we used to go blackberrying and we used to go potatoing and then beeting, used to go gleaning, used to like doing anything like that.[34]

Her aim was to earn some money for herself, and since she had no children she could probably afford the luxury of desiring some money of her own, but her husband deducted what she earned from her housekeeping money, and she thus lost her incentive to work in the fields. Blackberrying was considered suitable women's work by him, but nothing else. Most women, however, worked at stone-picking, fruit picking and gleaning to supplement the income of the whole house, and Ruby Ling has managed to buy a pair of cottages with money she and her husband have saved from jobs besides his full-time work at the Snape Maltings:

> Used to go blackberrying and sell them . . . People used to come round here with carts, you know, and buy the blackberries then, you see . . . I been potato picking, I been on a stack . . . when they were thrashing corn . . . I been doing housework. I done all sorts of things really, done nearly everything I think I could do in the world.[35]

Most women who worked were closely involved in the community; few needed to travel to factories, as employment was usually readily available on farms and in houses in the immediate vicinity. One of the younger women, Lil Durrant, worked solely on the land, as a couple of middle-aged spinsters in Snape still do, and housework was available and is now institutionalised in the home help system.[36] Ethel Pearce is still a home help, although she is in her late seventies, and many mature women in Snape and Blaxhall are home helps, including Lil Durrant, Dorrie Hart and Frank Reeve's wife. Some of the older women need a home help, but in the past would have been helped by family and neighbours. Bessie Hammond and Eva Ling used to do housework and be on call in Blaxhall to be present at births, to nurse the sick and to lay out the dead.

Ethel Pearce expresses the effect children had on her work habits:

> I went potato picking a little while but I couldn't keep it up, not with the children small, couldn't do it, could you? They were home from school. You got to be home, haven't you?[37]

Children limited her hours of work because she felt she must be at home for them, but she was able to work once the children grew. Work was more crucial than entertainment because it supplied food, and women could work before children were born, once they were at school, and after they had grown up. The work the women did both in the home and outside it was virtually full-time, and they therefore had less time

The Crown Inn, Snape, from an undated postcard, and The Crown Inn, Snape, and Snape Street, 1974

Ship Inn, Blaxhall

Cyril Poacher at Grove Farm, Blaxhall, 1974

Bob Hart singing at home, Snape, 1974

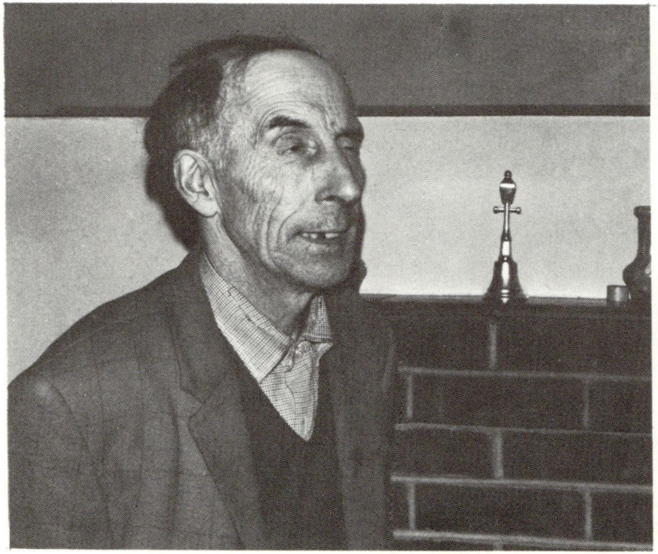

Ruby Ling singing at home, Snape, 1974

Clive Woolnough outside the Blaxhall Ship, 1975

Priscilla Savage and Wickets Richardson, Blaxhall

Blaxhall

Maltings (1974)

for entertainment than the men did. These families could scarcely spare enough money for one person to go drinking, so if one parent had to forgo the pub, it would be the wife. In this way, the pub reflects the whole organisation of British society,[38] which considers women more fortunate in their work than men,[39] and it is likely that in a society where such a view prevails the use of wages by men for drinking and the recreation of men in male company would be the norm.

Besides work for money, women had many tasks in the home: bread-making, beer-brewing, cooking, knitting, sewing and, of course, general housework. The preparation of food was an involved process during the early married lives of most of my informants, much as it had been for their mothers and grandmothers before them. Percy Webb describes his mother's baking enthusiastically:

> There were seven of us children and she used to cook twenty-one loaves of bread a week, and loaf cakes in a brick oven, which she used to heat with bushes, then when the ashes had got down, burnt out, you pulled it about with a thing they called a fork, rustle it up, and then – set it in there. Lovely bread that was, just as good then at the end of the week as it was at the beginning – better'n the stuff we get now.[40]

Priscilla Savage's detailed descriptions of bread-making and beer-brewing can be read in George Ewart Evans's *Ask the Fellows who Cut the Hay*; she was also adept at other aspects of household economy and worked hard to feed her husband and twelve children:

> My poor old father used to say when I had the children small, he said, 'Do that gel ever sit down and have a meal?' and I said, 'No, not very often, I got to see after them.' You know, I used to bake up five stone of flour twice a week. Bread and cakes – they were of the bread and then we used to get some currants and a piece of lard, and that there used to be what are called cakes. . . We used to fat a pig, and then a man used to kill it and dress it and then we used to have half of it and sell half then – people what was at the shop at Tunstall, they used to buy the other half and then they could sell it by the pound, and we used to . . . salt all the . . . leg and hand and a bit of the loin, we used to harvest that and make that into ham . . . that'd be ham, and the other used to be bacon, dear. When my mother used to do it, get so much salt and salt petre and she used to hang it up in the chimney to dry.[41]

Her children sometimes helped; once when she was ill, her son Percy made soup from two sparrows he had trapped and some vegetables:

> I was abed, I weren't well, and the doctor come. 'Hm, hm,' he said, 'what have you got in there, boy?' and he had got a twelve pints saucepan – I got it to this day, that hang in the shed – so he said, 'I'm making some soup for the boys' dinner.' 'Oh, well, what have you got in there?' He said, 'Two sparrows. Yes,' he say, 'I got some onions, carrots and turnips,' he said, 'in, and I got twelve swimmers' – well, that was dumplings, you see, what we call these here. And so the doctor said, 'Give me a cup, boy,' so he give the poor old man a cup and saucer, old man dipped the cup in and took it out, and he said, 'Give us a little pepper and salt.' Boy said, 'You won't need no pepper and salt.' And he say, 'They won't take no harm from it,' and that's all that was, two sparrows. They used to have bricks, dear, and they used to have one brick like that slanted, and they'd pull that down, that'd kill the sparrow, you see. They'd have a trail of wheat underneath these bricks here . . . That's how they used to get their living, dear.[43]

Vegetables were grown by each family, and exchanges could be made. A similar transaction was carried out by women when brewing and baking because yeast was an important commodity, and it was collected from one house after brewing to be used elsewhere for baking. Such domestic tasks were reciprocal and communal, largely dependent in the early years of the century on local produce, and were enforced by the general poverty of the area.

A woman unable to provide food, drink and other necessities had to be taught since there were no local shops to supply the basic needs of these villages. Thus, Blind Bess, coming from London, had to be taught by her mother-in-law:

> I never knew how to do it, not till I came down here to live. Used to have to make all my own clothes after I got down here to live. His mother used to think that a waste of money, if you went to a shop to buy clothes . . . I never done any beer, his mother did. I used to do wine . . . bake bread and things.[43]

Jobs in the home, the provision of sustenance and clothing were as demanding and time-consuming as the husband's job of bringing home money. The day-to-day life was close to needs and distant from luxuries. Entertainment must have been necessary to alleviate the careful wresting of a living from low wages and unreliable harvests.

For both men and women, church and chapel, clubs, village activities such as fairs (Snape used to have a horse fair) and harvest frolics have provided interest and entertainment. For men, the British Legion and quoits matches have flourished. A lot of women have been performers at village socials and concerts, at old folks' clubs, and at harvest suppers; some of these women have never or rarely sung in a pub, a few sing as often in pubs as they sing publicly elsewhere. One activity in which women played an important role was the harvest supper. Here, the economic role of the women combined with their potential as performers. Here is Priscilla Savage's description:

> Well, they used to hire the big room [of the Ship] and then, you see, the mothers of the men what were doing the harvest, they used to cook the meat and vegetables, and the women used to go and have the supper with the men . . . Used to have a singsong, my dear, and my father used to play what they called a concertina . . . The old people used to know good songs.[44]

Bessie Hammond describes a harvest supper in the parish hall:

> That's how I first come to have a little song in Blaxhall parish house fifty years ago . . . We had to do the supper for our husbands, and after the dinner was over and there was this little here get together, somebody said, 'Will Mrs Hammond give us a song?' Prissy told them, I think, that I used to be singing about there . . . and my husband didn't know and I didn't tell him anything. I thought, well I'll just give him a surprise. I said to Prissy, 'We won't tell him,' I said, 'he'll have a shock when I get up there,' I said, 'on that thing,' and he sat in the front and when they said this, I said, 'Oh aye,' I said, 'I'll give you a song.' Anyway, and of course I could sing better than I can now, and I got up on the stage – and you shoulda seen his face. He sat and looked at me. I thought, I reckon I shall hear more when I get home, getting up there like that, you know. I didn't. I was surprised when I come home. He said – 'Bet' – he always called me Bet – he said, 'You know what, I never knew you could sing like that, I never heard you before.' 'Ah,' I said, 'you didn't did you?' Took it all in good part, you know, and that's the very first song I ever sung up there, 'The Broken Doll', I sung it there, you know.[45]

The harvest supper in East Suffolk seems to have been a village celebration enjoyed by workers' families and the farmers. The women did most of the work for the supper, and were invited to perform in the singsongs afterwards and to dance with the men. Bessie Hammond's story illustrates how a woman could be championed by her friends on such an occasion and thus have her singing accepted by her husband who had previously been unaware of her talent, and who, it seems, might have been expected to disapprove.

A mainstay of village life was the concert or social, and women singers who did not approve of pub-going could perform here without fear of redress. Ruby Ling is a regular performer at these, so were Alice Messenger and Eva Ling until they gave up singing. Sometimes the village concert was organised by the Women's Institute or some other body, sometimes it was non-affiliated. Concerts organised by groups drew on members especially and on the general population as well, but the latter mainly as audience; village concerts in the strict sense of the word were open to everybody and were given impetus by a festival, a special event, or by a yearly tradition. Some organisations cross into both territories and run a concert *for* the village, as the British Legion now does in Snape. This is perhaps because village co-operation has broken down to the extent where an ordinary unsponsored concert would not get under way without an organising body. The organised concerts of the past, in Blaxhall for instance, are spoken of as a service to the community, deliberate attempts to entertain the village population in return for a small amount of money. Women played a major part in such events in Blaxhall and perhaps elsewhere, eventually forming concert parties which could travel to entertain.

The Women's Institute was a strong organisation in the villages, popular because it entertained frequently and included men in its social events, as Bob Hart relates: 'I always looked upon that as a good institution because when they had their party at Christmas, they could invite the husbands.'[46] Eva Ling was a member of the Blaxhall Women's Institute, and she describes the sort of concert they organised:

> Every month we used to have a concert to raise money for funds, and during the War when the boys were away, we used to have a whist drive or a concert every month, and we'd put that money away and when the boys came home that was divided out, they had a little bit of money each, you see. I was on the committee, we was a very good committee us women were, and we demanded that we were going to have this money. I belonged to the Institute, I was on everything . . .

> And then we used to get up these sketches out of a book . . . and Frank Reeve's mother, poor old Truey, she was very good at them when we used to get up the plays . . . I always used to sing 'The White Cliffs of Dover' . . . The young ones wouldn't take it up and we just finished like that.[47]

There were also concert parties that existed almost like clubs in their own right. Alice Messenger used to belong to one run by Mrs Thompson, a woman now living in Aldeburgh for whom Mrs Messenger was part-time housekeeper. Undoubtedly Mrs Thompson set the tone of these concerts, as she still does; they are primarily for charity, for old folks and the blind rather than for general village entertainment. These concerts came about because of an influence exerted from above, and the parties were largely populated by those women who had married into the village but were not natives, or by those who were not involved in the centre of village activities: although they gave some women the opportunity to perform, they did not function within the village traditions.

The Blaxhall Rovers was a concert party that sprang from village men and boys who travelled the area providing free entertainment and were often given alcohol by their hosts. Women were involved in the group mainly at the level of preparation and costume-making. Frank Reeve joined the Rovers when he was about fifteen years old, and he describes the sort of entertainment they used to present:

> Popular concert party, we had, very good. Lot of us used to lady impersonate and have very good times. I used to sing, I used to be one of the lady impersonators then – we tried to get three of us to do the lady impersonators, one to take the elderly lady, one to take the middle-aged lady, and one to take the young lady. Because we done an item once, a concerted item, and that was called 'Sitting on a Five-barred Gate', and that patter was made up, where the couples all met at the five-barred gate and there was patter in it. I remember I was dressed up as a young lady. I borrowed a pair of my sister's shoes and all very funny, you know, and very good, and it was something in those days which did stand in for people. I mean, they loved it, and they done something for themselves, you know.[48]

The fact that there were female impersonators implies that women did not take part in many sketches; perhaps impersonators were always used in comedy sketches and real women in serious sketches. It is interesting that women were made fun of in this way. The Rovers may have been influenced by music hall, where female impersonation by males, and male impersonation by females, took place, but Wickets Richardson, who organised the concerts, had not been to London at that time, and if he was influenced by hearsay knowledge of the music halls, he accepted what he wanted, or what was acceptable in Blaxhall terms. The Rovers were male, and when females were needed in sketches, male impersonation may have been both practical and a source of humour. It is possible that the three ladies Frank Reeve describes were modelled on local types, and men were able to vent anger or amusement on replicas rather than on wives and mothers. To make fun of someone or some group is to bring that person or group to one's level; the young men in the Rovers may have needed the catharsis of making fun of women in a society where women were frequently excluded from male activities and knowledge.

At home, the women had another audience. There, women who sang in the pub, those who sang at concerts, and those who never sang publicly could croon to their children or join in family singsongs around the fire. Home singing was a major entertainment on winter evenings, at family events like weddings, and at Christmas. At home, the women seem to have been as much to the fore as men in singing. Almost every woman I have spoken to in this area was sung to as a child and has sung to her own children; fathers also sang, and on such occasions families were close and bound together. Priscilla Savage and her husband, Robert, both sang at home:

> I don't sit and sing to myself now like I used to, but really our Dadda Bob used to – sat and sing songs and when we done them, we used to set and sing hymns. Well, that's the only pleasure we had, weren't it? I forget them 'cos I ain't got no children now and I don't set and sing to them now, like I used to. Well, 'sing to them', I used to make a noise, didn't I?[49]

Lenny remembers her singing to them:

> She used to have us around – you see them little footstools . . . we all had little footstools and we sit round her and she used to sing us all so we got so tired and then we faded off to bed.[50]

The Pub and the Home

Singing provided entertainment, lulled children to sleep, and cemented family solidarity, especially when the father was present. The home provided the primary audience of most women singers in this area, whereas the pub provided the primary audience of most of the men. The women's role was thus defined in the home, and the men were more free to form multistranded relationships elsewhere. The women's room in the Ship may have provided a necessary sanctuary where women could consolidate relationships with each other that helped immerse them in the village in a wider sense than through reciprocal economic arrangements and helpful neighbourliness. The women could thus form an awareness of themselves as a group, just as the men did in their frequent bouts of singing, dancing and drinking in the pubs. The men's mobility, and their common pastime of visiting several local pubs in one evening was generally beyond the bounds of married women. Women were home-centred, tied by families and public opinion, and thus pushed, paradoxically, into more active searching for extracurricular activities. Some, perhaps those from families of singers or those with sufficiently extrovert and assertive characters, found confidence in their performances of song at home and were thus encouraged to venture further. Those who objected to alcohol or the public house itself took to performing in village concerts or women's club concerts; those who did not object won their audience in the pub. Women who sang at home but not elsewhere, like Priscilla Savage, were sometimes religious, contented home-lovers. Sometimes they were simply too busy to sing elsewhere.

The pub became male territory, or was made so, perhaps by a man like John Hewitt, the pious landlord of the Ship. The presence of women there was an issue rather than an accepted fact. Subtly, by pressure of public opinion, and the established morality of the age, by pressure of laws and ideas about the role of women, some people were coerced into the belief that women belonged to the home and not in the pub. Surprisingly, sexual mores in Blaxhall and Snape even now are less stringent than the declared morality of the urban working and middle classes; perhaps this is because hypocrisy is seldom tolerated and behaviour therefore takes on a manifest existence in that it is what it is, a spade is called a spade. Sexual acts can pass as sexual acts and not as immoral acts. Many of the people in these villages have this straightforward attitude. It is strange, therefore, that there are clear rifts in local opinion about the place of women in pubs. Those who hold the view that women do not belong in pubs are generally concerned with the correct role of women; some of the women amongst them are home-lovers, some refer to the shortage of money. Generally, however, there is a prejudice at stake rather than a fact. The prejudice seems to result from a societal imposition or reaction to a looser morality, rather than from a long history of puritanism.

The general morality of a village may be shaped by the teaching of the church or chapel. There is a suggestion that in Blaxhall and Snape the people who regularly attend church or chapel are also those who criticise pubs in general, and consequently pub-going women in particular. This is suggested by behaviour rather than by statements. Stanley Day is a regular church-goer, and he supplied me with a list of 32 people who attend church regularly in Blaxhall; of these, 5 go to the pub about once a week and 6 go sometimes. Two of these weekly pub-goers are also singers, and none of the other pub-goers is a pub-singer. Eva Ling disapproves of women going to the pub, so does Alice Messenger, and both had connections with the church when they were younger. Priscilla Savage also believed her place was at home and she too had been a church-goer. The fact that present church-goers are not also the people who overtly express disapproval of women pub-goers may not be a true indication of the correlation between religion and a stricter morality, since those who disapprove of women in pubs may be prevented from attending church by old age and infirmity. Mr Day's list of church-goers certainly suggests that pub and church attendance do not usually coincide.

In general, those who disapprove of pub-singing by women are angered by the public house as an institution and also by the effects of alcohol. If the first attack is on the pub, then drink is used afterwards as a rationale for the outburst; if drunkenness is criticised, then the public house is mentioned scathingly as its source. Alice Messenger and Ruby Ling both abruptly say that they do not like the pub, and when questioned, they can give no reason for this. Pushed further, they mention drunkenness and its connection with violence. It is possible that many women suffered at home from drunken fathers and husbands and therefore turned against the source of the drink, the public house. There are many stories of violence in these villages; the stories describe public violence, but there must follow the suspicion that violence, or at least ill temper, occurred at home as well. Fights usually occurred during drinking bouts, tempers could be inflamed and be rekindled at home. In any case, violence does not always burn up its energy in action, and can be automatically triggered above a certain level of alcohol. It is possible that men did not want women in the pubs because pubs are neutral ground where men cannot be as freely dominant as they can be at home, and the incursion of pub into home (when the man arrives home drunk) or home into pub (when the woman goes to the pub uninvited by her husband) can result in conflict. The man's drunkenness may result from his fear of his wife, and her treatment of him may result from the fixedness and hopelessness of her lot.

Frank Reeve suggests a way in which women could have come to hate alcohol and its effects:

> I think that years ago too, if there was any trouble and the wife was there, the wife would often go and get in between and stop them and really do that herself. That was many years before my time. I don't remember a lot of those times.[51]

Alice Messenger also blames the violence on alcohol: 'They get a drop of beer and then the balloon would burst. That's when the fights used to happen on a Saturday night.'[52] It seems that questions about pub activities to non-pub-goers can lead to expressions of disapproval and to descriptions of the least attractive aspects of alcohol consumption. It is likely, therefore, that unpleasant experiences connected with alcohol, allied with a moralistic attitude towards drink, can lead to a denial of the pub as part of life. Another illustration of the association between violence, a manifestly wrong type of behaviour, and alcohol, an intrinsically neutral element, is the following exchange between Ben Ling and his wife, Eva:

> *B.L.* Used to be the Slenders and Smiths, they'd fall out about something, go outside and knock one another about there awful.
> *E.L.* Too much beer I suppose.[53]

Such assumptions are undoubtedly the result of experience.

Women were warned about the evils of alcohol and pub-going by their parents, and those who ignored the warnings deserved no sympathy. Priscilla Savage exhibits this knowledge of the evils of drink:

> When I first met my husband, my father said, 'If you get married, you don't want to stand and talk to him outside, you can ask him in,' he said, 'because', he said, 'if you have him come in,' he said, 'we'll make him welcome because', he said, 'you'll have a good husband.' I said, 'Yes, I shall never marry a drunkard if I know it, 'cos I think it's a sin getting drunk.' Because if they drink, they don't treat the wife as they should do, do they? I don't mind a man having a glass of beer, I aren't against that; but I don't like a drunkard, don't

> know how to behave, and there's some of them around here don't.[54]

Some women had good cause to dislike the pub and its alcohol because it not only deprived them of their fathers and husbands, but also caused the men to spend money needed for food, and it could make a man angry and violent. Those women who drank therefore deserved and received little sympathy from those who believed in moderation. Drunkenness was almost a daily occurrence in the villages, according to the older inhabitants, and its evils could therefore be witnessed often. Moderate drinkers, both men and women, could be misjudged by those whose principles kept them out of the pubs, and the creative activities connected with the pub, like singing and dancing, were overshadowed by the more conspicuous and destructive events like fights and brawls.

Priscilla Savage, a woman with principles about alcohol, had positive reasons for keeping away from pubs: she liked her home and children: 'The pub don't interest me, you see, dear. I'd rather go down to the chapel and hear the children say their pieces, I love to hear the children say their pieces.'[55] Men, also, could share such feelings, as James Smith describes:

> I was there in the Key one Saturday night, and all the children were being bathed at home, and I was drinking my pint, and they're playing darts, so I drank my pint and off I went, say 'I'm agoing,' stay home and help mother, so I got off it Saturday nights after a time, you see. Well, you see, there's more comfort at home than where the darts team is, isn't there?[56]

John Ling tells why he stopped going to the pub:

> That was mostly, I suppose, well, money wise, really. Better use for it. I still like going down, but of course, there's a difference between being single and married, I mean there's the money reason and then you got somebody else to consider, whether they fancy you sorta going out often and going to public houses and that.[57]

It is possible that women in the last thirty years have no longer thought it fair that they should stay at home with the children while their husbands go out. Some women seem to have found ways of coercing their husbands to stay at home.

A lot of women, however, have not exerted such influences on their husbands, and it is true to say that women have generally been regarded as second-class citizens in Blaxhall, and probably in Snape as well. Women have been informed of their role and made to believe it was pre-ordained; this role included keeping away from public houses. A typical version of the male attitude towards a woman is given in this account by James Knights of his wife:

> When I married, I married, and my wife was at home, she kept at home, she kept at home and done her work, she wasn't like they are today, pack the kids off to school, don't see 'em no more, not till nine or ten o'clock at night.[58]

The appropriate attitude of women, full proof of their acceptance of duty, is seen in the following statements, the first by Margaret Howell, the second by Eva Ling:

> I never have been [to the pub]. I don't like them. I don't believe in women being in pubs.[59]
>
> I had two sons, and that was my place to be at home. I wasn't brought up like that, you know. We were sorta isolated and I was never brought up to it, so I never used to go, 'cos that wasn't my line of life. My line of life was more at home doing sewing or knitting, that's what I used to like. . . It never appealed to me . . . other women never used to bother. I mean, if the children got up and got out, well that was nothing. But my mother drilled it into me that I wasn't to go to a pub when I came to the village, you see, and of course I never went.[60]

The woman's role as mother, by definition, excluded the pub from her social life since it took her away from the home where her centre was.

The definition and enforcement of the female role was sometimes subtle, through public opinion and pressure, and sometimes direct. It is likely that, in so small a community, neighbourly watchfulness and the creation of guilt feelings controlled much potentially rebellious behaviour. Priscilla Savage describes her own experience in relation to the Ship Inn:

> I never been used to the Ship . . . I never used to go there. I never used to go. I went one Sunday night for a walk with my brother. I said, 'I don't want no ale, I'll have a glass of ginger wine,' so I had a glass of ginger wine. When I went in, my husband was in the other room, he went home. I said, 'That's the first time, that'll be the last.'

> I never been in since. He didn't like women going into the pub. That weren't his idea, I suppose, he never used to use the pub a lot himself.[61]

Reg Jay's mother was not only kept out of the pub, but also forbidden to sing at home:

> If I sung in the pub, I didn't tell mother I sung, or father, you see. That's just how that carried on. I mean, they weren't cruel to us or anything, they were just poor. . . . I can remember when we was young, she'd sit and sing to us, nice sweet voice she'd got, which people round there'd tell you, and perhaps he'd be outside, and when he came in she'd whisper, 'Better shut up now, father's a-coming,' so we still got no forwarder from what we started from.[62]

In neither of these cases were the men cruel, but they simply had attitudes about the place of women. Geoff Ling puts it this way:

> Some women didn't like the entertainment, some prefer to go to the pictures or something . . . and some weren't allowed to go down. Bet that was a lot of the cases. I mean, they couldn't, they had to do what they were told, didn't they, I mean, they couldn't – their house was their castle, that's what they used to say, didn't they?[63]

Apparently the pub was the men's castle, and Stanley Day suggests that alcohol was actually one item in a man's armoury against his wife, and that it aided him in his struggle for power:

> Some of them used to be the masters, the men were masters. They didn't worry about the women. They used to go down to the Ship and have their pints and stop there as long as they wanted to, and either they'd get in the pony and trap, and pony would take them home, used to go back and forth so it could go blindfolded, and that's how they used to go.[64]

Men in the pub tended to behave as if they were at a secret lodge meeting. Indeed, the pub can become an institution to which the drinkers belong, to the exclusion of women. Wickets Richardson tells how he used to call on men to sing in such a way that their identity was hidden:

> Someone would ask, 'So and so will sing so and so.' I'd say, 'Order, please, Mr So and So . . . ' – wouldn't say his name in a pub or everyone would know he was there, including his wife – I said, 'Mr So and So sing by special request so and so,' and he'd get up and sing it, sit down.[65]

Basil Bennett describes how the introduction of women to British Legion outings actually killed the outings:

> I belong to the British Legion and I . . . join the Blaxhall Branch, and . . . when we first joined . . . we had enough for two buses to go to all the rallies, rally once a year at Felixstowe, Stowmarket, everywhere . . . that carried on for several years, and we had a lovely day, and the pubs were open all day for us. Best day of our lives. And then as the years went on they said, 'Well, why not have a ladies' section?', so they had the ladies section of the British Legion at Blaxhall. They formed that in January. Well, when the end of the year we had the rally, at Felixstowe, the ladies come with us. We were all . . . mixed, ladies and gentlemen, the wives and husbands, and of course, the old girls, they come out and they watched. They were open all day, and we were drunk; drunk, and they watched what them old boys had into them, and . . . – I shall never forget it – at the Martlesham Lion acoming back – they wanted to stop and have one for the road, and half got out and the women all stopped in. She say, 'I think you old men have had enough today.' And of course, we took a lot of cases with us on the bus, and of course – Ooooh, they set about them blokes, after they got home, and broke the Legion up. We never went to another rally, they disappeared out of the Legion, the Legion finished and the branch finished. I come back and joined Snape and we're still on the road. We ain't got no women in Snape . . . but – ooh, they put the damper on that, that won't do to have that combined. They just see it as how much we had. My wife weren't with me, but the others were, I'm sorry to say, and them old boys can drink, you know, we were drinking all day.[66]

The women may therefore be seen as dampeners on the men's activities, on their fellowship through alcohol. Secrecy, or the exclusion of women from men's socialising, may therefore have seemed a way of protecting what was valuable and enjoyable. Amongst the men who enjoyed the pub, women would have to prove they were 'real men' before they could be accepted; they would have to behave with as much bravado as the most fun-loving man and show themselves to be good sports, perhaps, as Robert Savage might have thought, they had to be 'loose' women; and they would have to forgo personal complaints about husbands being out at the pub and about the effects of alcohol. The men with moral objections about women in pubs would have to change their morality in order to live with a pub-going woman, but such a man would probably choose a home-loving and compliant woman. It is likely that there existed processes of selection in the pairing of male and female for marriage, based upon attitudes towards alcohol, public houses and the roles of men and women.

There may have been sexual reasons for the segregation of women from men. Many of the songs in the men's repertoires are bawdy: 'The Nutting Girl', 'As I Strolled Out to Aylesbury', 'Underneath the Apron', 'Female Cabin Boy', 'The Boy with No Shoes', 'Don't Do It Tonight', 'Little Ball of Yarn' and so on. On one occasion in the Ship Inn, Percy Ling felt he must curtail 'Don't Do It Tonight' because of the presence of a group of middle-aged women he did not know.[67]

> *Bob Hart*. I look around the company when I'm going to sing one of these here naughty songs, as I call them, I look round the company and if there's the young girls in there or anything like that, no. You get the real old-fashioned company agoing – I mean, they'd take anything. But that's very embarrassing – well, say there's a young girl in there about sixteen or seventeen and with her mother. Could happen, you don't want to sing these bawdy songs then.[68]

If women accepted the overt sexuality of these songs, perhaps they were allowed into the male society. Those women who were regarded as good sports, like Bessie Ling and Blind Bess, were encouraged by the men to perform, and these women's frankness and love of fun enabled them to break social barriers and become performers in a men's world. It is possible that the women's candlestick dance emphasised female sexuality and thereby condoned male/female sexuality. Bob Hart's description of the dance suggests the phallic and inviting nature of the dance; not only is it sexual, but it is also energetic and unladylike and actively rejects the notion of a woman as staid, legless, slow-moving:

> Ladies used to have long dresses in those days and, used to be their long dresses hanging on the floor. When they danced, they used to go through here [between the legs] and pick the whole dress up so they were holding the dress time they were doing it . . . That used to

be rather nice to watch . . . They used to all dance over that one candle, and 'course, when the candle went out, they'd all have to start all over again.[69]

It appears that in the last century, women in these villages were involved in pub life, and were later forced into a separate room by a stricter public morality, perhaps springing from the law excluding children from public houses and from contemporary discussions about the immorality of pubs and alcohol. The establishment of Saturdays and holidays as times when women were more free to go to the pub and to be with the men there eventually led, along with changing public opinion, to the abolition of the women's room, and the acceptance of women in the men's room. Women sang at home mainly, and also at village concerts and socials, but only those in exceptional circumstances have sung in the pub. Somewhat cut off from the male singing tradition, the women have different repertoires from the men, based on popular songs rather than on traditional songs. Different employment patterns enabling more travelling may have caused the repertoire differences. As always, repertoire is a response to life-style and situation. Even now, the evenings in the Ship are dominated by men, and those women who go are audience to the singers. This situation is a reflection of the role of women for the last forty years in the pubs and in the villages; at the moment there are no women singing with the men, and the men themselves are fighting perhaps the first direct enemy of their tradition, the young people and their juke-boxes.

Notes

1. James Knights, 11 Sept. 1974.
2. The women's room or back kitchen at the Ship is now the private kitchen of the Saunders family. In the Golden Key, the back kitchen was where the counter and bottles now are, next to the main bar or big kitchen.
3. Fred Pearce, Blaxhall, 23 June 1975.
4. Bessie Ling, Blaxhall, 2 Oct. 1974.
5. Ibid.
6. Ibid.
7. Bessie Hammond, Blaxhall, 30 Oct. 1974.
8. Stanley Day, 24 June 1975.
9. Bessie Ling, ibid.
10. Alice Messenger, 31 Oct. 1974.
11. Ben Ling, 2 July 1975.
12. Geoff Ling, 2 Oct. 1975.
13. Ben Ling, ibid.

14. Percy Ling, 2 Nov. 1974.
15. James Smith, Snape, 21 June 1974.
16. Lenny Savage, 1 Oct. 1974.
17. Bessie Ling, ibid.
18. It should be noted, however, that writing ability, especially ability to sign one's name, is not true indication of reading ability. See R.S. Schofield, 'The Measure of Literacy in Pre-Industrial England' in Jack Goody (ed.), *Literacy in Traditional Societies* (Cambridge University Press, Cambridge, 1968), pp. 311-25. The Blaxhall evidence still suggests that more women had literacy abilities than did men, but exact evidence is unavailable.
19. Ethel Pearce, Blaxhall, 24 June 1975.
20. Percy Ling, ibid.
21. Ben Ling, ibid.
22. Percy Ling, ibid.
23. Ruby Ling, 11 Sept. 1974.
24. Frank Reeve, Blaxhall, 24 June 1975.
25. James Knights, ibid.
26. Ibid.
27. James Smith, ibid.
28. Alice Messenger, ibid.
29. A distance of about one mile.
30. Stanley Day, ibid.
31. Margaret Howell, Snape, 8 Oct. 1974.
32. Alice Messenger, ibid.
33. This is no exaggeration. There is a statistical correlation between prostitution and domestic service in the late nineteenth century. See H.L. Beales, 'Victorian Ideas of Sex' in H. Grisewood (ed.), *Ideas and Beliefs of the Victorians* (Dutton Paperbacks, New York, 1966).
34. Bessie Ling, ibid.
35. Ruby Ling, ibid.
36. The home help system is a service of Social Security which provides help in the house for the elderly and disabled.
37. Ethel Pearce, ibid.
38. It is also possible that segregation in the pubs occurred so that the man, unseen by his wife, could spend more on drink.
39. For example, Josephine Klein, *Samples from English Cultures* (Routledge and Kegan Paul, London, 1965), p. 53.
40. Percy Webb, 19 July 1974.
41. Priscilla Savage, 11 Sept. 1974.
42. Ibid.
43. Bessie Ling, ibid.
44. Priscilla Savage, ibid.
45. Bessie Hammond, ibid.
46. Bob Hart, 5 Oct. 1974.
47. Eva Ling, Blaxhall, 2 July 1975.
48. Frank Reeve, ibid.
49. Priscilla Savage, 10 Sept. 1974.
50. Lenny Savage, Blaxhall, 10 Sept. 1974.
51. Frank Reeve, ibid.
52. Alice Messenger, ibid.
53. Eva Ling, ibid.
54. Priscilla Savage, 31 Oct. 1974.
55. Ibid.
56. James Smith, ibid.

57. John Ling, Snape, 1 July 1974.
58. James Knights, ibid.
59. Margaret Howell, ibid.
60. Eva Ling, ibid.
61. Priscilla Savage, 15 Nov. 1974.
62. Reg Jay, 25 July 1975.
63. Geoff Ling, ibid.
64. Stanley Day, ibid.
65. Wickets Richardson, 27 June 1975.
66. Basil Bennett, 2 Oct. 1974.
67. See Chapter 1, 'Men's Singing Institutions', recorded at the Ship Inn, Blaxhall, 19 July 1974.
68. Bob Hart, 17 July 1974.
69. Bob Hart, 5 Oct. 1974.

3 THE YOUNG PEOPLE

Introduction

The young people of this area of Suffolk have not, in general, carried on the local singing tradition. I do not know of any young women who sing, but there are a few young men who are either latent or active tradition-bearers. However, in most cases, there has not been a straightforward handing on of tradition, and changes have occurred. There are several identifiable groups, some distinguished by age as well as by singing habits.

The most common type of singing done by people aged from 18 to 44 is in country and western style; such singing may take place in the pub, in which case it is active, or it may take place at home, in which case it is a latent form of the local singing tradition since this tradition involves public performance. These country and western singers explain that they love the old songs as well as the country and western songs, and they link the two because both types of song tell a story; to them, country and western songs are the modern equivalent of the older men's traditional songs, since both are narrative forms. Since these are young men they feel it appropriate that they should sing the modern form of the old narrative song type, and it is possible that as they get older their repertoires will embrace several decades or even centuries of songs. There is no deliberate exclusion of non-country and western songs from their repertoire, although in most cases there is a comparative abundance of the more modern songs. A younger group of people, those between 12 and 20, know fragments of a lot of the old songs, prefer modern heavy popular music, and throw scorn on country and western. It is impossible to know whether any of these will become pub-singers in the old tradition in later life. The most unusual of the young singers, Clive Woolnough, stands on his own. He used to attend the Folk Club in Leiston, and he learned some songs there as well as learning several of his father's traditional songs. He occasionally sings in the pub, but his primary function there is that of chairman. He is the only young local person in whom it is possible to recognise the traces of the pub-singing tradition, and his uniqueness is a mystery. However, he does not sing often, and his chairmanship is often half-hearted. By far the largest group of youngsters includes those who know fragments and some complete versions of older relatives' songs, but who have never been known to sing in public. And true to form, as may have been suggested by the nature of the women's singing, there are no girls who show any signs at all of either knowing songs or of becoming performers. In general, there has been, throughout recent generations, a decline in pub-singing. The old singers report this impression over and over again, and it does not seem to be the result only of nostalgia, of glowing memories of a past imbued with community spirit, and the participation of the whole local population in local activities and entertainments.

Learning: the Family and the Village

Without exception the older singers, from James Knights born in 1880, to Geoffrey Ling born in 1916, sang in their youth. Songs were often learnt in the home from parents, older siblings and relatives. Some, like Bob Hart, still sing songs they learned at school ('The Death of Nelson', 'Roast Beef of Old England', to name a couple). Service in the First World War also added to the repertoires of those old enough to enlist: Percy Webb sings 'Broken Doll', 'MacCaffery', and 'O It's a Lovely War'; Bob Hart sings 'Break the News to Mother', 'Just Before the Battle, Mother', 'Keep the Home Fires Burning', 'No Man's Land', 'Pack Up Your Troubles', 'Take Me Back to Dear Old Blighty', 'When the Fields are White with Daisies' and others. Similarly, the Second World War provided songs for those men young enough to fight: Geoff Ling sings 'Suvla Bay', and several know songs that Vera Lynn made popular. By far the greatest number of songs was learnt locally, in pubs, where men would sing and listen to each other and learn each other's songs. This process involved transmission from old to young, and vice versa, and it was here that a latent singer could become active, where repertoires limited by family and occupation could expand and alter.

When singing was a major form of entertainment in the home and the pubs, as well as at local concerts and socials, those parents who liked to sing would encourage their children. James Knights's parents encouraged him, and singing was clearly a part of his life as a child since his sister had a piano and she used to play the melodies of all the songs that appeared in the *News of the World*, so that he could learn them. Reg Jay believes that he did not become a singer because he did not have the family encouragement and singing environment that his cousin Cyril Poacher had:

> Just as I'm setting here I couldn't think of a song, but [if] you walked out of that door and I got a screwdriver in me hand, then I'd

> start – funny, but that i'n't so with Cyril, because Cyril is a brought up family of singers, you see, and I think that's where the difference is made. That's like Alf, Alf Richardson, he was brought up, his family all the way through, all his brothers, all songs, and I think when you're brought up to singing that makes all the difference. We were very much restricted, you know, in the family . . . Now Cyril's father and mother, they were songsters, their family was, so that meant no difference to Cyril at all, whether he went in a pub or whether he didn't go in a pub, he would just set indoors and sing, but if we started singing indoors we get a cup flung at us or something like that, you see, so that was altogether different . . . So we still got no forwarder from what we started from. Only by later years having the old time gramophone and about eighteen year old sneaking into a pub and joining in with old timers . . . As I said, my family, we were brought up, we had no gramophone till later years and I think that's where it started, and if we sung indoors, mother would sing, but if we sung indoors he'd say 'Go to bloody hell with that singing, boy', like that, so we had no change. But with other families, that's like Geoffie, I heard him say he'd sat on his father's knee and he'd cut into it . . . 'Come on, boy, pick it up,' that's a wonderful thing. I'd 'a' loved to, I'd 'a' loved to learnt to sing when I was young, as I just told you, to go in the pub and give somebody some enjoyment with singing.[1]

Not all children were prevented from becoming singers by such active discouragement as Reg Jay describes. But he firmly believes that had he had the same upbringing as his cousins Cyril Poacher and Geoffrey Ling, he too could have been a singer. Given the necessary parental support, a child could develop an inclination for singing, as James Knights explains:

> I wouldn't sing if I wasn't in the mind, not bloody likely, girl, no, no. But you see, when I was ten and eleven year old I used to get up in concerts and sing 'cos that come to me all the time you see, so that was what I used to look forward for. That come to you, you see, like anything else would. O yes, I was always used to it, and of course with me abeing used to it I used to carry on with it, and the more practice you had, my dear girl, the better you got. You have to have the practice for it. If you keep singing and keep singing, well of course you can sing, but if anybody thought they could sing and if they had a go, well that gradually come to them. It did to me, and you see, with me sister having a piana at home, course that was

the very ideal thing for me. Cor. I sung hours to my sister, different songs, different pieces that we used to sing, you see, sung hours. Then, of course, when I went to a pub, well of course they used to want me to sing and I used to want to do it.[2]

Parental attitudes have clearly continued to influence the continuance of the tradition and its transmission. Bob Hart had a son, Claude (he died on 14 July 1966, aged 45), who was a popular local singer, well known for his performances of 'Two Little Boys', 'Sorrento', 'White Cliffs of Dover' and several comic songs. Frank Woolnough's son, Clive (born in 1947) is chairman at the Ship and a singer in the old style. Reg Jay has sons who sing at home and whose voices are admired there, but who are shy to perform in public. One of James Knights's sons plays an organ and sings in pubs, and Percy Ling's youngest son plays a guitar in a local country and western band and his other sons sing. Percy Webb's son, Vivien, is a harmonica player and is sometimes heard in local public houses. However, a lot of older singers have no children who continue the tradition or who show any signs of doing so in later life. The long family singing traditions of Cyril Poacher and Geoff Ling have not led them to produce any traditional singers; for Cyril, this may largely be due to the fact that all of his children are female.

Some informants attribute the earlier extent of the singing tradition to the closeness of the village community. Co-operation and chauvinism could provide a wider base for the continuance of local mores than could the family, and the condoning of singing outside the home in the social setting of the pub could function like a *rite de passage* for a young local man.[3] Once performing in the pub, this person was clearly one of the primary group, an adult perpetuating a local tradition and thus accepted by the already initiated. Thus the conservation of the musical tradition mirrored the conservatism of the community.

Geoffrey Ling regards his inclusion as a young man in the life of the older villagers as a result of the correctness of his upbringing, and as a parallel to his role within his family. As children grew beyond the family, the wider environment of the village could become a secure base or something to be shunned. Shunning, since it involved a rejection of parental and consequently of local values, could only lead to trouble. Geoffrey's initiation into the affairs of men led to his acceptance of the *status quo* and the core group's acceptance of him as an adult.

I was brought up properly, my parents did. I mean, if you swore in the house, you wouldn't say it only once, you wouldn't, and . . . you got to have your manners, yes, and you wouldn't answer back, you never thought of it. If you saw a policeman, that was enough, even if you hadn't done anything. I don't think there's enough discipline, I think that's the trouble . . . I mean, if you get somebody, if he don't do anything, if he don't take an interest in it, well all he think about is trouble, isn't it? But if he was to say, 'We'll have a little entertainment, I'll sing or I'll do a job or play a game of billiards, go to the Men's Club up there, up the parish hall' – they got one in Snape, haven't they? We used to go out at night and play a game of billiards, used to have tournaments. See, we used to play all them parlour quoits, darts. There was a billiards table; everything up there, cards, everything, whist drives, used to hold whist drives and get money together for the Club. Well, yes, there's none of that now, is there? . . . That's how you hear about me singing so much, see, 'cos the other ones don't, do they, they don't want to know. All they want to do is go and put the money in the juke-box. You can't do anything local unless you got a background. See, what it is, the youngsters today, they don't know anything about these old songs. They think it's a bit of recitation to them.[4]

Stanley Day, Geoff's cousin, shares many of these feelings, and is concerned with the breakdown of village community spirit, and the estrangement of young people and newcomers from the old way of life.

There's no kindness and thoughtfulness in this village amongst some people. Those days are gone. When I knew Blaxhall, I knew all my life, but I would like to see the good old times come back for the village. And of course we know you can't bring the dead back, but people what passed away, the elderly people, they were more considerate and they were more thoughtful and they were kind . . . As the old people of the village go, so that there age goes out . . . [the young people] seem to grow and leave the village to go further afield. But of course, they've got so now I think in the village, they've got a job and they've got cars and they've got a good wage, and of course night life, and they leave the village and go further afield and then come back home, I suppose in the evening, have a cup of tea, have something to eat, and go to bed and that's that. They don't patronise their village 'cos there's nothing here . . . But the people clung together more many years ago than what they do now. And they're not so helpful. Everybody's out for themselves. Whether that's the way things are going, hard times or what, I don't know.

> Like Blaxhall, it's a fine place. Some of the people are not what you expect to find. We know you can't live in the past – it's a possibility, though. I'm afraid those good days are gone, and not only that, as the people pass away, their property goes up for sale, and you have people come from away, they buy, which is only natural. I don't blame them, but they come in the village and they try to do good but they can't. They don't seem to take the people in the village like they should do. My grandmother told me you got to live in Blaxhall ninety-nine years to get initiated, and that's true, 'cos if the people in this village don't take to you, you might as well get out. Now, that's Blaxhall.[5]

The earlier days are clearly loaded with nostalgia for Stanley Day, but it is a wise nostalgia. His evocation of village life as it was is often poignant: the absorption of each person into this life was crucial to him: 'I'd sing. Cyril, Alf [Richardson], Johnny [Ling], Bob Scarce, George Scarce, Arthur Hewitt the landlord, myself, old Tom Curtis, whoever was in there. They took a dim view if you didn't – you was all one then.'[6] Thus, the singing of songs and the hearing of them must have been, in the youthful years of these older men, imbued with a sense of security, kinship and social worth:

> Me mother passed away, my uncle's pa, the Lings, all that generation of the Lings have gone, and, I'm another generation. That's another generation to carry through . . . The young people don't remember the times and the old Blaxhall people and the old Blaxhall songs and the good times and the good nights we used to have in the Ship, and the good days we used to have in the Ship, like dinnertimes we'd sing songs. I think that, well, the young generation, they don't know the songs, they don't know the good times, only the times what are coming along now. Which is pop music and folk songs which are coming back, you know, which were old time years ago, old times songs, and they're all coming back now, and the majority of the young generation are taking to them. But in our time of day, if a song came out, an old song, you sung it, and that carried on for donkeys' and donkeys' and donkeys' years. Like hymns . . . 'Abide With Me' is a Blaxhall hymn. Now why they should pick that hymn for Blaxhall I don't know, but that's a proper Blaxhall hymn and I think if you talk to anybody or go to a burial who has lost somebody, and they sing that hymn, you might sing the first two or three lines, but after that, you have a lump come to your throat,

that's a horrible feeling. You sing the first two or three lines in good spirit and good feeling, but after a while, they get to you somehow. I don't know. I've been like that, and I've spoken to several people who feel the same.[7]

The old singers could not have felt such nostalgia as young men, but the songs they sang then must have had the emotional aura of social appropriateness and approval. The process by which young singers became traditional singers may have been much the same for decades: newcomers to the adult world of the pub learned and performed current popular songs, and as the old men died, the new generation performed the traditional songs which they had long heard and learned but had sung only in other pubs or not at all. The local principle of song ownership does not make it impossible for a singer to perform a song commonly attributed to another, but such a man, especially if younger than the song owner, would be thought ill of by many of the pub-going audience. The simplest way, therefore, for transmission to occur through the generations was for the replacement singers to be present while the older singers performed, to have repertoires of their own made up of songs held in common possession (they were generally current popular tunes), and to sing the old traditional songs only after the older men had died. Thus, popular tunes prevented the new singers from becoming threats to the tradition-bearers, and acted as a sort of front to the learning process. In addition, they supplied the young men with a viable repertoire. And, by definition, they were also well liked, and often became favourites which remained resident in a repertoire expanded by the addition of traditional songs. Geoff Ling and Cyril Poacher explained their acceptance into the pub-singing life:

G.D. Does that mean you learnt some of the songs that were sung most?

G.L. Yes.

C.P. Yes. Well, you see, the ones we learnt are the ones he [Bob Scarce] sung the most. I mean, it wasn't no good hearing him sing one today, dinner-time say, for instance, and he didn't sing that song no more. I wouldn't learn that in a dinner-hour, but he used to sing this one so many times that you knew what you was going to have.

G.D. I wondered whether any of the old singers ever told you that you could have a song or something like that.

C.P. No, they didn't tell you. They weren't supposed to know you were learning on it, were they.

G.D. Well, what happened? Did you just never sing them when they were there?

C.P. No, not one of theirs.

G.D. Did you have to wait till they were dead?

G.L. No, no.

C.P. No, you sing it somewhere else.

G.L. But if he sang it, you wouldn't get up and sing it behind him, you see . . . If you got up and sang a song, well nobody need get up and repeat it, that's how it used to be.

G.D. But would you ever sing it in front of him? I mean before he sang it.

G.L. Not as a rule, no, not as a rule you wouldn't, no. We used to leave it to the old boys what sung them songs, you know, just so you could keep in good company, that's what they called it, good company. You didn't want to offend anybody. If Cyril sing a song, he'll sing a song. I'll sing a song, just like you ask us. That's how it was with them . . . Well, we used to sing the songs what used to be in the 1930s, the later ones, the popular ones, you see, like what used to come over the wireless, see, and then I got some song books there that were on a paper there, that's called *Fourteen Best Songs* – used to pick them out, you see, like, 'The Pale Moon was Rising above the Green Meadow', and all those ones, in the thirties, you see. Well, Bob's and that used to be all of the 1912s and that, didn't they, and a lot of songs come out just after the First World War, that's where they took 'em all from, didn't they, see.[8]

Stanley Day's descriptions of the old days in the Ship are as enthusiastic about the old popular songs as they are about the traditional songs:

> I think the progress is too quick. You can hear a song Monday and that's top of the pops. Next Monday there's another one get top of the pops. In that time of the day, those songs went on for months and months and months, and years, until a new one came out. I mean, if that was a good song, well, that stuck, and that was sung.[9]

Lenny Savage, like Cyril Poacher and Geoff Ling, sang the popular songs in the pubs when he was a young man, and his repertoire now, though small, is a mixture of these and traditional songs ('The Rose of Tralee', and 'Nancy from Yarmouth', for example):

> I was like the rest of them. I sung the current songs of the day – but

> they're all gone now. There's another one what Cyril sing – 'Riding Along on a Free Train'. There's another one. 'There's a Lamp Shining Bright in the Window' – that's another one. You see, the songs we sung when I was a young man – we had a concert party, the Blaxhall Rovers, and we used to go round.[10]

Whereas now older men object to most modern music, they did not object to the popular music of thirty years ago. The younger singers were thus able to supply the tradition with new songs in the old vein, and were also able to learn the old songs of their fathers and grandfathers.

The fostering of the young men by the old-timers gave the new pub-goers a non-active introduction to the singing tradition. A man who had not sung much at home had the potential of becoming a performer through his acquaintance with local music in the pub. As part of the audience he could join in with the choruses even if he never sang solo; and confidence gained through chorus singing could lead to solo singing. It seems that not many decades ago, almost all village men went to the pub, and there it was not liked if they did not perform. Chorus singing provided a role for those who could not be soloists, and thus enabled them to remain in the ranks of the older initiated members of the society.

Mrs Saunders, the landlady of the Ship, believes that the young people who join in now may be learning the old songs, even without knowing it, and may become singers later on:

> One gets the impression that the young people don't like the old people singing, and yet I have heard two or three of the young people in the village ask for an older one to sing – 'When are you going to give us a song?', you know, so I think they do enjoy it. I think the young people are coming to appreciate this sort of thing, and know that if they don't keep it going, well it's just going to die right out. I think this is a thing they're just sorta beginning to realise . . . I don't know whether there's many taking it up. They join in. Whether they'll carry it on I don't know. They probably will when all the old people are gone, and if they can memorise the things, I think when all the old people are gone, it'll be like a little spring of water that will gradually emerge.[11]

Learning: the Media and the Modern World

The arrival of the mass media may have had the greatest effect of all on the past tradition. Stanley Day, for one, laments that the pop songs of today pass quickly and have no meaning or value, whereas the old songs of his youth were true songs and stayed with their audience because the songs embodied emotions and knowledge relevant to these people, and became imbued with personal meaning. Modern society is a consumer society: materials are constantly replaced and the youth culture and popular culture depend on a rapid turnover of goods. Objects are created imperfect so that replacement will follow; songs are similarly short-lived and readily replaceable. Groups and pop stars rise and fall, and all but a few songs disappear into oblivion after promotion gives them a brief vogue. The isolation and stability of the old rural society was the antithesis of the modern consumer society, and as consumerism and change filtered into the older life-style, the *status quo* was upset, the local people upset, the traditions placed in jeopardy. Wickets Richardson ceased to be chairman at the Ship after 35 years when he realised there were elements of dissension in the pub;

> We used to carry on like that till they turned you out, then, at ten o'clock, and we had a lovely evening, but I kep' it up till what – ten years ago, yer, but you got, you know, so that when the sorta young ones come in they didn't want any old songs and that. They used to 'Oooh we don't want any of that,' see. I packed it up, I was no longer MC . . . Once you give an order, they were quiet, till latter years . . . Didn't stop going, I never stopped going. I used to join in with them when they used to sing, if I knew the songs. I used to join in with the chorus and that, yer.[12]

Things have turned full circle: in the face of opposition, and the comparative rarity of singing evenings, an old soloist becomes a chorus singer. He is on his way out of the tradition and all it stands for to him and others like him. He is a disillusioned man, and misses the old company he had in the pub.

Popular music now is not liked by the older pub-goers, but years ago the older men did not mind it, and learned some of the new songs themselves. The nature of this music has altered: there was not then the same commercial machinery behind the rapid output and promotion of both songs and singers. It seems that those songs (banal as many of them may appear) were of more universal appeal: they praised human, home-loving values, they mourned the sadness of war in a melodramatically direct mode which appealed to those touched by loss or injury. Contemporary commercial music for the last twenty years has concentrated on a youth cult, on romance, and on the feelings and importance of the individual. Pop songs largely exclude the parental generation (not to mention the grand-parental), and it is therefore likely that their appeal is limited. The usually rapid passage of these songs prevents their inclusion in local repertoires. Popular music of the present day serves no function in the pub-singing tradition whereas the popular music of previous eras did.

The incursion of the mass media into rural life has undoubtedly removed the need for people to provide their own entertainment:

> You see, years ago we had nothing of that. We never had a wireless or a television or nothing of that. You either gotta go to the pub to have a little enjoyment, enjoy yourself, or stop at home, and you got nothing at home to enjoy yourself with, see, so you gotta go there to have a drink and sorta liven yourself up and have a singsong, and that used to be the enjoyment. You had nothing else to do. But now, of course, they got television, they don't want to go out. Wireless and television. All they got to do is sit there and somebody else do the singing for 'em. That's the reason they don't.[13]

However, Mrs Saunders at the Ship acutely observes that the media have had one positive effect on the singing tradition: folk-songs have been made popular through their distribution on record, and consequently young local people are no longer so inclined to disparage the old men and their songs, and some have become involved in the folk-song revival. Cyril Poacher and Bob Hart have both made solo albums, and other singers have contributed tracks to anthologies produced by Caedman, Topic and Transatlantic.[14] The prestige that attaches, in the eyes of the young working-class people, to making a record in itself is almost certainly a factor in their increased respect for old singers, although the folk-song revival has not generally broken into the 45 r.p.m. market, which is still dominated by songs which are unsingable in terms of the village tradition, and with which the juke-box, as an apparatus, exclusively deals. There is a kind of local patriotism in Jack Saunders's playing these records in his pub, but there is an obvious irony in the playing of a pub-singer's record in the very pub where he performs, and the situation neatly epitomises the change in attitude towards singing which is happening in Blaxhall and Snape and which is already complete elsewhere.

The media have entered the pub to the chagrin of many older residents, and threaten the singing evenings. Reg Jay tells of his experiences:

The present day, the young boys go into a pub, and as long as there's music in there, juke-box, they're well satisfied. And if somebody else was trying to sing, they're interrupting . . . But the youngsters, I think if they'd got any leaders who would be interested in 'em like they were in our days – as I say, this village has got no one now . . . There were no juke-box in them days, so you just got to sit there and listen to accordion [sic] and the songs being sung, and with a juke-box in a pub for older people like myself, that's up the creek. That's just now agetting so I think the juke-box is going to ruin the music in pubs in time. I think the people will say, 'I can sit and listen to a record.' I mean, now they've got Cyril's record on and you come home and you don't go to the pub to hear it 'cos you just set down and put it on your record-player and you got it there.[15] So things like that may be doing harm to some pubs. I mean, if you can hear 'The Farmer's Boy', you don't want to come on a trip to hear it. You heard it once and you'll hear different things . . . I was in the pub a few Saturday nights ago, and he'd got 'em on. Well, other nights, you coulda went in there and said, 'Come on Cyril, give us a song,' but you didn't want 'em because you already got 'em on there, and I think that's the thing that's going to spoil it . . . I mean, you can just say to Jack [Saunders], 'Put Bob Hart on,' and he put Bob Hart on, I mean, you go to Snape, say, 'O Christ, we heard you, you had your chips,' so you go back to almost square one . . . As I say, that's no good now, because you go into the Ship, the record is on, so when he come in here, you say, 'O, don't want you Cyril, 'cos we heard the bugger in there' . . . I always thought how lovely it is to set down there and to hear somebody play an accordion, and the people singing, and now you go in there, that's all a juke-box, two bob in there, and there's some squit on there you don't understand nothing about, and I think the youngsters put the money in and they don't know what they'll get at all. Well, if he'd a given the two bob to a bloke would play an accordion, then he'd a got somewhere with it, but youngsters are youngsters.[16]

I asked Mrs Saunders what she thought the effect of the juke-box and of the fruit machine in her pub might be:

Fruit machine we've had in about seven or eight years, I should think. The juke-box was installed I should think about two years ago, mainly because there was a lot of youngsters using the place. They're quite a long way from any dance halls, discos. During the week when

> there was no singing, they liked a bit of music . . . We've got the controls behind the bar, so that if it's too loud or annoying, we can turn it down. When we have our live music, we just switch it off. Just wait until somebody has played their records and just switch it off . . . No one has made attempts to ask for it after then, therefore it does show that they appreciate the old people singing, and the old folk-songs. Probably they prefer them to the others. It's a sort of go-between, you know, just something to keep them occupied when there's no live music. No one wants it then. That's like going to a theatre show – that's much better live than it is on film, isn't it? . . . This was a thing went through our minds for several years before we actually got it put in. Would it go down? Would there be any sort of controversial sort of element come into it between people that wanted to sing and those that wanted to listen to it? . . . Everybody accepted it providing it's under control and you can turn it off or you can turn it how when you want it . . . The landlord's got to make a decision if it's on or off.[17]

It is often the case, however, that the juke-box is not switched off when people want to sing. On 5 September 1975, by nine o'clock Percy Ling, Cyril Poacher and Bob Hart were ready to sing but the juke-box was still playing loudly. Percy wondered whether to ask the landlord to switch it off, but was afraid to; Cyril called to Mr Saunders to switch it off, and the other singers and Oscar Woods, an accordion player, mumbled complaints for a good half-hour before it was finally switched off. The young people at the other end of the bar complained and pulled faces, and were very noisy while the singers tried to perform. There was no order even though Clive Woolnough occasionally called for it. If he was acting as chairman then, he did so in a perfunctory manner and had scarcely any effect at all; he was with the young people, whereas the singers were all at the other end of the room. He did not participate in the singing, and played darts throughout the evening. On other occasions, although more order was given, the singers had to wait a long time before they could begin singing. Thus, whereas in the past, older singers included youngsters in their performances, and initiated them into the tradition, it now appears that the majority of the young people in their teens and early twenties are in opposition to the older generation and often make it virtually impossible for singing to occur in the pub.

There were numerous social events at which singing used to occur in these villages: at any of these it was possible for a young singer to become a public performer. Clearly the local singing tradition was tied up with the pub and the drinking of alcohol, but a teetotaller was not excluded by his principles from singing since there were plenty of other opportunities for performance. Non-pub singing was more open to women than the other tradition and, as has been shown, some women found their way into pub-singing through prior public appearances at concerts, socials and such events. Young men were included in older men's activities at quoits matches and other sports events; in this case, a youth might be invited to a game for the first time, and thus be given the right to join in with the other events following, a drinking bout and a singsong. The age at which a youth began to attend the Men's Club might also have been a watershed between immaturity and adulthood; his acceptance into the club by older members was an acceptance of his maturity. Stanley Day recalls the past order:

> Then once a week, they used to have concerts and mothers' meetings and do's up the parish room, and everybody was in, everybody would mix, farmers and people, and they was always there to give you a helping hand, but nowadays everybody is out for themselves.[18]

The society was hierarchical, with the farmers and churchmen in the highest position. And within the confines of the village itself, there was another hierarchy amongst the people: age superior to youth and male superior to female. Some women were able to break barriers and enter into the men's world, but there was a steady dominance of men over women, and the entry of a few women into the pub-singing tradition was not part of a process of transition. The dichotomy between age and youth was a self-perpetuating state of change, wherein young people were absorbed into adult life through behavioural as well as biological changes. Non-biological change was often formalised into a *rite de passage*, such as marriage; less obviously, the arrival of the age when drinking became legal could, in the case of males, be such a rite. And besides the first legal entry into the pub, and the ceremonies of buying drinks and consuming them, performance was a clear indication of the individual's establishment in the primary adult male group of the village. Women were similarly initiated by marriage, by motherhood, by attendance at women's clubs, and, in fewer cases, by pub-going. Whereas different generations were subsumed into the pub society, different sexes were not so easily absorbed there. However, some families went to the pub and, as we have seen, many people remember very happy times there with all types of people mixing.

It is a fact that there are a lot of bachelors in Blaxhall, presumably another function of greater female mobility, and several of them are singers (Freddy Ambrose, Arthur Drewery, Abraham Ling, Alderman Ling, the late Bob Scarce, amongst others). Possibly the singing tradition continued in their hands because they had nothing to stop them from going to the pub often. They started to go to the pub as young men and have continued to do so.

However, the twentieth-century shortage of women in Blaxhall cannot entirely account for the male domination of the singing tradition, since it would seem that in societies where the sexes are unevenly balanced, the less numerous sex usually becomes the more powerful because it has bargaining power. In Blaxhall, the tradition could have continued as it did because of the large numbers of men with few commitments other than their jobs. After their introduction to the tradition as young men, there was little to entice them away. Now, the young men are confronted with a barrage of new sounds and sights from the media and from fashion magnates, they have added mobility, they are largely forced out of the village in search of work and they are consequently more likely to meet women from elsewhere who may become their wives. Introduction to the singing tradition is therefore not likely to have much impact, as other life-styles will appear more attractive, and, in any case, they may be living away from their village in a house with wife and television. The unmarried people who go to the Ship do not like their juke-box being switched off so that the old men can sing, they mostly work out of Blaxhall, and there is litle to make them follow in their fathers' footsteps. Mrs Saunders describes the clientele thus:

> Summertime it'd get quite full. Wintertime you'd probably get about a dozen that'd sit around the fire. Mostly the bachelors would come down. There's quite a lot of bachelors that sit around the fire on winter evenings . . . Probably you get the married people come in and have a drink and go home again. But the bachelors were the ones who were there until closing time. You know, they used to sit round the fire, and some of them used to bring in chestnuts in and roast, they had a lovely time. I used to enjoy going and sitting with them, you know, talking to them. There wasn't much else for them in the area, and they sort of discussed things, had a laugh and a joke. I think they really enjoy themselves.[19]

The learning of songs was partly by chance but it was also the result of diligence. It is likely that if songs are not being learnt now, it is because there is no reason for young people today to feel dedicated enough to bother. Those who use the Ship as their local pub have often either broken away from the village and live elsewhere, or have come from elsewhere for the evening. They do not sit with the old men and thus they do not necessarily listen to their songs. The closeness of the community has been shattered; old men can no longer take boys under their wing and teach them the old songs; nor do they work together in the fields as they once did, thus nurturing another bond of contact. The few children there are in the village have to travel to school by bus; when they leave school they are once more forced out of the village to work, and the village has consequently opened up and the old traditions are therefore not as strong as they were.

At present there is very little for the young people in these villages to do. Bob Moore, the landlord of the Golden Key, Snape, arranges a dance once a month in the village hall.[20] His pub has some fruit machines, a soccer table and a darts board which young people from the age of fourteen upwards use. It is common for those under the age of eighteen to go to this pub, perhaps because Mr Moore's young children are usually in the bar. Bob Hart's grandson, David, and a lot of his friends go there about once a week.[21] These lads are not interested in girls so they do not go to dances; their recreation is mainly in the Key, eating crisps, drinking Coca-Cola, and playing with the machines, or they attend local football matches, support Ipswich Town Football Club, and sit on their bicycles outside the Snape fish and chip shop. These boys also have a shed in the Harts' back garden, where they tell jokes (often bawdy), talk, laugh, smoke, eat and drink. Some of their discussions centre on the old people in the village, and on what they know of local singers, including those in Blaxhall. Few of them have been to Blaxhall and they regard it as a slum about which jokes should be made:

Adrian Last. Blaxhall – never heard of the place. That's where all them niggers live, outbacks.

Christopher Berry. Those cavemen.

A.L. They still got candles in their bedrooms, they haven't got electricity.

Stuart Haggard. One of them came out of his cave the other night – 'I invented the wheel.'

C.B. If you walk through and you blink, you miss it. And if you've good eyes, you'll see it . . . There's a big oak tree and that hides everything.[22]

They imitate Bob Hart singing 'What a Funny Little Place to Have One', and they imitate his ordering a half a pint of bitter and a cheese sandwich at the Key. They especially make fun of the old men who get drunk, and their slurred songs. It is almost as if singing is regarded as one of the old men's idiosyncracies, along with urinating on the way home from the pub, bicycling up the Snape Hill and having to get off to walk, going bald, deafness and obesity. These signs of old age are often talked of by these boys in the same breath that they talk about singing. They are well acquainted with a humorous oral tradition about long-standing local inhabitants. They tell the story that one old man lost his hair because he was afraid of having to join the army. They say another is known to have a permanent barrel of beer in his house. None of them admits to liking the old songs except for the funny ones, and they think that all of the songs would be more bearable if the audience were totally drunk. They associate the songs with old age, its concomitant physical decline and with drunkenness.

Two of these boys, Adrian Last and Christopher Barry, sometimes entertain the others with mock folk-songs such as 'Margy on the Farm' and 'Little Old Tree', which each boy makes up, by himself, in the style of one of the old singers. These parodies are often bawdy or underline the banal humour of some of the old men's songs; the gap between youth and age is emphasised when teenagers extemporise bawdy songs (modelled on those the old men sing) which suggest, through parody, that the old men's vicarious pleasure is (or will be) for the youngsters a reality. None of them seriously considers that he might be a pub-singer in later life, although Paul Rumsay makes intelligent comments about the old singers and may well be attracted to the songs though loath to admit it because of pressure from his peers.

Those of drinking age in Snape usually go to the Golden Key, as the Crown Inn and the Plough and Sail are regarded as unwelcoming by these young people. At the Key on Saturday nights there is usually singing and music, and a local country and western band will play and the audience will join in and make a great deal of noise. Some of the older singers, like Percy Ling and Dowey Bloomfield, go to these evenings, and if one of them sings, there is an obvious gap between his type of performance and that of the guest artists. It seems that the old style of singing there will die with the old men, but it could be that some, among the audience for the country and western and popular music, are silently learning the old songs.

MARGY ON THE FARM

as sung by Christopher Berry, 25 June 1975

2. And then there were Bill.
   Old Bill, he come down from the town,
   And he went along to Margy.
   He said to Margy, 'Get them down.'
   But Margy said, 'You get back to town.'
   So poor old Bill, he went back to town,
   And there he went and he wept and he died,
   Only 'cos Margy wouldn't get them down.

3. And then there were Bri.
   O then there were Bri.
   O Bri he did, he come from the town,
   He went along to Margy,
   And he said to Margy, 'Will you take 'em down?'
   Old Margy say, 'Not for you,
   No, you get along back to the town.'
   Poor old Bri.
   Old Bri, he went back along to the town,
   And there he wept and he cried,
   Until he finally died,
   All because Margy wouldn't get them down.

4. And then there were Joe.
   Now, Joe, he didn't come from the town,
   He come from the road down from the farm.
   Now, he went up to Margy's place,
   Said to her, 'Will you please get 'em down?'
   And so she did.
   Poor old Joe he went back to his house,
   There he wept and he finally died,
   All because Margy got 'em down.
   'Cos he got too much.

Poor old thing, he got too much,
That bloody well killed him. [spoken]

LITTLE OLD TREE

as sung by Christopher Berry, 25 June 1975

In Blaxhall, the juke-box is of prime importance in attracting young people to the pub, and they sit at the end of the long room near the juke-box. The darts board is also at that end of the room, and when there is a darts tournament, some of the older singers (Percy Ling, Cyril Poacher) do not bother to go to the pub. Reg Jay says, 'I think singing is dying out in pubs, in a lot of places, I think darts could overtake singing and that, weekends.'[23] Certainly the players are all young. The fruit machine is as popular with the old men as it is with the young people, although some think it a stupid waste of money. With their little bit of gambling, their sport, their music and their girlfriends from other villages, the young men of Blaxhall and the surrounding area seem at the moment to have little impetus to become singers in the old mould.

Tradition: the Old and the New

The few young men who do sing are folk-club members or country and western singers; a few more are latent tradition-bearers. It is significant that most of the latent singers are younger than the active singers; confidence through chorus singing and maturity may turn them into public performers. David Hart's friends Adrian Last (his father sings popular songs at village concerts) and Christopher Berry (the parodist) could possibly develop into pub-singers. Reg Jay says that his son, Ivan, has a good voice and knows some good songs, but is too shy to sing publicly.

The biggest body of younger singers like country and western. Arthur Drewery, who is not young but is of the middle generation which has supplied very few singers in the area (Geoff Ling and Cyril Poacher are the major exceptions), sings in a country and western style, and knows songs such as 'Blackboard of my Heart'. One of Percy Ling's sons plays in a country and western band, and the landlady of the Ship has noticed the popularity of country and western music:

> It seems to me to go from pop music to country and western, from country and western back to folk music. In other words, the stories have come back into the songs again. The beats of the pop music and the jumble of the pop music has died a bit. Country and western took over a little from that so that you got a story to the melody and then that has stepped to folk music again. There again, you've got a story to folk music haven't you. So I think this is where it's sort of gradually coming back. I've noticed this.[24]

John Ling, born in Snape in 1938, gives a similar description of country and western music:

> Well, I learnt most of them off records, you know, and I did know one or two of me father's, and the ones I knew from him were mostly country and western style, but I never heard them on record, 'I Had a Home Down in Texas', and . . . there were three or four I know like that, they were more or less of the country and western style, though they were old songs . . . The country and western I always did like it, singing, and as I said, I like these old sorta songs what were sung in the pub, but I never followed up any sorta urge to learn those, but I did like the country and western style. I suppose the trouble with the old songs mostly is, you never hear them with music, that's just solo voice, unless there's somebody can play them on some kind of instrument in the public house itself, because all the other ones what I got on the records, they come with the music built in . . . How I think of it is, I don't mind some of the pop music, but with some of the pop songs, there's no sorta meaning or feeling to them, but with the old songs and with country and western the thing that tie them together is both the types seem to tell a story. I mean, if they wasn't put to a tune or anything and somebody just spoke 'em, that'd be like somebody telling a story, but with the new songs, there's just a load of words and noise just mixed up, which don't make no sense, if you listen to them, but with the country and western and the old songs, I think they're more or less a way of expressing an opinion in more or less a story type. That's the connection, I should think, between the two. I should think if you listen to most of Mr Hart's old songs, there's a kinda story about one thing or another to 'em, and I think that's the same in country and western. I don't mind some pop music, some I like just for the tune, and some I don't mind just for the words, some of it's just bright and gay, but a lot of it I don't like.[25]

Jake Foreman, a singer of similar age in Snape, also prefers the country and western style, and uses its characteristic delivery when he sings songs like 'Old Shep', 'Missing in Action' and 'The Wild Colonial Boy'. Both of these singers were initiated into the local pub-singing tradition in the traditional manner.

> *Jake Foreman.* Well, I used to – you know, they used to have an old piano going, used to get them asinging, and people just turn round and said to me sometime, 'Well, how about singing a song?'

and I just started like that. What I can remember about it I really don't know . . .

Mrs. F. Right from a little tiny boy really he picked up bits and pieces and sung quite a bit. He was quite small, and when we had company he used to stand here and sing to 'em.[26]

John Ling. My father used to go in the Key with an accordion [sic] and sing and play . . . I was very young then, I mean, don't know whether I was really allowed to be there, but I used to go, and listen, be in the passage – 'course, the pub's had passageways taken out now, made into big rooms . . . When I was young, they used to have a darts team at the Key where Father used to go, and there was his mate, sorta right from school days, Fred Belman, he used to get up a darts outing, and we used to go – that used to be Yarmouth every year . . . they'd sing, you know, and when they used to sing 'Flanagan's Band', they used to stand up, you know, and play the instruments that comes in the song. When the bus moved along they used to wobble, and they used to have a good laugh on that. Darts team from the Key. And I always remember that though I were very young at the time, I was about thirteen then . . . I used to go there [The Golden Key] and he [father] took his accordion [sic] and I used to have a bit of a singsong there.

G.D. Do you remember the first time you ever sang down at the pub?

J.L. No, not exactly. That was mostly, um, instigated by me father when I went with him, and then he used to say, 'Go on then boy, give 'em a song' – 'course, he knew, like, I used to just sing at home, I liked having a singsong to meself, and I suppose the first song what I sung I suppose was 'Rose Marie', what Slim Whitman sang, but I should think that was before he made it a hit. I heard it sung by somebody else, and well, I just started from there. When I used to go in after that, they used to say, 'Give us a song,' and then somebody musta liked it, and they say, 'We'll sing so-and-so,' and that, you know, and that's how that starts. Once somebody hear you, I suppose if they like it, then I suppose they get in a jolly mood in the pub. I don't know whether that sound good or not, but they just want somebody to sing and they'll ask anybody. I suppose that's how that first started, when me father would craze you to get up and sing.[27]

Jake Foreman and John Ling knew old songs learnt from their

fathers and other older singers (Jake learned some from Violet Ling, Percy Ling's late wife and John Ling's aunt). But they tend to prefer and remember newer songs in the country and western style. The link between the old songs and the country and western is that both types tell a story, and for younger singers living in a peer group in a changing society, it would have been important to sing current songs or to use a current style, rather than to sing only the songs known by the older people. They also had a choice, because they had radio and records to keep them informed of exotic musical ideas, whereas most of the old singers had no choice at all. Before the days of juke-boxes in these pubs, John Ling and his friends used to take a record-player to the pub:

> We used . . . to get in that room, mostly all the young ones, and we used to have a sort of singsong to the record player, and, ah, that's how I picked up most of the country and western to start with, with Slim Dusty, sing 'A Pub with No Beer', and that's where I started picking those sort of songs up.[28]

This was the parting of the ways: a modern electronic communications machine was introduced into the pub by these young people at a time when they might otherwise have remained with the older tradition. They sang *with* the machine. They were thus straddling the old and the new, and it is not yet clear whether the pub-singing tradition will ever return to what it once was in Snape.

Clive Woolnough, born in Blaxhall in 1947, now married and living in Chillesford, is an enigma. Like other young people in the Ship, he plays the juke-box, although he prefers country and western music to rock. His father, Frank, and uncle, Dick, are both singers, although Frank will warn his audience that he has no tune, only the words. Clive has learned songs from his family but also from other singers in the pubs and from folk-club singers. He claims that he sings in the pub when he has had enough drink to make him merry and in the mood, but I have never heard him sing a complete song. He used to go to the Leiston Folk Club, but now rejects the style of singing that he heard there, preferring the straightforward pub-singing style to the nasalisation of the Folk Club. Bob Hart makes similar comments about the Folk Club style:

> That started recent years. I mean, that sound so dreary nowadays, folk music . . . in fact, some of those musics what you hear, it seems as though that person's in pain what's saying it . . . [29] I don't know what they do to the music today, that all seem pulled about . . . he'll

tell you all about the song and then he'll sing it – well, its a good job he told you something about it because plenty of times I can't understand it. Not that class . . . it used to be just plain singing in my time and you could understand it . . . loud and clear, that's what I used to like to hear.[30]

It does not seem that the local folk clubs will immediately provide the pub-singing traditions with singers in the old style; Clive Woolnough got his impetus from his family and village background rather than from the Leiston Folk Club. But as songs circulate once more, young local people may again carry on the tradition unbroken, put it back into the pubs, and close up the growing gap between the old singers and the few young singers who perform occasionally. Clive's position as chairman in the Ship may help to encourage others of his own age to sing, but it is not clear how seriously he takes this job, and he certainly did not follow through his calls for order on the last two occasions when I was in the Ship. He has, however, an awareness of the nature of the tradition and distortions of its style, and it is possible he may become a key figure in years to come.

Mr Wickets, Alf Richardson, he pack it up, you see, and they used to come down here for a singsong, a lot of people, and they could never get order, you see, so generally I – Cyril or somebody asked me if I could get order, so I shouted order and that and they always asked me to get order from then on, you know. I suppose that must be three or four years now I suppose. We always used to have a singsong in here, you know, years ago. I always had a singsong, ever since I was a boy, but more regularly I suppose that's since I was around twenty. Used to come in here when I was seventeen, eighteen . . . Why me? Probably because I got the biggest mouth, you know . . . Not many young ones in the village. I think there's a lot know the songs and they like the songs, but they just haven't got the beverage enough to get up and give one, you know.[31]

Although Cecil Sharp believed the English folk-singing tradition to be on the decline almost seventy years ago, and the generation of singers he recorded to be the last, the tradition has obviously made a lie of his prediction. There is always a danger that on each examination of the tradition, it will appear to be in its death throes, when in fact it may continue, perhaps in slightly different form. The tradition in Blaxhall and Snape is by no means dead, but it is necessary to look to the young people for signs of its continuation. There are indications that the singing may spring up in a new generation: Geoffrey Ling and Cyril Poacher, two of the few singers in their generation, sang popular songs in the pubs when they were young men. At this time, they were learning the old songs and performing popular songs and the songs they had been taught by their fathers, mothers and grandparents. It is possible that the present younger generation is similarly learning songs and will later perform them. A chronological development of latent tradition-bearer into active tradition-bearer may also exist within this tradition. Undoubtedly, modern popular music, records, radio, television and the juke-box have intruded upon the local pub-singing tradition, but they will probably not kill it. What is happening now may be an exaggerated version of the transmission process in these villages anyway, and there is a fairly strong possibility that the singing will go on.

Notes

1. Reg Jay, 25 June 1975.
2. James Knights, 4 Oct. 1974.
3. Women were apparently largely excluded from this system.
4. Geoff Ling, 2 Nov. 1974.
5. Stanley Day, 24 June 1975.
6. Ibid.
7. Ibid.
8. Geoff Ling and Cyril Poacher, 17 Nov. 1974.
9. Stanley Day, ibid.
10. Lenny Savage, 30 Oct. 1974.
11. Mrs Saunders, Blaxhall, 3 July 1975.
12. Wickets Richardson, 27 June 1975.
13. Ben Ling, 2 July 1975.
14. These records include: Bob Hart, 'Songs from Suffolk', Topic Records 12TS225; Bob Hart, Ernest Austin and Percy Webb, 'Flash Company', Topic Records 12TS243; Folk Songs of Britain series, Caedmon, re-issued by Topic Records; 'The Larks they Sang Melodious', XTRA, Transatlantic Records XTRS 1141; Cyril Poacher, 'The Broomfield Wager', Topic Records 12TS252. A disc of Ling family singers has since come out, featuring Percy and Geoff Ling, and Geoff's late brother, George (Topic Records 12TS375).
15. Jack Saunders, the landlord of the Ship Inn, has a portable record-player behind the bar on which he plays Cyril Poacher's record, amongst others.
16. Reg Jay, ibid.
17. Mrs Saunders, ibid.
18. Stanley Day, ibid.
19. Mrs Saunders, ibid.
20. Bob Moore ceased to be landlord of the Golden Key in mid-1976 and left the area.
21. Because of the nature of this study, based as it is on field-work, these facts are no longer true as the boys referred to have now reached manhood.

22. David Hart and friends, Snape, 25 June 1975.
23. Reg Jay, ibid.
24. Mrs Saunders, ibid.
25. John Ling, 1 July 1975.
26. Jake Foreman and his mother, Snape, 4 July 1975.
27. John Ling, ibid.
28. Ibid.
29. Bob Hart, Crown Inn, Snape, 23 Apr. 1974.
30. Ibid., 5 Oct. 1974.
31. Clive Woolnough, Blaxhall Ship, 2 July 1975.

PART TWO

4 LEARNING AND THE SINGER'S ROLE

The Choice to Learn and the Choice to Perform

Before anyone can begin performing, he must serve an apprenticeship in the singing tradition and acquire a repertoire. Songs are learnt in the social and musical milieu in which each potential performer finds himself, by whatever methods are most appropriate at the time. First, he is passive and listens to songs, in the pubs or on radio, television and records; the second stage is active, and the singer is invited to perform and is then recognised and treated as a performer. During his life as a singer, he continues to learn songs aurally and also visually, from texts, in order to expand his repertoire without transgressing the rules of song ownership.

Singers commonly forget where they learned their songs, and they simply know that songs are 'picked up' or that they 'drift in' or 'creep in'. If a singer 'picks up' a song, he is the recipient of it and in this sense he has at least partially chosen to learn it; at times, though, it is through repeated exposure to a song that a singer will learn it, and his acquisition of it is therefore largely passive. Bob Hart says, 'If I didn't like them, no, they'd still creep there . . . Some of those come drifting along, like "My Souvenirs". First heard it I don't know where, I couldn't tell you. That's just drifted in.'[1]

Singers have varying opinions about the amount of choice they exercise in the forming of a repertoire. Some choose to learn only those songs which they like and wish to perform. Bessie Hammond describes how she chose to learn songs:

> There's a song come on the wireless, I sit and listen and take it all in and perhaps that'd come again and I'd pick that up and the tune and I'd start singing it – that's how I got it . . . Isn't because I've ever been trained or took much notice of it, no. If I heard something what I liked, I'd keep listening to it till I got it, see? That's where it all sprung from.[2]

Cyril Poacher says, 'That take some doing to learn them all, don't it? I choose the ones I like best.'[3]

A singer's liking for a song is not the only reason for his learning of it. If it is a song which normally gets good audience response, that is stimulus enough to encourage a canny singer to want the song for himself. A popular song is a sure way to the heart of an audience, and clearly songs which a singer likes are songs which he will wish to perform: the acquisition of a repertoire is thus dependent on the taste of both singer and audience.

A perpetuation of local taste goes on since those songs frequently heard are likely to be those which are passed on. Geoff Ling and Cyril Poacher discuss this:

> *C.P.* I choose the ones I like best.
> *G.L.* And not only that, you see, like we just said, you see, nobody ever wrote them down, so the more you heard them singing, the more you used to pick them up.[4]

Popularity therefore controls transmission and the content of the tradition; performance results in transmission: 'Well, you couldn't help what learn them if you was in the pub and they had a singsong nearly every week, you couldn't help what pick them up, could you?'[5] Aurally learned songs therefore pass into a singer's repertoire and it is then his decision whether or not to perform these songs. He is likely to learn those songs which he hears most frequently and to which he offers no resistance; he may choose to learn some songs for positive reasons, such as personal appreciation of the song or understanding of its popularity with audiences, or he may find himself knowing songs which are central to the local repertoire and familiar through repeated performance.

Because a singer establishes himself only through continued exposure to the tradition, it is inevitable that he may learn songs that he may actually not like. The singer in this case has the choice not to sing such a song, although he may remember it and be able to perform it on demand (to folk-song collectors, for example).

Alternatively, once a song is learned, the singer may promptly forget it if he finds no use for it or does not like it; this is the song which is only a potential item in his repertoire. Except as fragments, these songs are unknown factors since they have disappeared in the process of selection that occurs both at the level of choosing to learn songs and also at the level of choosing to perform songs. Again, a song may even be memorised without the singer's knowing it, and since he does not feel the urge to perform it, he does not actually know he has learned the song (and so a field-worker is unlikely to find out). The knowledge that a song is learned comes from a conscious attempt to perform; in confronting a song as a possible addition to his repertoire, the singer brings it to the surface of his mind. In this way, he knows that he has learned the song. His acknowledgement that he has learned a song usually also means his acknowledgement of its place in his repertoire. He accepts his learning of it and accepts his performing of it.

Bob Hart learned so many songs through his involvement in the tradition that he could not possibly perform them all often enough to keep them all memorised, and an inevitable process of natural selection has occurred in his repertoire: those that he liked most he performed most and they were the ones he knew best; reciprocally, those which he performed most he liked most because he felt confident in performance of them. Others subsided into the backwaters of his mind and were not frequently performed because he forgot he knew them; forgetting he knew them, however, did not mean he had forgotten the songs, which could be called forth by reminders and chance thoughts, as is the case with 'All Getting Older Together'. There are other songs that he chooses not to sing, although he has not forgotten that he knows them, for example, 'Eat More Fruit':

> You go off a song, you don't worry about it . . . I think that's all right, that'll pass, but as a song, it's not a song . . . I think a good song is, you know, when you get down to the real old fashioned ones like 'General Wolfe' and that sort of thing. They're the old songs what I like.[6]

Percy Webb similarly describes his rejection of a song:

> Like, my wife's mother learnt me 'Female Cabin Boy' what Bob sing. I don't like that much . . . I don't know. I never sing it, anyway, I never took much interest in that to learn it, you know. If I hear a good song, I'll pick that up then, I'll pick up a good song, I'll take an interest in it. I don't like to hear Bob sing it either, not much.[7]

In performance, then, the singer exercises greater choice than he does at the learning stage. The songs which he hears most often are generally the easiest to learn, whether he likes them or not; songs he likes or desires can be learned deliberately. Taught songs and learned songs can be rejected completely by the singer when he forgets that he knows them, or he can choose not to sing them, although he is aware of their presence in his memory. In a singer's life, therefore, there are songs of varying status: there are those learned deliberately which are either heard often and are therefore normally learned aurally or are heard seldom and are normally learned visually. There are songs learned largely involuntarily, which are either heard often, learned and performed, or heard often, learned and discarded, or heard often, learned and remembered but not performed. The songs in a singer's life therefore form an anti-repertoire, an active repertoire and a passive repertoire. The first is a collection of songs he has stopped himself from learning, has forgotten after learning, or has discarded after learning; the second is the body of commonly performed songs; and the third is the collection of songs which can be called up for performance by recording companies and field-workers, but which it is unusual for the singer to choose to sing for his local audience (unless such a song re-emerges through a reminding stimulus, an odd request, or a challenge).[8]

When a potential singer has learned some songs well enough to perform them, he is then in a position to become a singer – some learn their songs after hearing them several times, and some claim to be more adept at this than others. Chorus singing in the pubs is an aid to familiarisation since it not only makes the words easier but also gives singers vocal involvement in the performance.

> I picked up ones sorta off Percy Ling's wife. I learned one off her hearing her different times. You join in the chorus, you obviously sing the verse, and you join in with them and you gradually pick up the song after a time.[9]

Tune, rhythm and first line are also mnemonic aids:

> The thing on it is, if you can get the beginning of the verse, that's the only way, and you can rhyme it; you see, like Cyril say, we heard so many and you see, to get these things right, like that is now if you going to start them well you want them right, otherwise there's a lot of misunderstanding that, you see.[10]

'Rite de Passage' and Singer's Role

The bulk of a singer's songs, then, are learned early in his singing career, and provide him with his identity within the local tradition and give him his performance rights. His early methods of learning are used throughout his life, and are added to as he experiences new places, entertainments and media. As a young singer equipped with the core of his repertoire, he passes into the mature world of the adult singing tradition by a *rite de passage*. In Suffolk, young people are introduced into the world of pub-singing and social singing as performers once they have mastered songs. The descriptions of the learning process – the repeated exposure to performances of a song, familiarity with a song through chorus singing, knowledge of the tune and gradual assimilation of the words – belong mainly to the apprenticeship of the singer.[11] At this time, he is part of the audience and his familiarity with the songs grows; in the second stage, his partial learning is completed and he learns more songs; in the third phase, he is invited to sing. Beyond this time of admission into the performing tradition, he continues to learn songs, but his repertoire is crystallising throughout his apprenticeship.

The commonest pattern of initiation of males into the pub-singing tradition is for the boy to have attended the pub on several occasions, to have learned songs either there or in the home, and to be requested to perform by an older person such as his father or the pub landlord. Here is James Knights's introduction to singing:

> Well, I first started to sing, I was ten years old when I sung in a pub. I was with me father and mother, and of course you could go in any age, take any children in at any age that time of day, so there was a singing contest on at this pub. They called it the Wagon and Horses. There was a singing contest on, and they were getting on with the singing, they'd sung three or four different people had been singing, and when I got in, I'd been in once or twice before, then they – my mother wanted me to have a sing, you see, if I would, and I used to have to – so I sang – they asked me to sing, the landlord said to me, 'Are you going to give us a song, Jimmy?' I say, 'I don't know whether I know one.' He say, 'You do,' so I sang a song what they call 'Sweet Genevieve' – and I sang this song, and of course, old landlord and landlady gave me the first prize, they said that I beat the lot. I was ten year old then, that was. Used to be a nice little song that was.[12]

John Ling and Jake Foreman[13] were both initiated into pub-singing by older people, in John's case by his father; they both attended pubs for a time before they were requested to sing, and they both had a particular song to perform and others to increase the repertoire as demand for performance continued and their singing role was established. Introduction to performing occurred for Bob Hart in a work situation: at sea, it was common to sing while the nets were being hauled, and group singing as well as solo singing occurred. The transition from group singer to solo singer is not as significant as the transition from non-singer to singer, and in the work situation, Bob Hart began to sing alone, and continued to sing solo in the same group of fishermen at concerts on shore. From here, he continued to sing alone at local pubs and social events once he had left the sea. Bessie Hammond became a singer through initiation into social performance,[14] and her adoption of the role as singer at this particular concert was a surprise even to her husband. Learning is a prerequisite of performing and performing is a prerequisite of role; all acceptance and understanding of role and performance rights come necessarily from singers and audience. The tradition, comprising singers, songs and audience, provides the environment in which a new generation learns and grows and continues.

A lot of the singers were born into singing families, and here they learned songs from parents, relatives and siblings. Sometimes such learning was incidental to a child's involvement in family activities, and sometimes it was deliberate and songs were taught. The songs learned at an early age often became some of the best known in a singer's repertoire, as Cyril Poacher indicates:

> 'The Nutting Girl', I learnt it off my grandfather, 'The Nutting Girl', and in fact I learnt five of them off my grandfather . . . 'The Nutting Girl', 'Joe Moggins', 'Young Man from the Country', and 'Once I had Plenty of Time', and one more – oh, 'Nancy from Yarmouth', yes.[15]

Alice Messenger relates how children were not always involved in family singsongs when they learned the songs:

> I used to pick them up, pick the tune up, then get the words and there you are. See, when I was a child – they used to have orgies or something, Saturday nights, indoors, and I used to lay awake and listen to the singing. When my aunts and uncles all came from London, you see, for a holiday, they used to go over to the Ship and come back with all these stone jars of beer and suchlike. Gallon jars, and bread and cheese and onions. You could smell it, lovely smell. They'd be there till three or four in the morning, singing. That was the family get-together, and of course I was in bed, but that didn't matter because I weren't asleep. Far from it. That's how I learned a lot, like that.[16]

Percy Webb describes a similar situation with the child learning songs unbeknown to the parent:

> I – I sung from when I was eight. My father taught me a lot of my songs. See, he used to play a concertina and accordion, and I used to sit under the table and listen to him, and I picked all them up, so one day when he was out, I sung one of his songs. He say, 'You don't want to sing that old song,' he say. That's what he said. I say, 'Why, that's all right,' and of course the other chaps said, 'Yes, go on.' 'Go and Leave Me if You Wish it' . . . But then he used to teach me a lot 'Dark Eyed Sailor', 'Sailor Boy' . . . [17]

Seomtimes the contact between singer and child was extremely close, and the child as audience learned the songs, as Stanley Day describes:

> He, [Cyril Poacher] sit on grandfather's knee, and he's only a young little babe, little boy like I was, and grandfather used to have a stone jug of beer, and he used to give Cyril a swig and a puff of his pipe and he used to sing all the old songs to him, and that's where Cyril learnt them from.[18]

For children not from singing families, it was more difficult to learn songs, as Reg Jay and Stanley Day often complain. Percy Webb was fortunate in that he learnt many songs from his father, but was also in contact with non-family tradition-bearers from whom he learned and by whom he was taught songs:

> He [father] used to have some chaps work with him when I was a boy, and they'd be asinging – these songs – that's how I learnt . . . 'It's Only a Beautiful Picture in a Beautiful Golden Frame' – I learnt that off some of them.[19] Like it? It's a good song ['Green Grow the Laurels'] . I learnt that off an old hurdle maker, you know, what used to make the hurdles to hold the sheep, you know, for my father, and that's how long ago I learnt that. I liked that soon as he sung it. I thought, 'Well, I'll have that,' so I did[20] ['I Came Home Late Last Night']. An old fisherman learnt me that on Bawdsey beach, that's a good old song, that is . . . We were on the beach, we came from Thorpness. They had their houseboat on the beach, and they used to go out in front of Bawdsey fishing, along the shore you know, getting lobsters and catching all kinds of fish. Mostly they caught flat fish and at night time they used to give me half a bushel of fish,

> and you know, to take home. I had more fish 'n I could eat, so I used to give it away to neighbours, and after tea they said, 'Come back after tea, we'll have a singsong'. Got in this boat and I stopped there till about ten or eleven o'clock singing these old songs, you know, what I knew, and he taught me that one, I laughed when I heard him sing that. Nice chap . . . I was working down there then. I lived there. Well, he got one field off the sea, like, and used to go down there very often. That was Bawdsey Hall, 1910 to 1914.[21]

Bob Hart did not come from a singing family, although his mother sang hymns on Sunday evenings to her own accordion accompaniment, and he began formulating his repertoire at the age of fourteen when he went to sea. He had also learned a few songs as a boy from workmen on farms, just as Percy Webb did:

> A man by the name of Larkins used to sing 'Lincolnshire Poacher'. He was a horseman . . . Well, he used to sing it in the evenings sometimes. You see, in those days there weren't a lot of entertainment, but there used to be a bank somewhere or a nice clear space somewhere where they could sit down, used to lay on the grass or sit on the grass singing. No money to go to the pub with.[22]

Although Percy Ling's parents did not sing, he knew a few songs before the time of his marriage; possibly, he learned these from other pub-singers rather than from his own grandfather or uncles, since these songs are relatively modern ('A Group of Young Squatties' and 'Sweetheart in Spring') and the Ling family's repertoire is generally older and traditional rather than popular. A later important source of songs for him was his family by marriage, and it is likely that he found his identity as a singer through his wife's singing abilities and the songs of her father:

> 'Flanagan's Band' . . . That's my wife's father's father's song. My wife's father used to sing it, I learnt it from him and I sing it, you see, yer, I do, and – 'Go and Leave Me if You Wish it'. That's my wife's mother's mother's song and my wife's mother used to sing it, my wife used to sing it, you see. That's how they come around.[23]

The misfortune of being born into a non-singing family does not necessarily forestall the career of a potential singer: other people, older relatives, workmates, friends and family acquaintances may lead the young person into the world of singing by giving him the opportunity to enjoy and learn songs or by teaching songs to him. School also provided songs for those who did not receive stimulus in their own homes to learn songs as well as for those who did, and introduced some children to public performance.

The Consonance of Life and Repertoire

Any singer's repertoire is a reflection of his life. When the young farm labourers of Suffolk joined the army in the early war years, it was for most of them their first journey out of East Anglia. Suddenly they came into contact with another world, and just as their own had been, this new world became a great source of songs for many of them. On leave and after they returned home for good, they could perform their newly learned songs for the old men and familiarise themselves with the songs they had known as boys. Most of the songs they learned while away are still performed occasionally, though more often in the company of other war veterans than before general pub audiences or at folk clubs.

Songs learned in wartime were often functional, in that they encouraged men to continue marching, they raised morale, and they also allowed satire and dissent to be expressed. These are the songs that are still remembered and sung. Here is Percy Webb's account of the song, 'MacCaffery':

> We weren't allowed to sing that really in the army, you know. They wouldn't let you sing it, you know. *But* when we came out of the army we used to sing it. I learnt it from an Irish chap who knew it, and, I used to get him to sing that very often, and he would, you know . . . We weren't allowed to get up in the barracks and sing it. That was in 1915. Paddy, I used to call him. He was a cook, and he used to go on the beer a lot, you know. When we went on an outing, he'd get drunk, then he wouldn't be like to get up next morning, you know, wouldn't like to get up much, so he'd ask me, 'Come on, old mate,' he said, 'will you mash the fires in the morning?' If I was the corporal of the guard, you know, I'd get up early and make it for him, then go and call him, take him a cup of tea. Yer, I got on well with Paddy . . . In France that was . . . anyway, near the Arras-Cambrai road, that was . . . He come to England and joined it [regiment], in the machine gun company we was in then . . . I used to go in his dugout and he'd sing to me in there . . . They said that was a crime if you sung it so we never sung it, you know, at least I didn't. I waited till I got home, then I sung it . . . That's a good song, you

> know, that's a meaning in that, a meaning, got a meaning to it anyway.[24]

'MacCaffery' is a song which crystallises Irish dissent, since MacCaffery is a young Irish soldier sentenced to death in the British Army; Percy Webb learned his version from an Irish soldier in the British Army, to whom it was probably as ethically vital as a political treatise. MacCaffery's trial was held on 15 December 1861,[25] and Percy Webb learned the song in 1915. To him, Irish-British dissent was certainly less relevant than the dissent of corporal against officer, and the harsh treatment of the young soldier by the army and the law. Although Percy Webb does not specifically state his case when talking about 'MacCaffery', he calls it a meaningful song, which suggests that he sympathises with its sentiments and its ethical standpoint.

It is clear from his own descriptions of his army experiences that he felt angered by the humiliations, ill treatment and lack of respect that young soldiers suffered; war itself was horrifying to him, and it is simple for soldiers in the face of war to feel hatred towards those in power whose positions protect them from proximity to wartime realities:

> Them Kensingtons, not one of them came back, no. So when we was going up there even, there was an officer blew all to smithers. They picked him up in a sandbag, you know, and there was another bloke stood up in the trench like that with his head off, and 'course, we had to go by there, and my coat caught on a nail, where the shell had bust the trench in, and I kep' going, I kep' going, I ran off, and ah – all mud up to here. Oh, that was rum. And then you froze at night. You got in a little hole you dug like you might dig in that wall like that and just hang your waterproof sheet at front and get in there . . . A place called Catterick Camp, that's the worst camp I ever went in my life – we was bearing the soldiers out every day – you won't remember that, I don't expect. That's when that 'flu epidemic was on, and ah, we used to have to have this here potash stuff up your nose every morning. And we was bearing one every day. Then you had to go on the funeral and fire the rounds, you know. One old doctor, he said, 'There ain't nothing the matter with you, you go home and go to bed.' Went to bed, he was dead next morning. He didn't know much. 'Cos you see, them old army doctors, that's like the dentists in the army – they pull your head off, they don't care, no. I know an old sergeant-major when we first joined up, he said ah, I got my hat on the wrong side, you know, cocked over there.

> He say, 'Where the hell d'you think you're going to, the fair?' I say, 'No, no, I don't think so.' 'Well,' he say, 'Well, you broke your mother's heart but you won't break mine.' Cor, they was some strict. Cor, we called 'em bees knees.[26]

Bob Hart remembers songs they sang on the march:

> I used to sing it ['What a Time'], you know, walking about . . . Out in France. We used to sing all sorts on the march. I mean, you could march to that, swinging along . . . I believe I first heard it ['Seventeen Come Sunday'] in hospital during the First World War, and that wasn't me asinging, 'cos I couldn't sing then. I'd got a broken jaw, but . . . that's where I first heard it . . . But we used to have little concerts. We used to pick some of those up, you see;[27] I've got one here about 'Pack Up Your Troubles'. Did you ever hear that one? . . . That's actually from the First World War, that one, and that's on a rough idea of how they went on . . . we used to sing it on the march, this one. That was a new song come out and we used to sing it when we were marching . . . We used to sing this one ['Long Trail Awinding'] . . . we used to sit and sing that very often, this one . . . when we were on the march. We used to have ten minutes' halt, we always used to sing something. Back on the side of the road, we used to sit on the road actual and put our feet up on the bank. You'd be surprised how soothing that was when you started walking again. Yes, that's how we used to rest, ten minutes every hour . . . That ['Tanks in Picardy'] was another First World War song. Hindenburg and little Willie . . . I learnt it in the First World War, yes, that's how we picked them up.[28]

These songs have clearly fulfilled functions for First World War soldiers: a good swinging rhythm provided a suitable beat for marching ('What a Time'), and bright songs must have cheered up the marchers ('Pack Up Your Troubles'); nostalgia ('Take Me Back to Dear Old Blighty') and stoicism mixed with self-pity ('Long Trail Awinding') at least turned attention from aching feet and limbs, and the songs were a constant reminder of England and therefore a source of hope. The men who fought and marched were likely to retain songs of the war in their repertoires since these songs encapsulate a critical stage of their lives and are full of the emotions of patriotism, nostalgia for good times and good comradeship, hope and despair with which these men became imbued.

Normality returned when men came home and took up work in their villages once more. Songs were once again sung by them in the pubs, and they became audience once more for the singing of the older people. A lot of singers, all of them men, acknowledge the pubs as their greatest source of songs, directly, or by way of fathers, grandfathers and uncles from the pub-singing tradition, and sometimes they remember the pub where they learned a particular song and the singer from whom they learned it, for example:

> Do you know I learnt that ['Two Little Girls'] off a blind man called Ali Storey, and Lenny Savage, they all knew him, he used to live in an old hut at Farnham, just at the back of the Farnham George on a meadow there, and he used to sell cottons, ribbons, garden seeds and all little things like that. He used to come round, and when he used to take the seeds out, we'll say you ask him for a packet of carrot seed, he'd shake that, he'd put it back if it wasn't carrot seed, pick another one up and shake that. If that shook right to him he'd give it to you and that was carrot seed, or whatever you asked for. And that's the truth, that is . . . He used to come in the Ship to sell his seeds, either there or Farnham George. I heard him in Farnham George and in the Ship, that's where I learnt that off him. He sung it a couple of times down there, I heard it a couple of times up here. I sung it myself after that.[29]

The Search for Songs

An unusual stimulus to learn a song is recalled by Reg Jay:

> I learnt to do that ['The Farmer's Boy'] off a fellow just before the War [Second] in Wickham Market. He were in a pub, and he bet me, I believe, half a crown that I couldn't learn it within a month, and I met him in Aldeburgh and he said about the old song, 'Shall I sing it?' and I said, 'No, I'll make a noise,' and I picked up from there.[30]

This challenge to learn a song, with a financial reward, underlines the relationship between the singer and the learner; presumably, as Reg Jay implies, successful learning of the song gave him the rights of the song as well as the half-crown. Performance of such a song is difficult at any time but especially after an evening's drinking, and Reg Jay's performance, habitually begun five minutes before closing time, is a challenge to his learning of the song and a test of sobriety and mental agility. Such a challenge is a type of pact whereby the singer offers a means by which the other man can approach him and match him. It is also a way of transferring song ownership, by setting a task for which the reward is money as well as the rights to the song.

Oral transmission occurs throughout a singer's life, but non-aural learning appears to be more common after maturity than in the apprenticeship stages, probably because of the constraints imposed by song ownership. The singer then finds it necessary to move further afield outside the limits of aurality in his search for new material, and recorded and printed songs often supply him with what he wants, as well as those songs with which he comes into contact only infrequently. If the desired song is one not often performed in the local pubs, a singer may decide to write it down for himself over a period of time, or have it written out for him:

> Well, that is the way really to learn a song, write it out. You know, you got no copy, but you hear somebody sing a song and you write it out. Well, that might go weeks and months before you hear that song again, then you learn that verse the best you can time they're a singing and write it down. But to write a whole song out – don't know. Well I heard him [Bob Scarce] sing it, you see, different times, and, uh, when I sang a full verse I'd write it down and then start on the next one. The tune is there, you see, you know the words, well it's, it's all right.[31]

> Yes, well, I have had songs wrote out for me. Yes. Well, I mean, if you go say about twenty mile away and there at a pub and you hear a song and you like it – there ask 'em to write it out and give 'em a pint of beer, they'll write it out for you, and sing it to you, if you give 'em an addressed envelope.[32]

In many instances, such as those suggested by Bob Hart (with an extensive repertoire) and James Knights (who may not be able to return to a pub in order to learn a song heard there), the needs of the moment overrule any fidelity to aurality. It is certainly not the case in Suffolk, anyway, that the use of print, writing and recorded music is generally frowned upon; but there are some singers who take pride in memorising ability and dislike a too easy passing on of songs to younger people. The challenge issued to Reg Jay is an extreme example of this attitude.

One of the commonest ways in which traditional singers have learned their songs is from song sheets and song books. Broadside publication has been crucial in the continuation of song, as indicated by Henry

Burstow's repertoire, which closely follows the song catalogues of Such and Fortey.[33] James Knights's repertoire is largely made up of songs published in the *News of the World* and of songs learned from song sheets; because his sister played the piano, he learned, with musical accompaniment, a song each week from an early age:

> I learned it ['Sweet Genevieve'] from a song paper, because when there was anything like that going about or any murders or anything like that, you see, they always used to have a song about it. I think they [song sheets] were about three pence or four pence – now you get a penny song book with fifty songs at the music shop, yes, big volume, for about sixpence . . . My sister was always on the lookout for old and new songs, you see, and . . . where I got a lot of good songs from was, we used to have the *News of the World*, there was always a song in there every Sunday, and the music to it, in the *News of the World*. I used to always harping on and she'd say, 'Boy, d'you want to hear the song in the *News of the World*?' – she'd get on the piana and play it and if I – sometimes I used to say, 'I don't want to hear that, I don't care nothing about that, I – I don't like the tune on it,' or something or other, and if that was anything I liked . . .[34]

An equivalent of this form of learning was used by Ruby Ling when she was in service in London:

> I used to live in London when I was in service, and me and my friend, we used to go to my friend's aunt in Hendon, and you see, that's when we used to sing all the songs, you see . . . We heard this song – she used to treat us to all these different plays, you see, and when we used to go, we used to hear these songs, and then, you see, we used to buy them, and then we used to sing them, all the different things, and that's how we got all our music, and if we saw a nice bit of music – we got it, and my friend could play it on her aunt's piano. So that was really how I got to more singing, you see. That was what it was.[35]

> *Wickets Richardson*. I used to get most of mine out of *News of the World*, Sunday morning, well every Sunday there was one in there, and I used to cut it out, and the wife used to plaster it on brown paper so I could stand it on the piano, you see, and practise, you know, once or twice a week. I couldn't afford to buy any.[36]

For those without a piano, song sheets were vital for words, and tunes were commonly known because people were singing the songs:

> You know, we used to buy these song sheets at a penny for twenty songs on it, and I wished I'd a saved some of them, I just didn't, well, I didn't know then, did I . . . When I was a kid went to school, we used to buy a song sheet, yes . . . The boys used to run the streets with them, from the shops, you see. They used to play the old music halls' tunes, that's how we used to pick the tunes up . . . You'd hear them asinging practically anywhere, uh, pubs, you see, they were new songs to the pubs . . . The boys used to whistle – you don't see the boys go whistling about now – they were always awhistling tunes.[37]

An authoritative text allows singers complete memorisation of songs, gives promise of accuracy, and fills in gaps left by partial aural memorisation. Lenny Savage describes the way in which he completed his learning of 'The Dark Eyed Sailor' from a printed text:

> I learnt that off a periodical, and I got some of that song but I hadn't got the lot. You know, I'd got about two or three of the verses, and . . . I know somewhere, either in a train or somewhere, I picked this book up what was left in the seat, and there was my song in the middle of it, and this old boy was asinging it at an old party, so I whipped them two pages out and I'd got it, so that's where I learnt that from. But my grandfather used to sing it, you see, so that's where I got the start from, but of course, not being very old, I couldn't remember the whole lot right through.[38]

Pragmatism is therefore crucial in the singer's search for songs. He uses whatever devices are available to him, including texts and recorded music, either to increase his repertoire or to refresh it. Once he is established as a performer with songs of his own, his place in the tradition is partially controlled by the constraints of ownership, and for diversity he must look outside his immediate circle and beyond his traditional means of learning, as local singers have always done.

Notes

1. Bob Hart, 17 July 1974.
2. Bessie Hammond, 2 Oct. 1974

3. Cyril Poacher, 17 Nov. 1974.
4. Cyril Poacher and Geoff Ling, 17 Nov. 1974.
5. Lenny Savage, 1 Oct. 1974.
6. Bob Hart, 9 Sept. 1974.
7. Percy Webb, 27 June 1975.
8. More can be read on this subject in Roger Abrahams, 'Creativity, Individuality, and the Traditional Singer', *Studies in the Literary Imagination* no. 3 (1970), pp. 9-10, and Kenneth S. Goldstein, 'On the Application of the Concepts of Active and Inactive Traditions in the Study of Repertory', *Journal of American Folklore* no. 84 (1971), pp. 62-7.
9. Jake Foreman, 4 July 1975.
10. Geoff Ling, ibid.
11. An extended analysis of the apprenticeship phase and learning occurs in Albert B. Lord, *The Singer of Tales* (Harvard University Press, Cambridge, Mass., 1960) pp. 21-5.
12. James Knights, 11 Sept. 1974.
13. See Chapter 3, 'The Young People'.
14. See Chapter 2, 'The Women'.
15. Cyril Poacher, 10 Sept. 1974.
16. Alice Messenger, 31 Oct. 1974.
17. Percy Webb, 19 July 1974.
18. Stanley Day, 24 June 1975.
19. Percy Webb, ibid.
20. Percy Webb, 24 June 1975.
21. Percy Webb, 15 Nov. 1974.
22. Bob Hart, 15 July 1974.
23. Percy Ling, 2 Oct. 1974.
24. Percy Webb, 24 Apr. 1975.
25. Gerard Corr, 'Private MacCaffery's Revenge', *Lancashire Evening Post,* 17 Dec. 1973.
26. Percy Webb, ibid.
27. Bob Hart, 17 July 1974.
28. Bob Hart, 20 July 1974.
29. Cyril Poacher, 26 June 1975.
30. Reg Jay, 25 June 1975.
31. Bob Hart, Crown Inn, Snape, 13 July 1974.
32. James Knights, ibid.
33. A.E. Green and Tony Wales, Introduction to *Reminiscences of Horsham. The Recollections of Henry Burstow* recorded and edited by William Albery, (Norwood Editions, Pennsylvania, 1975).
34. James Knights, ibid.
35. Ruby Ling, 31 Oct. 1974.
36. Wickets Richardson, 27 June 1975.
37. Bob Hart, 25 June 1974.
38. Lenny Savage, 1 Oct. 1974.

5 SONG OWNERSHIP

The Flexibility of Song Ownership

Most of the singers have an idea that certain songs belong to certain singers. Some believe that there is nothing to stop any singer from singing any song, whereas others decry the practice of performing a song commonly sung by somebody else. Very few, however, deny that there is such a thing as song ownership, and discussions about it attempt to define the ethics of ownership rather than dispute the principle. Even those local people who do not sing in or go to the pub know about song ownership:

> *Chris Messenger*. They all had their own songs, didn't they?
> *G.D.* Did people mind if people sang their songs?
> *Alice Messenger*. O, they didn't like it, did they?
> *C.M.* No.
> *A.M.* Oh, no.
> *C.M.* Mustn't sing anybody else's song.
> *A.M.* Your own song, they called for you, you go into the Ship, I heard 'em say, you go into the Ship, and they call a song from so-and-so and they had their one song to sing and that was that, weren't it? And if they sung anyone else's that was warfare straightaway.'[1]

Bessie Hammond adamantly denies that people resent song poaching:

> *G.D.* Did people worry if someone sang a song that belonged to someone else?
> *B.H.* Oh, no, no no. No, never worried them, no, there weren't that, no.[2]

And Abraham Ling logically regards strict song ownership as a barrier to transmission:

> *G.D.* Would the old singers mind if one of the young ones picked up one of theirs?
> *A.L.* Oh, no, no. Oooh, a lot of them used to learn them, that's how Cyril came to get a lot of my father's. He learn them off him, and Father didn't mind.[3]

It is clear that singers value differently the implications of song ownership, and, as we shall see, are likely to allow modification of rules when this is to their own advantage. Bessie Hammond's attitude is exceptional rather than common, and possibly results from the nature of her own repertoire. Her songs are popular and were learned at her home in Yorkshire, from the radio, with female friends at work during the First World War, and in a canning factory in the 1920s. She did not learn or wish to learn the songs of Blaxhall pub-singers, and had a small but satisfactory repertoire by the time she started singing in the Ship during the Second World War. She was not receiving her songs from local tradition, nor was she dependent on the local pooled repertoire, as hers was partially established by the time of her marriage and move to Suffolk from her wartime work in Blackpool. The exigencies of transmission, learning and song possession were never apparent to her since she did not experience them herself. Abraham Ling, however, is a member of a local prolific singing family and although he does not sing now, he once did a little singing. His attitude is one of tolerance and expedience; his concern is with the passing on of the tradition and the obvious need for incursions on individual song possession for the continuation of the tradition. He also admits freely that he never was a real singer, and for a long time refused to see me as he did not regard himself as a useful informant on song, and always referred me to his cousins, Cyril Poacher and Geoff Ling. He is certainly not an active tradition-bearer, and scarcely a latent one, and like Bessie Ling, therefore, has never been caught up in the building of a repertoire from local material, and the personal transactions undergone in the process.

Utilitarianism such as his, though, is visible in some active tradition-bearers, perhaps the most notable being Cyril Poacher. Often attached to this utilitarianism is a partial denial of the correctness of the principle of song ownership, an assertion that all songs belong to everybody. Or the singer may feel as Abraham Ling feels, that a song is to be performed, and the association of singer with song comes about merely through frequent performance, and frequent performance merely through a personal liking of the song. Perhaps Jake Foreman shows a modern understanding of song ownership which is not possessive but purely the result of circumstances:

> *J.F.* Normally they always ask me to sing 'Old Shep'. That's the one I sing, and another one they usually craze me to sing is 'Rocking Chair'!
>
> *G.D.* Are they your favourite ones?

J.F. Well, they're just the ones I know well and sing those ones really. If I get a few drinks and get going, I can sorta think 'em up more quickly, like old fashioned songs, they come to you more then really.[4]

Although acknowledging that some songs belong to some singers and that it is unfair to perform another man's song in front of him, several singers will deny the wrongness of such acts in principle, although they may well object to specific instances. Geoff Ling thinks that if someone sings another man's song, the end may justify the means: 'Well, that don't make no difference, do it? Well, they do pick it up, but there's some sing it better than others.'[5] Percy Webb gives an explanation of the modifications allowed to the principle of song ownership:

G.D. Do you know 'Underneath the Apron'?
P.W. I can sing it but that's Bob Hart's song.
G.D. Will you sing it?
P.W. Yer, I'll sing it. [sings]
G.D. Where did you learn it?
P.W. O I learnt it down there. [Butley Oyster]
G.D. Who from?
P.W. Well, they say that was Bob Hart. But a mate, Peter Benstead, he learnt that off Bob Hart, and Bob said, 'Don't sing my song' . . . 'cos he thinks I'm giving his songs away. Well, I told him then, they weren't his songs. They were sung to him from other people, 'cos a lot of Blaxhall old people learnt him a lot of those songs, yer.[6]

Although he regards 'Underneath the Apron' as Bob Hart's song, and respects his right to it by not singing it often, he also dislikes what he thinks of as meanness on the part of Bob Hart when he becomes possessive about his songs; he then turns on him with a denial of song ownership. The tradition must allow transmission, which necessarily involves disregard of song ownership, and within these bounds singers can function until one oversteps the unspoken rules by being either too possessive or too free with other people's songs. Bob Hart is both principled and tolerant in relation to song ownership, and borrows from others when he sees fit; he understands the circumstances in which borrowing is acceptable:

G.D. Do they sing any of the songs that you sing?

B.H. No, not many of them, no. Only what they've picked off me.

G.D. How do you feel if you hear someone else singing one of your songs?

B.H. Oh, I don't mind, I don't mind that, but I never sing one of their songs. Ah, did you ever hear that one about the dog – 'Old Shep' – you heard that one, didn't you?

G.D. Yes, you sang that. You said that was really someone else's.

B.H. That was, yes.

G.D. If you learnt a song from somebody, would you sing it in front of them or not?

B.H. I would if I'd asked them first, though, if I liked the song.[7]

The Restraints of Song Ownership

People have to learn songs in order to be singers, but it is not appropriate to learn a lot of songs from one repertoire, and especially to sing these songs in front of the song 'owner'. The compromise between learning to keep the tradition going, which could not but encroach on someone's songs, and learning and performing at random and learning at will, which involves widespread and thoughtless usurping of another's repertoire and performing potential, becomes clear in relation to specific transactions:

B.H. As we were placed on a Saturday night, we had all our own songs, and though I picked these songs up, some of them off Jack Harland, I wouldn't have sung them if he was there. We each had our own songs.

G.D. And what happened if you did sing them and he was there?

B.H. Well, that's, I dunno, that's something you wouldn't dream of doing. I mean, we used to have the same old songs on a Saturday night.[8]

In a village pub with regular customers and regular singers, individual repertoires were known. Singsongs were thus limited beforehand and singers would know from those present what songs were likely to be sung. The learning process went on because of the frequency of performance (in combination with personal taste), but a singer did not need to perform a newly learned song in front of its original owner. It is the stage beyond learning, the decision to perform, which reveals the problems of song ownership. Bob Hart understands that he will learn songs on frequently hearing them, and so do most of the singers, but it is the choice to sing the song, and in what company, that matters in terms of song ownership. The relationship of the closed group of pub-singers to the songs, then, may be visualised in this manner:

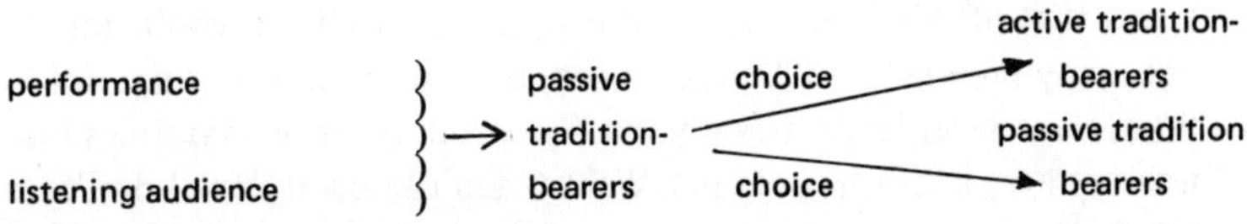

The opening up of song ownership to allow the transmission of songs and the continuation of the tradition is one step in the direction of anarchy. With no rules, songs can be taken over and performed at will. Cyril Poacher's reply to a question about performing other people's songs is, 'Can't stop you, can they? They can't stop you.'[9] He has made one long-playing record,[10] and it was necessary for him to sing a song normally performed by his cousin, Lenny Savage, in order to have enough songs for the LP:

> I sung one of them there in Blaxhall Ship, and Lenny say, 'What chance have I got, you took my songs?' I say, 'I ain't took only one.' He say, 'Well, I haven't got any chance,' but he have. I took only one of his . . . 'The Dark Eyed Sailor'. I took that one . . . and Webby took two of mine [for a record]. In fact three. He took 'The Yellow Handkerchief', he took 'Nancy from Yarmouth', and he took 'The Nutting Girl' . . . I don't know many more'n fifteen. Well, I might know a couple more, but that take a lot of finding, fifteen.[11]

In pub performances, too, he has annoyed others by singing one of their songs and thus prevented their full participation in the singing; in these cases there is not the prestige of making a record at stake, and a free utilitarian attitude is shown in defiance of the ethics of song ownership and transmission. For all his bravado, however, he too has complaints against others:

> I say 'The Nutting Girl' is my song, but that doesn't stop Webby from singing it. I can't help myself, can I? Webby sung it, he sung it on a record, and he say he learnt it off his grandfather, and he didn't, he learnt it off me and he sang it, but there was nothing I can do about it . . . No, I couldn't do nothing about it . . . That in't the form, you see.[12]

And he exhibits prime possessiveness in relation to 'The Maid and the

Magpie':

> Now, you said you were talking to Alderman Ling, well, his father, I learnt that off his father. A lot of people want to but I won't sing it, not many people know that, only me, they never picked it up, did they, they never learnt it, only me. Sung it in there several times but nobody ever learnt it, only me. Webby don't know it, 'cos I don't sing it.[13]

Here is a man who knows there is nothing to stop him from appropriating anybody's song, and who will do so for personal gain, but who resents other singers claiming his songs and who even goes so far as to sing a song infrequently in order to keep it for himself. Cyril's objections arise from confusions over a song's provenance; he believes that the singer who first knew a song has a right to that song. He does not consider that two singers could learn the song separately. A problem of song ownership is that the provenance of the songs is not known, and local ownership is also in dispute. Percy Webb believes 'The Nutting Girl' to be his song just as strongly as Cyril Poacher believes it to be his, and neither wonders whether the other learned it separately as a young man from older singers. Such argument is common, and the obvious solution is not considered valid.

Bob Hart also shows the double standard in the functioning of song ownership, in that he takes the songs of others but objects to his own being taken. However, he does not sing his 'stolen' songs (which include 'Old Shep' from Jake Foreman, and 'Flanagan's Band' from Percy Ling) in front of their owners, and not often in public anyway:

> I never like to step on another man's ground. I don't think Jake'd mind if I sang it, but he'd rub it in. Stealing his song, I 'spect he'd say. When he do sing, he generally bring that song into it. Well, I'd hate to spoil his night. Whether he'd be the same with me, I don't know. I think he would.[14]
>
> When I did sing 'Old Shep' when he wasn't there, I told him I used his song, that night. 'That's all right, boy, that's all right,' he say.[15]

Similarly, Percy Ling will not sing 'Old Farmer's Servant' for me when I ask him to because of his conviction that it is Bob's song, and his refusal to sing it in his own home with only me present exemplifies the division between knowing and singing.

The problems of song ownership arise only in the process of transmission. Singers pick up songs through their frequent experience of performance, and also request specific songs from singers who then agree to give them the songs, usually in written form. Sometimes a singer will not pass on his songs, and Percy Ling often relates how Bob Scarce refused to write out any of his songs for him. Such a refusal seems to be the result of a personal dislike or mistrust, although the old man must have known that Percy Ling could learn his songs by hearing them over and over again. It is strange that the song he is best known for and the song he probably sang most often,[16] 'When Paddy Stole the Rope', is one that no one in Blaxhall or Snape now sings. But some of his other songs are still sung, notably by Percy Ling ('The Boy with No Shoes'), Cyril Poacher ('Bonny Bunch of Roses', 'Australia'), Clive Woolnough ('The Larks They Sang Melodious') and Bob Hart ('Australia'). Singers know that their songs can usually be learned after a few hearings, but the formal giving of a song is a chosen transmission and not one due to frequency of performance.

Whereas Percy Ling requested a song and was refused it, Bob Hart believes that Cyril Poacher is trying very hard to learn one of his songs aurally, but has not asked for it to be given to him. Bob does not feel as Bob Scarce felt, that his song should die with him, but there is an edge of resentment in his voice when he tells about this:

> You heard Cyril ask me to sing again last night. I know what he's on, he's trying to learn that song, 'Banks of Sweet Primroses'. He's after learning that. Well, of course, I don't mind now I got to the age when they have got to keep agoing. But when I get up to sing in there [Ship], he always say, 'Let's have the "Banks of Sweet Primroses",' and not only is that a bit annoying, but you make up your mind what you're agoing to sing next. I sing that every time I go to Blaxhall Ship, and I know what he's adoing, he's learning it from me asinging it, not as I grudge it.[17]

Bob Hart has written out songs for people, and talks of 'giving' some of his songs to Percy Webb:

> I gave Percy that ['Underneath the Apron'] Well, I say I give it to him – he wanted me to write it out for him and 'The Old Farmer's Servant' was another I writ out for him. He say, 'I don't want them to sing in public,' he said, 'They're nice songs,' he said, 'and I like to know 'em.' He done nothing else but sing them in public ever since, which I don't mind.'[18]

I just wrote them out for him. That's the easiest way out.[19]

There is a more formal giving of songs which Lenny Savage has experienced, and because he is thus the rightful possessor of a song, he is incensed when Cyril Poacher begins to perform it and thus usurps his status. Apparently, Cyril learned 'Nancy from Yarmouth' aurally from Fred Ling, whereas Lenny was given it. Lenny has related this event several times, and each telling further explains the situation:

> That 'Nancy from Yarmouth' – there was only one man ever sung that and that was this Freddy Ling what lived here, and he sung that, and I used to take him out on British Legion rallies. He used to be with us and us four – there was Bob Hart, Percy Ling, myself and Basil Bennett, that's four – and invariably sometime in the evening we'd get around where they were having a little singsong, and if not, we have a little singsong coming home, and if that was any distance, all had a drink or two, and if we hadn't finished singing when we got to the dispersal point, got up on the hill there, we'd stop and finish it there – you know, amongst ourselves, and that was an unwritten law in villages that you never sang another person's song – if that was the only song that he sung. If you did, you was a poacher, you poached 'em, you see, because that was recognised as their song, and they called on that man to sing, they'd expect him to sing it and if he sung another one, they'd probably give him a few minutes grace and go around again and have that one what he normally sing before he went. Well.
>
> Freddy Ling used to sing that song, and no one else sung that song, only him and he was a sailor, and he was the only one used to sing that, and I sang that a time or two, when we went out on outings, sang that a time or two with him, and he said to me – they called on him in the Ship to sing, and he was getting on now, he was a Blaxhall man born and bred, and he said, 'No,' he say, 'I got somebody else here', he said, 'will sing that as good as me.' 'No, there's nobody sing that like you,' and I kep' on about it. I said, 'There ain't nobody can beat you at that 'cos you're the only one that sing it.' Well, eventually I did sing that for him. 'Now,' he said, 'you can have that one.' I wouldn't have dared to sing that, not if he was in the pub . . . Cyril Poacher wouldn't dare to sing that song if Freddy Ling was in that place, but I know what happened, I set in the Ship and old Webby said, 'Come on, Lenny, give us a song,' and I didn't feel like singing, he say, 'Come on,' he say, 'Give us "Nancy from

> Yarmouth".' Well, Cyril heard me sing that previous Sunday, see, so he say, 'Well, I know that one.' I say, 'Do you, Cyril?' He say, 'Yes,' he say, 'I know that well.' About ten minutes after that they called on Cyril to sing and he sang 'Nancy from Yarmouth'. Well, that was it. I just don't sing that anymore in Blaxhall Ship, and I'll bet you tomorrow night if I were to be sitting there and they crazed me to sing and wouldn't sing, he'd get up and sing 'Nancy from from Yarmouth'.[20]

Lenny has a good reason to adhere to the rules of song ownership: if a singer has a small repertoire, he cannot afford to have his songs taken from him in his lifetime, as this leaves him with very little to perform and thus undermines or even destroys his position as a singer in the local community:

> There was certain people, their repertoire was so small, they probably only knew two songs right through. Well, if they got a singsong going and this fellow arrives, and they'd already had that song, he weren't going to sing that a second time were he, not the same session anyway, so that halved him for a start. If he didn't know another one, well, they had to pass him, didn't they? Some are lucky enough to know five or six, but like I say, through the years some of them have picked up other songs, what these other people used to sing. That doesn't matter if they're dead and gone, that's a good job too, they in't lost 'em, have they, but for them to sing a song of one particular person, and that's the only song he sing, I mean, that's stealing isn't it, more or less, isn't it?[21]
>
> That'd be different if you knew a lot of songs . . . That wouldn't matter, no. No, they weren't copyright. You weren't born with them, you'd only inherited them, or picked 'em up somewhere.[22]

Bob Hart is able to be magnanimous about Percy Webb's singing 'Underneath the Apron' and 'Old Farmer's Servant' in front of Bob's own audience because Bob knows a hundred songs, and Percy's effective repertoire is much smaller. This explains the difference in attitude between Bob and Lenny.

Song Inheritance in the Community

An important criterion in disputes about changing song ownership is whether the new singer performs the song as well as his predecessor. Cecil Sharp's only direct reference to song ownership in *English Folk-*

song: Some Conclusions is in a discussion on the accuracy of the oral tradition. To Sharp, a singer's loathness to sing another's song is due to his fear of distorting the record, or of being inaccurate; but Sharp does not seem to see that the singer may also genuinely dislike singing another man's song because the convention is that he should not do so.[23] Inaccuracy, however, is a problem of which some singers are aware, and it is one of Lenny Savage's concerns:

> I mean, a lot of times when I hear one get up and make a fool hand of it, where the original bloke sitting in the place coulda sung it properly. Well, that wouldn't a done years ago for anybody else to sing anybody else's song. Probably been a fight, or they'd ask was he trying to get into his pram or his coffin, you know. That wouldn't go down too well . . . The original people what sung the songs coulda beat their arse off.[24]

Once a performance has begun, however, it is accepted by the audience, and singers do not try to give a second better performance. This implies an appreciation of content in peformance and, furthermore, that in any song session content should be maximised. It is interesting that repetition from one session to another is acceptable, indeed expected if not positively valued, as if the notions expressed in song require frequent restatement, but the session itself is self-contained. Repetition of one song in a session, in so far as it prevents in itself the performance of another song that *adds* something, is not only redundant but actually counter-productive. Geoff Ling's earlier quoted statement[25] suggests that quality is also important in performance, since it may justify one man's rendition of another man's song, but such justification for song-stealing is worked out by the singer before performance and the audience knows nothing of it and has no control over it. An audience can, of course, express dislike for one singer's performance of another singer's song, but disapproval does not act as a deterrent in this tradition, perhaps because performance of the song itself is highly valued and because the audience is less aware of song ownership than are the singers and, *as a whole* does not disapprove on these grounds. If the original singer dies, however, there is little to stop the second singer becoming accepted owner of the song since there is no longer any precedent, and in any case, the audience would rather have the inferior version than none at all. Bob Hart does not like the way Percy Webb sings his songs, but there is nothing he can do about it:

> He don't sing either of them, not to say, as I like to hear 'em sung . . .

> That's not his fault, but I was watching him last night, you know, 'cos his voice is going fast – he used to be a good singer.[26]

> He don't sing 'em exactly right now . . . Slightly different in places . . . I've noticed a big difference in Percy, and he's only seventy-seven.[27]

For the group, song ownership functions as a control on the variety of songs performed. In a close-knit society where singers and audience are relatively constant, repertoires of all the singers are known and an evening's entertainment can therefore be approximately predicted once the singers are assembled. Mervyn McLean cogently writes of the New Zealand Maori that:

> Once song loss has begun in a community, other factors begin to operate to hasten the process. Foremost amongst these is the matter of song ownership and an associated reluctance to allow outsiders to learn the songs. Songs may be owned by individuals, by families, or by tribes.[28]

If singing in Suffolk is on the decline now, and if singers do have smaller repertoires than they once had, it would be reasonable to suppose that song ownership does exist primarily to protect the small repertoires, but from singers in the group as well as from outsiders. If there were no principle of song ownership at work, any singer could learn the songs of any other and thus those with better memories would become the only singers in the group, and at the moment it is apparent that people prefer a variety of singers, some able to sing only one song, to one singer knowing all. Song ownership protects those who know few songs and also ensures that there are several singers to listen to, each singing different songs. Familiarity with the locally sung songs is important to the audience, and song ownership allows the audience to know the song possibilities in any evening. It is apparent that a singer who knew a song long before another does not necessarily have the right to claim ownership of it. A singer with an extensive repertoire is likely to have a large number of songs which he does not often perform, since he does not have time to do so. The alternating of songs in such a case may occur in cycles: he sings ten songs alternately for several weeks, and then ignores them and performs another ten in the following weeks. This is certainly the pattern of Bob Hart's performances. What happens is that people forget that he knows some songs, and do not request them any longer, so that a new singer singing one of these songs (learnt, in fact, from Bob) may be acclaimed as its owner. A large repertoire is, as Bob Hart often points out, a disadvantage since he cannot possibly keep practising all of his songs, whereas someone with five or a dozen can. A repertoire can thus be both latent and active, and some of the songs known and not performed can become part of the active repertoire of another singer. Song loss does not therefore occur, although song ownership changes. But the group continues to perform the same songs and to maintain the number and variety of its singers.

Song Inheritance in the Family

The villages are made up of families which are related by blood and marriage, and many of the singers are related to one another:[29] in Snape, George and Basil Bennett are brothers related to the Savages by marriage; in Blaxhall, Alice Messenger comes from a singing family – she was born a Ling but says she is not related to the other Lings. Dick Woolnough, who died in February 1976, lived in Snape; his brother Frank lives in Blaxhall, and Frank's son Clive is the young chairman at the Ship. Percy Ling's wife, Violet, was a Ling before she married, and these Snape Lings are singers; John Ling is her nephew. Reg Jay's mother's family, the Baileys, were singers, although his father's disapproval of singing prevented him from becoming a prolific singer. By far the greatest number of singers are Blaxhall Lings: Cyril Poacher, Geoff Ling, Priscilla Savage, Abraham Ling, Wickets Richardson, Stanley Day, Percy Ling and Lenny Savage. Most of these singers have, as Lenny Savage expressed it, 'inherited' songs, and disputes over song ownership therefore arise within families. Songs can be held in common in a family with no ill feeling, and passed down by understanding rather than by formal giving. Reg Jay's explanation for the paucity of his repertoire and underdeveloped singing ability is that he was not brought up in the kind of singing family that Cyril Poacher was brought up in. A singing family would clearly have its own collective repertoire, and its members could identify themselves as singers, whereas Reg Jay was prevented from doing so by his father.

Lenny Savage. They had a song that was handed down from their parents. The ones who sang the most songs were the ones who travelled most, a lot brought songs home from the wars didn't they, some were regular soldiers, they got billeted around. Same as these fisherman, a lot of these songs were glorified sea shanties, a lot of 'em were Negro spirituals, you know. They used the same tunes and put their own words to them – 'row you buggers, row,' or something like that . . . that would be handed down to them if their parents were singers, or gifted singers, and they'd got big families, and they scattered around, they moved around, and nearly all got a song different to their brothers or fathers, weren't they – if they learnt their father's song or mother's song, that was probably the one they's plump for – went down all right – because normally they'd ask them to sing that one, wouldn't they, if that was their favourite.[30]

It is natural for any singer to know the songs of his parents, and there are very few local singers who did not have at least one singing parent. Songs were also learned from grandparents, aunts, uncles and siblings. Outside the family group, young singers had to be careful about which songs they performed, but in the family, transmission was encouraged. The acknowledged habit of the young men[31] singing popular songs in the pub whilst learning the old songs exemplifies the difference between learning songs within the family and learning them in the public house.

Cyril Poacher recalls being taken on to his grandfather's knee at about the age of eight and being taught 'The Nutting Girl'; Geoff Ling learned songs from his mother, Susan Poacher, and Lenny Savage, Stanley Day and Wickets Richardson heard the songs of their parents, aunts and uncles, and were encouraged to sing them. At home, then, song ownership was suspended in order to allow the transmission of the song inheritance. Once children knew the songs, ownership was endowed by their place in that singing family, and the audience could then come into play and prefer one performance to another.

Lenny Savage. Well, like Geoffie [Ling], cousin Geoffie. He sang that 'Green Bushes'. Well, he sing that in the Ship, but if his brother George from Romford come down on holiday, you never hear Geoffie sing 'The Green Bushes' if his brother George is there because George can sing it better'n what he can. George can sing it exactly like his mother did. Geoff can sing it but he ain't got the same rhythm, you know . . . He [George] got a different kind of voice, and more mellow, you know.[32]

Almost everyone to whom I have spoken in Blaxhall has mentioned that they prefer George Ling's singing of 'The Green Bushes' to Geoff Ling's. They begin by praising Geoff as a singer, and then say that George is better, at least for that song. Cyril Poacher also sings it, and it will be interesting to see whether, since George died in September 1975, Geoff or Cyril is credited with the better performance of it. When the provenance of the song is so bound up with its place in one family's repertoire, preference for one singer's performance may be inseparable from allocation of song ownership. If people now prefer Geoff's singing of 'The Green Bushes' to Cyril's, they may still regard the ownership as familial rather than individual. When George was alive, everyone referred to the song as Geoff's until George was mentioned. Close family transmission gives song ownership a wider application than it has in the case of individuals; George's performance was preferred, Geoff's was enjoyed since George no longer lived in Blaxhall, and Cyril's was allowed because of the family ties. However, the song is associated with Geoff's mother, Susan Poacher, and this is a closer relationship than that between Cyril and Susan. The aunt/nephew relationship is not likely to persuade Blaxhall people to regard the song more as Cyril's than as Geoff's now that George, its preferred performer, is dead. In the case where there was no direct singing descendant, however, the rights to the song would undoubtedly have gone to Cyril Poacher.

Conclusion

Song ownership, therefore, exists as a means whereby songs may be learned and transmitted in a controlled manner. Songs must be learned, from contemporaries and younger people as well as from older singers. The act of learning is accepted and goes on quietly throughout performances, whereas the act of performing a song for the first time is a conscious decision to take on a song and make it one's own. Local ethics prescribe that such performing should take place only after a formal 'giving' of the song by the original singer, or in his absence, or after his death. Encroachment on another's repertoire is allowed where that repertoire is sufficiently large to be unaffected by a few losses or where there has been a handing on of the song. Singers may sing another's song after acknowledging the true ownership of the song in public, or requesting permission from the owner before a performance at which he will not be present. Singers thus have ways in which they can perform the songs of other people without disobeying the rules of song ownership. Songs can be wholeheartedly given, as in the case of Freddy Ling and Lenny Savage, or songs can be given with certain attached rules, as in the case of Bob Hart and Percy Webb, and if the rules are broken the original owner has cause for complaint. Songs can be held in common by more than one singer, where a song has been given but not given up by the owner, as is the case with 'Underneath the

Apron' and 'Old Farmer's Servant', which both Bob Hart and Percy Webb sing, but which were Bob Hart's to give. Songs can be borrowed, so that the owner is acknowledged and there is no threat to his ownership, as with Bob Hart's borrowing of 'Old Shep' from Jake Foreman. All of these are legitimate transactions. What is not allowed is for a song to be taken. The taking of a song involves the performance of a song learnt aurally and with no giving involved, where no owner is acknowledged even if he is present and about to sing, and where no apologies are made. This is the ultimate transgression against the laws of song ownership. Other complaints are about specific faults, such as a bad performance of a co-owned song, the breaking of a personal agreement not to sing when the giver of the song is present, and disputes over ownership of co-owned songs.

Song ownership is an important control on the transmission of songs in this area of Suffolk. It operates at the levels of the individual, the family and the singing group. Cecil Sharp writes:

> His songs are his own, the creations of his own class; he is proud of them; they are exceedingly precious to him; they have come to him as an inheritance, and he rates them at a high value.[33]

This assessment tends to regard the singing community as entirely homogeneous, battened against the outside world. Song ownership functions dynamically within the community itself, though its controls may derive power from an awareness, by comparison with popular or serious music, of the uniqueness of the local blend of music and community.

Notes

1. Alice and Chris Messenger, 31 Oct. 1974.
2. Bessie Hammond, 2 Oct. 1974.
3. Abraham Ling, Blaxhall, 1 July 1975.
4. Jake Foreham, 4 July 1975.
5. Geoff Ling, 2 Nov. 1974.
6. Percy Webb, 24 June 1975.
7. Bob Hart, 9 Sept. 1974.
8. Bob Hart, 5 Oct. 1974.
9. Cyril Poacher, 10 Sept. 1974.
10. 'The Broomfield Wager', Topic Records 12TS252.
11. Cyril Poacher, ibid.
12. Cyril Poacher, 26 June 1975.
13. Ibid.

14. Bob Hart, 17 July 1974.

15. Bob Hart, 20 July 1974.

16. It is possible that he was best known for this song precisely because nobody else sang it, and this may have caused his possessiveness about it.

17. Bob Hart, ibid.

18. Bob Hart, 9 Oct. 1974.

19. Bob Hart, 13 July 1974.

20. Lenny Savage, 18 July 1974.

21. Ibid.

22. Lenny Savage, 30 Oct. 1974.

23. See Cecil Sharp, *English Folksong: Some Conclusions* (EP Publishing, Wakefield, 1972) (first published 1907), p. 23.

24. Lenny Savage, 18 July 1974.

25. See above, note 5.

26. Bob Hart, ibid.

27. Bob Hart, 5 Oct. 1974.

28. Mervyn McLean, 'Song Loss and Social Context Among the N.Z. Maori', *Ethnomusicology*, vol. 9, no. iii (1965), p. 302.

29. See genealogies from the Blaxhall parish records in Appendix III for exact family linkages of some singers.

30. Lenny Savage, 30 Oct. 1974.

31. See Chapter 3, note 8.

32. Lenny Savage, 1 Oct. 1974.

33. Sharp, *English Folksong*, p. 131.

6 AESTHETICS

The Primary Aesthetic: Performance

It is not the nature of such a tradition as this to produce a separate and self-conscious system of aesthetics, and although the singers and the members of their various audiences have formed opinions about performance and the qualities of individual performers, there is not a readily verbalised set of judgements to be found in any one informant. Aesthetic criteria are integral to the tradition and are consequently social as well as artistic by nature, and it is only by sifting the evidence of performance, attitude and dialogue that the folklorist may arrive at an assessment of traditional aesthetics. The danger is, as always in fieldwork, of supplying the informants with an answering terminology and of stressing aspects of the tradition to the extent that these aspects then loom larger in the minds of local people than they did before. By observation and in conversation, though, the life force of the tradition and the primary aesthetic emerged, that performance is good in itself. This is the first consideration, the platform for the ritual of contact, of continuance, of conservatism, of unity. After this, there are personal preferences, both for singers and songs, and for points of style and technique. However, any performance is accepted, and the social bias of the local aesthetic is underlined every time a singer stands to sing before his fellow men.

Singer, song and audience are central to a discussion of the tradition and its aesthetics, since not only are they the context of the tradition but also the tangible tradition itself. Alan Dundes suggests[1] that efforts should be made to elicit the meaning of folklore from the folk, and this he terms 'oral literary criticism'. The tradition is studied in terms of the performance situation, which in this case includes singer, song and audience, the wider village context, in which singers and audience exist in other capacities, and the information which people are willing to give about song, which is oral literary criticism.

The critical criteria of serious[2] and popular music are not generally appropriate to the local singing, which is by its nature conservative: the songs last for years, and people go on requesting them. Traditional music exhibits a closer link between audience and performer than do popular or serious music; the village singing is not for gain, for the profits of an entrepreneur, and the songs are not replaced in a search for new products. Stars are not being made, and there is a high tolerance of bad performance. The relationships of singer and audience in the local pub are not dependent on a newspaper advertisement, on payment of money, or on a publicity drive, but are multistranded and mostly exist before and after the singing event as well as during it. Consequently the aesthetics of a local singsong are bound up with the performance rather than with pre-defined ideas about style and technique. Performances are compared to those of earlier singers and of the same singers when younger; preferences result from such comparisons and also from personal liking. Local opinion may gather around one singer and become a consensus of approval, but most songs are liked as there are songs to suit most needs. There is no concern for the artistic criteria of correct phrasing, descriptive ability, imagery, key control, organic form and originality, although specific criticism is made of non-emotional delivery of what is regarded as an emotional song, and of gross lack of accuracy. Efforts are made to give reasons for preferences but in fact these can seldom be satisfactorily verbalised. Performance of any kind is appreciated, because it is entertainment, because it occurs in the warmth of a social environment, because without it the tradition is no more.

When asked who the best local singer is, most informants name Bob Hart, Geoff Ling or Cyril Poacher; singers who are now dead are usually referred to as well. Often, no reason is given for any preference: the person in question is known as a 'lovely singer' or a 'good singer', for example:

> Brother-in-law Arthur Smith, he used to be one of the best singers, and dozens of them about here who could sing, lovely singers they were. Tommy Curtis was another one, Benny Ling down here – he's still alive but he's getting on now. Geoff Ling. But they nearly all used to sing, you know. Arthur Smith was a lovely singer, he been dead some time now.[3]

Some informants take the question further and enter into a discussion on singing quality, and if the informant himself does not move into such a consideration, he is not likely to make more critical comments when he is questioned further. To some people, the description 'a lovely singer' is sufficient and needs no further explanation. The most frequently heard singers are generally those who are preferred singers: excellence as performers derives from the fact of performing. The earlier stages of introduction to the audience, usually after introduction to a family or peer-group audience, and acceptance of the young singer by the audience, are lost to us. We now have singers who are accepted by virtue of what they do rather than by virtue of how they do it, but there are also qualitative distinctions made among them.

The recognition of performers as good, by nature of their performing, is the primary critical standard in the local tradition but secondary standards are important too, and indicate the concerns of singers and audience. These critical standards are prescriptive as well as descriptive, and serve to maintain the *status quo* of singing style and choice. Elements of delivery are analysed to the extent of isolating those characteristics which make the tradition what it is; thus, deviant styles of delivery can be checked, at least by close participants, so that the norm is kept in mind. External influences upon performance are noted, and the unavoidable effects of old age. Songs serve social and personal needs, and delivery should be appropriate to the emotions contained in the songs. These are the secondary considerations which audience and singers will talk about amongst themselves and when prompted by a field-worker. But any comments made are in relation to the total performance structure, and do not undermine it or the wish for performance in any way.

Secondary Aesthetics: Voice and Delivery

The most common appreciation is of a good voice. A singer must have an acceptable voice in order to fulfil his function as a performer:

> I believe you gotta have a voice to sing them, you know what I mean. You can't just stand up and shout, you gotta have a voice, ain't you, yes. I sing. I don't know whether I gotta voice, I can't hear myself can I? What do you reckon? You reckon I got a good voice? O, you do.[4]

Frank Reeve, a chorister who has learned singing, recognises that the local singing tradition requires a certain type of voice:

> Well, my voice is never suitable for them [old songs] I think. See, when you get like Cyril Poacher, when he sing a song, he sing a song that's very suitable to his voice, and the type of song that would go down to a lot of people today who like to hear the old way of singing and also the old songs which they used to sing. I've been in a choir, most probably my voice has got stronger, and I haven't quite got that kind of voice that they have in a public house, you know,

> although I always go down well with people, and they always like to hear me sing a sacred tune.[5]

His singing is regarded as different from that of the pub-singers – it is more 'highbrow' – but his performances are enjoyed all the same. In local terms, a good voice is not a tutored voice, but a tuneful voice. It is likely that any voice at all would be praised for singing and enjoyed, but a tuneful voice will be remarked upon in its own right, as a gift somebody has:

> Aaron Ling, and Abie's father, Aldie Ling's father, they were all singers, all singers. Old Bob Scarce was my favourite, Arthur Richardson was, Cyril was, so was Percy [Ling]. Not because they were relatives but because they had good voices.[6]
>
> Well, Sid Messenger got a wonderful voice, he's dead now, poor fellow, but he sang some nice songs, like 'Would you Mind Passing me the Salt?', that's a good song.[7]

Priscilla Savage has a more definite reason for liking a singer: 'A man named John Smith . . . he'd got a beautiful voice, man's voice, you know, heavy, yes.'[8]

A good tune is appreciated, and Geoff Ling suggests that a process of tune selection occurred whereby local singers accumulated a number of good tunes, easy to pick up and easy to follow:

> Nearly all of these songs, they rhymed, you got 'em to rhyme, see, and then once they put a tune to 'em and that's how they went. That's how I've got these here good slow singing tunes, 'cos if you got these here quick ones, you wouldn't be able to cope with them, and more wouldn't they [the older singers and audience].[9]

Like Frank Reeve, Alice Messenger has been in the church choir and has thus learned some formal singing techniques:

> *A.M.* Well, there's a certain way to sing, keep in time with the music and notice all the stops and suchlike. Charlie Richardson, he could [sing]. Wickets' cousin. He been dead years. He been in the navy, you see, and he got a good naval voice – you know, gruff sort of voice.
>
> *G.D.* Why were they good?
>
> *A.M.* They could sing.

Chris Messenger. Got a good tune, you see.[10]

The landlady of the Ship:

> I like Geoff Ling's singing, because in my opinion Geoff, although he's got a forceful voice, it's in tune . . . Geoff Ling I like to hear sing . . . We used to have Bob [Hart] from Snape, he's another one, he'd come and give us one, he's a good singer what's well in tune. To me, it's got to be in tune otherwise it's just something that I can't stand, you know, it just grates . . . Percy Webb – I don't quite understand his singing, I'm afraid. I'm afraid I can't sort of get along with his type of singing, not Percy. It's not a melody, is it, there's no real melody that goes with his song . . . It's sort of rather uninteresting tone to his voice. I don't know what it is, it's just something that doesn't attract me at all.[11]

Clearly, people find it difficult to express their aesthetic reaction to singers and songs, and those with some musical training or knowledge give fuller accounts than others, but in total are just as confused and impressionistic. This is hardly surprising since this is also the situation in which musical scholarship finds itself, give or take a measure of verbal eloquence. The fact that a man lifts his voice in song, thus transforming himself from speaker, has social implications for all of those who hear him. The singing voice is the vehicle of the tradition, the means by which it flourishes, and is separated from the everyday voice by its disguised and dramatic character[12] and the immediate role change the man undergoes as he stands to deliver his song. Musicality exists to a greater or lesser extent in his performance and is appreciated to a greater or lesser extent by his audience, although there is a consensus about the quality of pleasantness of voice since this inevitably attracts audience to singer and thus imbues the traditional performance with immediate involvement and acceptance.

The songs usually tell stories and it is therefore recognised that pronunciation of the lyrics should be clear. This is one critical criterion widely accepted and mentioned:

> To speak clear, to sing clear, rather. We was always taught that at school. We had a school master at school who used to take great interest in singing, and the words had to be exact and distinct, so you could understand what you were talking about.[13]

Poor pronunciation can mar performance:

> I like to listen to anyone asinging as well as singing myself. I 'spect I get as much fun out of that when I go to the folk club at Leiston as anybody, because I listen to every word, and that's why I don't like, you know, this 'ere guitar, in't it? There's plenty of those lines you can't understand what they say – well, that's not singing if you can't understand the song. They might just as well have a Frenchman asinging it. I like a song with a story in it.[14]

Discussions about specific singers can lead to the establishment of qualitative criteria:

> Well, I liked Mr Ling always singing, because he was very easy going with it and he'd always stand very erect when he sang and you could always hear every word that he said. That was Mr Ben Ling, he's now about eighty-odd.[15]

> You . . . should pronounce every word distinct so any – anybody – we'll say, down at the bottom of the yard, can hear you and understand it.[16]

Pronunciation of the words must be clear because the song is telling a story, and the story can be lost by poor singing. Clarity is necessary for a good performance:

> The young people of today have changed a lot to what that was when I was a young person, in the singing. I suppose that's because the songs have changed. Loud and clear, that's what I used to like to hear – well, I do now if anybody's singing. Not too loud, but, ah clear.[17]

A comparison with folk club performance, most often heard in the area at Leiston and Butley, although the young singers do visit pubs in Blaxhall and Snape, oftens leads to notions of a natural style which is present in the older singers and absent in the younger singers:

> There's a very few people sing a straight song today. I mean, if you get a bloke asinging, he's got the music with him. I think that spoil the song. I'd rather just hear the plain song, but of course my voice is not so strong as it used to be.[18]

> What they sing at Leiston now . . . I have a hard job at Leiston too – you see, they play a tune or two on their accordion, or whatever they're playing, then they start singing, because that's . . . I don't know what they do to the music today, that seem all pulled about . . . he'll spend five minutes tuning up and then he'll tell you all about the song and then he'll sing it. Well, it's a good job he told you something about it because plenty of times I can't understand it, not that class . . . it used to be just plain singing in my time and you could understand it.[19]

> [I like them to sing] just ordinary, like how we sing about here, like our own language. Like a lot of singers, they put it on, don't they? If they belong here, real Suffolk, well, people where I go now, they like you to sing in the old Suffolk way, you know, not think you come from London or somewhere. I think the singers in folk clubs today, they sing a lot different to us, you know, right up and sing too high for them.[20]

Clive Woolnough feels the same way as the older traditional singers, and has had experience of the Folk Club in Leiston himself:

> I like to hear the songs sung just by an old boy or somebody. I don't like going 'wah', they never used to do it years ago, they just sung in their natural voice, you know, and that's how I sing. Just blurt it out, just how it come fashion . . . I always say that the majority of young ones, they don't sing in their natural voice anyway, not folk-songs. They sorta 'wah', you know, this sorta thing, you know, and come out all – 'I was an old bachelor boy.'[21]

Frank Reeve has an idea of what good local singing is and bases his concept on the practical considerations of audibility, which also means communication between the singer and the audience, and on the aesthetic consideration of an emotionally sympathetic rendition of the song:

> Well, I think sing the song with ease and really express it. I don't think in the pub it's very natural to do a lot of actions, and look up when you talk about the sky and all that sort of thing, but stand erect and make sure your words can be heard so that people know what you're singing about, because there's always a story behind it, and unless you really get the words clear you can't really understand what the song means. They're quite difficult really, some of the old

> words, but I always enjoy them. But I think that's the main thing – get up and make sure you're looking at your audience, and as I say, expressing yourself but not to do too much moving about. Keep erect so that people can hear what you're talking about. And never pitch it too high.[22]

The most eloquent evocation of good singing comes from Cyril Poacher:

> To sing, to sing and sing decent, you know what I mean when I say that – I mean, to sing just like that [waving motions from hand to mouth]. You don't want me to tell you because you know. He [Bob Hart] don't force his voice, do he, that just come from him like that. I heard him at dinnertime, he sung me 'Primroses' which I wanted him to sing. He got right out on it, and he's the best singer for – you know, just singing without forcing his voice or shouting, he's the best singer I've ever heard, myself, and I reckon I can sing, but I'd give him preference to me, yes I would. I reckon he can sing because it – it come and he don't raise a hair, it come like that. He's the best singer I ever heard yet and I aren't saying that because you're staying there, but, ah, I mean it, and he know I mean it if you tell him. And he – he don't shout or – like I do sometimes, and I don't shout right a lot – I usually sing pretty fair. But Bob is a good singer and I like to hear him sing in company, 'cos he sit there as I say – well, he did Friday night – he sit there beside you and he didn't make a murmur, and that just come like that – I heard him today and it just come like that.[23]

A relaxed strength of voice is a recognised quality, and many old men lament that they have lost it:

> I never used to sing on a mike because everybody used to tell me I never wanted a mike. I could sing – I could get upstairs without a mike, and I could make people hear too, and that's the truth how I say it. I – I could do that job, but I don't do nothing now – I don't sing now.[24]
>
> If my voice was a little stronger, it'd be better wouldn't it?[25]

Bob Hart enjoys strong singing: 'There were some jolly good singers, yes. Ah, big strong healthy chaps, you know, they used to really let it go, yes.'[26] This is by way of contrast to the gentler, and in his opinion, inappropriate, style of folk-club singers, whom, as we have seen, Clive

Woolnough also criticises for their affectation of a nasal tone. It is possible that Bob's preference stems from familiarity with functional songs, with robust musical accompaniment to heavy work on the fishing boats in his early days, but it may stem from an aesthetic appreciation of straightforward male singing, such as Priscilla Savage admires.

The domination of the aesthetic by performance means its domination by the idea of male superiority, since performance is almost exclusively the right of the males, or of women who are in effect honorary men. The favoured performance-style is identified as a masculine style: Bob Hart talks of 'strong healthy chaps', Priscilla Savage of a man's 'heavy' voice, Alice Messenger of a 'good naval voice'. The 'naval voice' is probably a cognitive paradigm of the preferred masculine style, cognitive because this is a cultural definition. Women do not, by virtue of their sex, sing less powerfully or less tunefully than men, and the male dominance of leisure and the masculine attribution of the preferred style both derive from the culture's concept of men and women. It seems, therefore, that it is not the style itself that is an index of social relationships, as Alan Lomax's essays on cantometrics have suggested,[27] but rather what people say about the style, the oral literary criticism of the Snape and Blaxhall tradition.[28]

What can be lacking in a strong performance is emotional honesty. The songs must be sung with feeling, as they were in the old days:

> Well, they put their hearts into it, you know, and they stressed their feelings in the song. You know, they sorta brought the words out, and there's feeling in it when they sung it there, and meaning in it. Some you get now, in the present day, there's no meaning to it, and no feeling to it. Songs they sing, they had more feeling to them, and more go in them than today. You see, if you go into a pub, you get the old-time singers, you seem to attract people more than modern songs. I mean, they'll go miles to hear an old country song. But songs today are all right I suppose for the generation, but *they* were good songs.[29]

Lenny Savage is critical of performances which lack feeling:

> A lot of these put too much voice in and kill it, don't they? They kill the actual song, they don't put any feeling for the song at all, so that's why I just let them get on with it.[30]

> I like them real old ones, what are sung with feeling in them. I can't bear to hear 'em shout. They should be sung as they should be sung

> if they're going to – I suppose some of them shout to get above the others . . . that's all right, if that's your type of voice, you can't help it, can you, but there ain't no need to blaw, which I suppose a lot on it could be the brewer, couldn't it? Wonderful saying they used to say – 'Give it mouth.' To me that never appealed, to give it mouth except what you might get on some high notes later in the evening, but I mean that's more like old army barracks, you know, mess room stuff, to my idea. That's like 'Nellie Dean' at turning-out time, isn't it? Everybody is in the same.[31]

The first principle so far, then, is performance, the willingness of someone to entertain. Secondary to performance are aesthetic considerations which depend for their singling out on the specific relationship between singer and audience: since the songs tell stories, the words must be pronounced clearly, since the stories are songs, the basic musicianship of keeping in tune is required of the singer. Beyond that, however, the considerations of art music go by the board, since all musical concerns are subordinated to the requirements of narrative performance. Thus, tunes should be clearly defined in their tonality and phrasing, and moderate in tempo which is in any case objectively a function of performance style rather than of melodic structure. There is an ambiguity of attitude as to whether tunes exist in themselves and impose attitudes on the singers (as Geoff Ling believes), or whether singers impose their attitudes on the melodies (as criticisms of Percy Webb suggest), and it is therefore of little consequence whether melody or singer is the more imposing since in performance tempo and phrasing are determined by the singer and not by melody. With story occupying such an important place in song performance, perhaps because in this society tale-telling is not common, musical accompaniment should not predominate (note the frequent adverse comments on guitars and accompaniment in folk and popular music.[32]) Nor is bravura performance and virtuosity an aim, but rather the ideal combination is strength of voice yoked with sympathetic feeling, and a kind of power (associated with masculinity) held in restraint yet produced in a relaxed way.

There are certain physical characteristics which change the quality or type of performance: excitement, drunkenness, lack of wind and old age. These four factors are often mentioned by singers and audience as effective on performance. Excitement goes hand in hand with drunkenness, and these are controllable factors, whereas lack of wind and old age are beyond the control of anybody and are therefore treated with understanding and tolerance. It is clear also that in a tradition held mainly by the older men, all of these physical factors are permanently present, since pub-singing is a local male prerogative, and lack of wind and voice are concomitant with the age of the traditional singers. Pride is taken by some in the ability to sing without the aid of alcohol: Cyril Poacher, for example, regards this as proof of his true singing ability. But generally, singers recognise that alcohol helps them to sing. It is when moderation is passed by that criticism is made of poor performance through drink. Cyril Poacher estimates the effect drink has on his own and Bob Hart's singing:

> The trouble is, now, there's a lot of people can make a hell of a lot of noise when they've had some beer, if you understand my meaning. Now Bob Hart ain't like that and I'm not like it, 'cos if you was in the Ship at seven o'clock and you asked me at five past to sing you a song, I'd sing it, and sing it as it should be sung. So would Bob Hart.[33]

Similarly, Bob Hart: 'I can sing with it and I can sing without. I sing better without a drink, yes . . . I don't know what it is, give more attention to it, I suppose.'[34] Lenny Savage is an advocate of a drink before a sing-song ('they generally warm them up a bit first');[35] so are Clive Woolnough and Jake Foreman, and the behaviour of most of the other pub singers suggests that they feel the same way: 'When I'm sober I try and sing a little bit better than what I can do and mess it up. And if you had just a few, you sorta sing more natural, I think.'[36] Since it is largely a pub-singing tradition, the consumption of alcohol is bound to have effects on the choice of song, on the confidence of people about to perform, on their performing abilities, and on the pleasure of the audience. David MacKay's thesis, 'The Tradition of Pub-singing in the Villages of East Suffolk',[37] states that alcohol can increase musical variation, especially in the case of Percy Webb. The examples given are of a performance of 'Wheel your P'rambulator' in Clopton Crown on a Saturday night and at home on a weekday morning, and of 'The Nutting Girl' verse by verse in Clopton Crown. MacKay suggests that alcohol encourages a certain creativity and that pub performances are superior to and more authentic than performances at home, but it must also be noted that any pub performance before a familiar or even unfamiliar audience is bound to be better than a performance before a fieldworker. However, MacKay's point is valid since alcohol is a stimulant and so is audience, and variation is as likely to occur when a singer is excited as it is when he has a lapse of memory or a need to censor or to elaborate.

Lack of wind has struck some of the singers and makes them more critical of their own performance than they might otherwise be. Lenny Savage often will not sing because of his asthma, and George Bennett is convinced that his wind is all right, but that he would have made a real singer if he had a good set of teeth:

> I don't think that man Bennett has got much the matter with his lungs. He got good lungs – he isn't short of breath, no. He'll go acarrying on another thirty years, yer. At your service, thank you . . .[38] I believe in the past if I'd been more cultured and had a tidy teeth in, I believe I coulda been passed for a singer.[39]

Only too often the singer clearly recognises the general decay and decline of old age, not only in older men (as is the case with Cyril Poacher's descriptions of Bob Scarce and Percy Webb), but also in the case of younger men (as with Bob Hart's description of Percy Webb).

> *Cyril Poacher*. Bob Scarce weren't very good, tune weren't very good, but the words were very good. That's like Percy Webb, he's all right, but I think he's had it, to tell you the honest truth. I think he's got past it. Well, Bob Hart said to me at dinnertime, he said, 'I think Percy's got past it,' and I think so too. No disrespects to him, though, I mean, he tried to sing Friday night, but he'd no idea of singing, oh no.[40]
>
> I don't think Percy was so good last night, he's getting feeble. Pity too, because there's a bit of fun in him.[41]
>
> *Bob Hart*. Percy's getting past singing. He used to be a fair good singer, but if you notice if he come to a high note now he shout it. He . . . don't let the song float, he just shout that out and get past that into another, like I do sometimes.[42]

It is particularly sad when a very old man like James Knights knows that his singing has become worse, and almost stops singing because of this awareness:

> I got no interest in it now, dear. No, I got no interest in singing now, and in fact I don't sing. One time o' day, it didn't matter what I was doing, I was always singing. I got a damn good voice . . . my voice

was always in tune, you see, would be. That's the thing, you want to practise a lot, to keep the voice goin', you do. I've known when I've been orf it a month and ain't sung a song at all, well, you feel such a fool, your voice ain't there, you can't get it. But if you're asinging about all day long and asinging of a night as well, well, your voice is always in tune. It's just like an old fiddle, you've got to keep it in tune. No, that is so, dear, I found that out, different times, when I haven't done any for a long time. When I used to be following the plough all day long, I used to be singing all day long. I've heard 'em say this – 'Know where you've been aploughing today, I know the field you've been in.' Yes, well . . . that's what I liked, I loved singing, always anxious to get hold of any fresh song or anything. Well, they class me as a good singer anyhow, that they did. That's the reason how I sung at so many concerts . . . Well, I haven't got the interest in it, dear – I've got old, dear, because, you see, my dear girl, I ain't got the voice. I don't call myself a singer now . . . No, I don't. O dear, no, no, no, no, no. No, I'm only just sort of a bumble bee hummer, that's all.[43]

Song Content: Truth and Meaning

The singer's delivery of the song, his clarity, tunefulness and sincerity are all important features in a consideration of the aesthetics of the local tradition. In performance, singer and audience are in a relationship where the technique and physical conditions control communication. It is also the content of the songs which indicates local aesthetics, the preference for certain subject-matters, and especially for truthful songs which have a meaning. Songs of sexual fantasy are enjoyed mostly by the men, and the songs are sung with a male propensity for outlining the most desirable type of woman and sexual behaviour. Women also enjoy these songs if they are women who attend the pub regularly, since by their going they declare their broadmindedness. Censorship may occur in the case of obscene songs like 'The Lobster' and 'Don't Do It Tonight', but it is most likely to occur in the presence of non-local women. The nature of the favourite songs is often humorous or sentimental, expressing the two poles of human emotion, the range of human experience, and the breadth of human communal response.

A lot of people show a preference for comical songs, perhaps because they demand least of an audience, allowing, as they do, emotional anarchy rather than emotional sympathy and empathy; and the role of comic singer is therefore a fortunate one. Women singers like Bessie Ling and Blind Bess were comic not solely because of the nature of their songs, but also because, by virtue of being female, they were forced to be more sporting and fun-loving in their adoption of the pub-singing role than men were. By entering the pub and singing there, they were marked as good sports, and they therefore took on an aura of fun, which is closely allied to comedy. Reg Jay feels that singers exist to entertain and, consequently, they should be pleased to cause laughter, as he is when he sings his only song, 'The Farmer's Boy':

> If you're laughing, that's what you're singing the song for in my opinion. I mean, if you sung religious songs, they'd all moan or say something, wouldn't they, but to sing a comical song or a straightforward song, soon as you start laughing, first thing they say, 'They take the mickey out of you.' You're singing that song for the enjoyment of them and that's why I think the young ones are gone wrong . . . Well, if you go into a pub, that's what you like, a good comic song, and Cyril a got 'em and so has Geoffie, I mean like 'Take the Chains from off my Heart and Set me Free', which Geoffie sing. Well, people are interested in that.[44]

Bob Hart regards Percy Webb as a humorous performer but has doubts about the efficacy of his behaviour during a funny song: the singer must make little of himself in order to give his song full benefit, and Bob Hart definitely adopts this deadpan stance, whereas Percy bellows with laughter throughout his funny songs when he is drunk:

> Last night he was in that sort of laughing mood . . . I mean, he spoilt it. We're the ones should laugh. He shouldn't laugh . . . Well, the audience should see the funny side. I mean, you got that song, and you're asinging that to make them laugh, but if you laugh yourself, that take all the picture out of it. I don't know how I shoulda got through these last years if I hadn't a took up singing, you seem so far away from everybody, but if you can do something to amuse them, that's all right.[45]

People can be amused by a song even to the extent of forgiving a technically poor performance of it, and it is clear that content is thus maximised in comedy, and the individual performer and performance is of less significance.

> To me, it's just got to be in tune, otherwise it's just something that I can't stand, you know, it just grates. But I don't mind Percy [Ling]

> singing out of tune a bit if it's a funny song, you know.[46]

Humour, and its association with anarchy, thus suggests a certain lifting of restrictions with regard to delivery: although the performer may enhance his image in his comic presentation, the content of his song and the shared jollity of its existence dominate the performance.

At the other end of the scale from humour is sentiment, and in these two types of songs the range of human emotions is expressed. When a young man moves into adulthood as a singer, he may well adopt the role of singer of sentimental songs, or of comic songs, and thus identify himself strongly with one emotional genre, or he may choose to mix the songs of his repertoire and thus reflect a more varied response to life. Some singers say that they prefer sentimental songs: 'Well, I used to like to sing all sentimentals, not this dirty old poked up muck, I didn't like to hear that. I used to like to hear sentimental songs. Did you ever hear Harry Lauder sing?'[47] Percy Ling's sentimental songs are appreciated by the landlady at the Ship Inn:

> Percy can sing some nice little songs if he doesn't go off on a dirty song . . . He can sing some nice songs, Percy can. One or two nice ones I think he sing with a lot of sincerity. Don't you agree? They're nice sincere songs and I think he sings them with sincerity.[48]

He himself recognises the value of having such songs in his repertoire, for just as a funny song attracts the attention of the audience away from his technique, so does a sentimental song:

> O yes, I ain't got no voice, look, I ain't got no voice to sing. I don't think I'm very good. I won competitions, but . . . you gotta consider these things, don't you? Well, if you sing a song . . . a cutting song, what go down deep in the hearts of people, they think more about that than they do the singing. You know what I mean, you know, like 'I Had a Home Down in Texas', that go down in people, don't it. That's a real song find. And so is 'A Group of Squatties' – 'one is my mother, God bless her I love her,' you see, you gotta think of the type of the songs.[49]

Percy's pragmatism only partially disguises his real commitment to his sentimental songs, since he appreciates their truth as well as their power of attraction, and his understanding of the polarity of humour and sentiment is instinctive, in response to audience, rather than intellectual. Repertoire reflects the stages of a singer's life, and the emotional environments in which he has found himself, and the consonance of repertoire derives from the consonance of the individual's life. Simultaneously, because many of his experiences and many of his songs are shared with many of his contemporaries, his repertoire constitutes a reaching out to them whereby his individuality can likewise be brought into consonance with that of others.

W. Roy MacKenzie, in *The Quest for the Ballad*, writes that only when an old and familiar audience hears an old and familiar song by a familiar singer will a true ballad be experienced and the social significance of traditional singing be realised. Most Suffolk singers like a song with a story, and generally a truth or meaning is looked for in the songs.

> *John Ling*. I mean, if they wasn't put to a tune or anything and somebody just spoke 'em, that'd be like somebody telling a story, but with the new songs there's just a load of noise and words just mixed up, which don't make no sense if you listen to them, but with the country and western and the old songs, I think they're more or less a way of expressing an opinion in more or less of a story type.[50]

> *Clive Woolnough*. I always like them a little bit jolly so they got a little bit of life in them – some I like that are slower, but as long as they tell a good story, you know, they must tell a good story. If I can't follow it, you know, I don't like it.[51]

> *Chris Messenger*. Those old songs have a meaning in them, really.

> *Alice Messenger*. What I like about the old songs, they've got a story behind them. Some of these things modern songs, you don't know what they're singing about.'[52]

The specific meaning of any narrative song is carefully listened to.

> *Arthur Drewery*. I give order for all of them. When they say 'Give order,' I listen to all of them, 'cos the majority of them have got a song with a meaning to it, so they're good solid songs, you might say.[53]

> *James Knights*. Folks don't want to hear those old songs, do they? They're the best old songs there is. I tell you what there is about

> them when you're singing those bloody old songs, there's some sense in those songs, ain't there? A lot of thèse bloody songs what they get up now, that's a lot of bloody gibberish, they're amaking up all this bloody old – there's neither tune nor nothing else there.[54]

Sometimes it is not a specific meaning, though, that is noted, the evocative power of the song, as in Bob Hart's understanding of 'When You and I were Seventeen':

> That came out not so wonderful long after the First World War, and ah there was a young couple, a young courting couple, but ah the boy died eventually, and, ah, what happened to the girl I don't know. They were – they sang it together on the – we had a little do on at Blaxhall, not in the Ship, that was on fete day, and they'd got a stage outside and that was very nice, that was . . . O they make me feel sad, yes. Ah, that song do bring me back memories, you see, 'cos that little girl died what was in that one . . . Died before they got married, I can't think of the – I can't think of the names even. I can picture the man – can't think of his name. He was relation to somebody at Blaxhall, but Blaxhall are nearly all relations, you know, Smith and Lings, that what that's composed of.[55]

As we shall see, for Priscilla Savage, talking about songs evokes memories of her dead husband; and for Stanley Day, the old songs evoke past village life, its closeness and security, and his childhood holidays in Blaxhall:

> When I go down there [Ship] sometimes and I hear the old songs, you know, you sort of sit there and you're miles away, and somebody'll sort of say, 'Hey up, you,' like that. Well, you're in a daze to them, but you're not in a daze to yourself 'cos your memory is going back to the relations and the things where you were and what you were doing when that song's being sung, many many years ago, you see, and that all comes back into your mind and then you're concentrating on that in thoughts and that because that song has brought them to you, brought your thoughts back, but nowadays, you know, you can sing a song what you like, I don't think that's got no feelings or no memories to that song like the good old songs used to have years ago.[56]

Stanley Day goes on to talk about 'When it's Lamplighting Time in the

Valley', and associates it with Cyril Poacher's mother, Susan, Stanley's aunt: 'that's got feeling 'cos that was Cyril's mother's song.' In turn he is reminded of his childhood and his aunt's kindness to him. The evocative power of the song, its association with a particular person, is important in the present (song ownership – Cyril now sings this song), and also in the past (the powerful associative feeling in which the past emotion is made present). Such evocative power and association is unavailable to strangers in the audience and to young uninformed local inhabitants.

Similarly, a song like 'Don't Go Down in the Mine, Dad' means a great deal to the Yorkshire woman, Bessie Hammond, as she explains:

> We were kids at home and that's a good meaning song, that is, 'cos that's just how it is in the mines, in't it, the way that song goes. Yer, I remember when we were kids, there used to be an accident in the mine, it's true, you'd see 'em going to the pithead, and . . . they'd let you know when there was a disaster in the mine, you know, love, and you'd see all the women and sweethearts and that and the families going to the pittops and seeing who come up in the cage and who's hurt and who weren't and that's just how that song goes. There's something in that song, I think, if you know what I mean, and I can remember when we were kids, my father was a miner, we were all miners . . . Them days there was nothing else to do. They went in the pit when they were fourteen, left school and went down in the pits. There weren't no like there is now, take a job, you know, and pick your own job. That's all there was so they were brought up to it – never knew no different, did they? There's a bit of meaning to that, isn't there? When my father used to come home from t'pit, you know, he worked down t'bottom of pit, me father did, some of them were on the top, he was on the bottom, and we heard them talk about it, used to walk miles down these here pits to get to their jobs when they got to bottom of pit, and you could see the pit cages . . . When he come home, he used to say to me mother, 'Emma, what sorta day has it been?' 'Course, you can't see in a pit, can you? Said, 'What you talkin' about, father, it's been a nice day.' 'Aye, lass,' he said, 'you don't know,' he said, 'when you go down that pit we don't see daylight till we come home on the top,' and as I got older I could see what he meant then.[57]

Mrs Hammond regards 'Don't Go Down in the Mine, Dad' as a true song because it matches her own early experiences of mining life, and the song clearly has strong emotional associations for her. Percy Webb finds that his singing of 'Old Shep' produces a strong effect on his audience, especially female, and the emotional overtones of the song are less specific than those of Mrs Hammond's mining song and perhaps therefore more universally appealing. Her song has a moving story, the context of which has added significance for her, and Percy Webb thinks 'Old Shep' may also be very moving because people make it relevant to themselves rather than allow it to spell out generalised emotions. The worth of her performance of 'Don't Go Down in the Mine, Dad' is that it touches her very deeply, and her sincerity is bound to communicate itself with her audience. 'Old Shep' serves a more direct function of having immediate emotional impact on an audience with little effort on the part of the singer:

> That make the women cry when I sing that, a lot of 'em, you know. Touching song . . . O, that's a true song, and they don't like you to sing it down here. I sang it once or twice. They say, 'That's a sad song.' That's why they – the women, you know, cry. There's a woman up at Orford where I sing it – she don't like to hear it. She cry every time. 'Course, that got meaning, you know. They got dogs themselves and faithful animals, and that make it like that I suppose. My father had three, nice dogs they was, wouldn't let nobody come and attack my mother, you know, or us. Didn't like a policeman, didn't like a tramp. That wouldn't let them in the gate, see. He stood that high – collie – used to lay on my mother's bed. You see, lambing time my father used to be away all night with the sheep, and he – it used to lay on her bed – there weren't nobody'd go there.[58]

Another form of truth in songs is appreciated by these people: songs are believed to affect real life and to reflect it. This is a reason for consonance of themes in individual repertoires and in the local repertoire. An example of belief in a song is expressed by James Knights:

> There's . . . this little old poacher song what I sang –
>
> O I like me wife, me pipe, and me glass,
> Carry through my long life do I pass,
> Jolly and free and it just suit me,
> And out with me gun in the morning.
>
> . . .

> Who'd lay in bed when the lark sing high,
> Up in the blue and cloudy sky,
> Gay as a bird o'er the fields I go,
> Back I return in the sunset glow.
>
> My dear little wife, she crossed the stile,
> She welcomed me home with a loving smile,
> Perhaps other women would fairer be,
> But she is me own and she just suit me.
>
> Then I like me wife . . .

> . . . I sung it in here one night, in this Lion [Little Glemham] here. Head gamekeeper here from the estate here was in there. He said, 'Here,' he say, 'I'll give you a bloody good drink to shut that up.' He didn't want to hear that, you know, 'cause that was atelling them how to go on, you see, telling the poacher how to go on . . . Poor old Jack Bayfield, he didn't like to hear me sing that. That was telling on them way to get after the pheasants, you see.[59]

Priscilla Savage likens Bessie Hammond to a song character and thus suggests that a song's proximity to real life could ensure its popularity; the relevance of songs, their ethical and emotional truths, is important:

> That one Mrs Hammond sang, 'left me like a broken doll'. One night up at the parish hall when she first married and come down here, they ask her, would she please sing them a song? . . . of course, her husband did leave her like a broken doll [he died young]. Poor woman, she did have to work hard, and she's a nice little woman, she used to live next door to me twenty-nine years.[60]

Thus songs can have specific evocative powers or contain generalised emotional truths, and such songs are appreciated by the singers and audience of this East Suffolk tradition. Herbert Halpert, in 'Truth in Folk-Songs', posits the theory that the old songs are still sung because the folk-singer believes strongly in the factual basis of his songs.[61] The old songs, passed on mainly by oral transmission, are part of a heritage from parents to children, and the truth of the songs is in their lineage. Truth in itself becomes a principle of aesthetics, as Halpert suggests.[62] Besides a belief in the historicity of song events, for example, in 'Bold General Wolfe', there is a belief in the truth of song emotions. This trust in the emotions of a song is necessary before the song is accepted into the local repertoire. Trust is the root of all feelings of nostalgia that singers and audience have for the communal singing of the past: the proliferation of singing then strengthened social ties through the communicative act of performance and the adoption of songs of emotional truth. Presumably, such truth was one criterion in the selection and popularity of songs.[63]

Song Performance: Unity and Fellowship

As stated earlier, performance or the principle of entertainment is the prime concern in this tradition, and other considerations are secondary. These are villages where people have long had to make their own entertainment, both in the home and at social gatherings, and consequently most people appreciate a performance of any sort, and there is a flexibility about their preferences.

> *Ben Ling*. I used to like to hear all of them, weren't any favourite about it, they all used to try and do their best, yes.[64]

> *Wickets Richardson*. I ain't got no favourite singers, dear, no, no. I haven't. They were all good, more or less, then. Plenty of songs, plenty of singers. We was noted for that. They always said, 'If you want a good evening, go to Blaxhall Ship.' Saturday nights and holidays, August Bank Holiday Monday. It was a smaller place then, all round sit and listen.[65]

Similarly, the singers may be aware that they are not the most musically or technically proficient, but they will tend to oblige with a song.

> *Arthur Drewery*. There's some people down there [The Ship] can't sing. I don't profess to be a singer, but as I say, I just like to join in for the fun . . . O yes, I always have done [sung] in the Ship, yes. I've always had a go, cause a bit of amusement or something like that. They say, 'Come on, we'll have a song all round,' and most of 'em have a go.[66]

At home, singing could provide comfort, community, diversion, love and peace, and it involved the participation of adults and children in a reciprocal hearth-centred activity. Lenny Savage describes his mother singing to her children:

> I mean . . . I'm going back to the days when there was Abie, Daley, me, probably Russell, there was probably four boys like that, you see, and we'd all be sitting round this old fireplace on little stools and that was the days of candles and oil lamps, you see. Father'd be alambing, you see, sleeping in the hut, so used to huddle us around the fire and that was where she used to sorta try and sing to us, that was only more or less to try and kill the boredom so we didn't fight or anything like that, we'd be at one another's throat. Or else there weren't enough light to do anything else.[67]

Priscilla Savage also sang songs with her husband, and there is in her description an air of love and nostalgia, an indication of the face-to-face nature of leisure in the home in these earlier days before radio and television provided a mass outward-looking, separately experienced form of entertainment: 'Our Dadda Bob used to, used to sit and sing songs and when we done them, we used to set and sing hymns. Well, that's the only pleasure we had, weren't it? Yer. Poor old boy.'[68]

A singer who is warm and obliging is well liked; he conforms to the principle of performance.

> *Reg Jay*. Wickets was one of the leading singers in there. I mean, you'd bring a crowd in, and perhaps you'd say, 'Go on, Wickets,' and he'd sing. Then he'd say. 'Ladies and gentlemen, my friend Mr Bob Smith will now sing,' and Bob, and that's how that would carry on in this particular pub. I liked them best 'cos they'd try to help you, you know what I mean. Like Alf, he used to sing a song, 'Airman, Airman, you don't put the Wind up Me'. Amy Johnson and all such times as that, and he'd go into a pub and he'd say, 'Hullo, how are you getting on, give us a song, give us so-and-so,' and I'd probably say, 'Give us "Airman",' and then he'd sing it, see, so I think to myself that the proper singer in Blaxhall Ship in my time was Wickets, 'cos he helped you and they all helped you and you helped them.[69]

In the pubs, singing can produce a great deal of fellow feeling so that it is appreciated as entertainment, given obligingly, and accepted tolerantly and gratefully. Communities can be strengthened by the singing situation, especially since people come from the surrounding district to hear local pub-singing, and a singer who is warm and obliging is well liked; he fulfils the expectations of his role. The singing can thus be a giving, a consolidation of feelings amongst people who know one another in other, more general, contexts, a celebration of a way of life, a recognition of quiddity, and a reinforcing of unity in a small area infiltrated and surrounded by the encroachments of modern life.

Notes

1. Alan Dundes, 'Metafolklore and Oral Literary Criticism', *Monist*, no. 50 (1966), pp. 505-9.

2. 'Serious' music refers to music that is taught in academies, performed in concert halls for paying audiences, composed by artistically self-conscious people. The term is unsatisfactory, obviously, deriving as it does from precisely that cultural bias which the study of traditional music must avoid, but there is no satisfactory term available.

3. Fred Pearce, 23 June 1975.

4. Percy Ling, 9 Nov. 1974.

5. Frank Reeve, 24 June 1975.

6. Stanley Day, 24 June 1975.

7. James Smith, 21 June 1975.

8. Priscilla Savage, 15 Nov. 1974.

9. Geoff Ling, 17 Nov. 1974.

10. Alice and Chris Messenger, 31 Oct. 1975.

11. Mrs Saunders, 2 July 1975.

12. For an excellent explication of the functions of disguise in traditional drama, see Simon Lichman, 'The Marshfield Paperboys' (PhD dissertation, University of Pennsylvania, Philadelphia, forthcoming).

13. Alice Messenger, ibid.

14. Bob Hart, 13 July 1974.

15. Frank Reeve, ibid.

16. James Knights, 11 Sept. 1974.

17. Bob Hart, 5 Oct. 1974.

18. Bob Hart, 15 July 1974.

19. Bob Hart, 5 Oct. 1974.

20. Percy Webb, 16 Nov. 1974.

21. Clive Woolnough, 2 July 1975.

22. Frank Reeve, ibid.

23. Cyril Poacher, 10 Sept. 1974.

24. James Knights, ibid.

25. James Smith, ibid.

26. Bob Hart, 25 June 1974.

27. Alan Lomax, 'Song Structure and Social Structure', *Ethnology*, vol. I (1962), pp. 425, 451; 'Musical Style and Social Context', *American Anthropologist*, no. 61 (1959), pp. 927-54.

28. For more on this subject, see my article, 'The Aesthetics of a Singing Tradition' in John Blacking (ed.), *The Ethnography of Musical Performance*, Queens University Papers on Social Anthropology, vol. 5 (forthcoming).

29. Stanley Day, ibid.

30. Lenny Savage, 1 Oct. 1974.

31. Lenny Savage, 30 Oct. 1974.

32. For a singer whose musical consciousness is of a linear sequence of individual tones supporting individual words or parts of words in a narrative progression, the synchronic clusters of tones produced together, or in the

kaleidoscopic effect of an arpeggio, by a guitar or free reed instrument, may be rather confusing, especially as the instrument's performance moves forward in clusters rather than with the fluid progress of the voice.

33. Cyril Poacher, ibid.
34. Bob Hart, 12 July 1974.
35. Lenny Savage, 1 Oct. 1974.
36. Clive Woolnough, ibid.
37. David McKay, 'The Tradition of Pub-Singing in the Villages of East Suffolk' (unpubished BA dissertation, Institute of Dialect and Folk Life Studies, University of Leeds, 1971), pp. 20-1.
38. George Bennett, Snape, 3 Oct. 1974.
39. George Bennett, 14 Nov. 1974.
40. Cyril Poacher, ibid.
41. Ibid.
42. Bob Hart, 25 June 1974.
43. James Knights, ibid.
44. Reg Jay, 25 June 1974.
45. Bob Hart, 12 July 1974.
46. Mrs Saunders, ibid.
47. James Knights, ibid.
48. Mrs Saunders, ibid.
49. Percy Ling, 16 Nov. 1974.
50. John Ling, 1 July 1975.
51. Clive Woolnough, ibid.
52. Alice and Chris Messenger, ibid.
53. Arthur Drewery, Blaxhall, 30 June 1975.
54. James Knights, 16 Nov. 1974.
55. Bob Hart, 15 July 1974.
56. Stanley Day, ibid.
57. Bessie Hammond, 30 Oct. 1974.
58. Percy Webb, 19 July 1974.
59. James Knights, 4 Oct. 1974.
60. Priscilla Savage, 31 Oct. 1974
61. See Herbert Halper, 'Truth in Folk-Songs' in John H. Cox (ed.), *Traditional Ballads, Mainly from West Virginia* (National Service Bureau Publication No. 75-5, New York, 1939),p. xiii.
62. Halpert, 'Truth in Folksongs'.
63. For example, Roger Abrahams, *A Singer and Her Songs. Almeda Riddle's Book of Ballads* (Louisiana State University Press, Baton Rouge, Louisiana, 1970), p. 112.
64. Ben Ling, 2 July 1975.
65. Wickets Richardson, 27 June 1975.
66. Arthur Drewery, ibid.
67. Lenny Savage, ibid.
68. Priscilla Savage, 10 Sept. 1974.
69. Reg Jay, ibid.

EPILOGUE

Thus this description and its commentary come to an end. All that the anthropologist and field-worker can do is to represent, as faithfully as possible, the events in their spatial and temporal contexts, to show the movements of people in and out of the institutions, occasions and situations offered by their social milieu, and to suggest a theoretical approach to these dynamic community interactions. The pub, principally, provides a meeting-place for the men of these villages; and here too the women have formed their own society and eventually been taken into the larger male-dominated one; and young men have learned the ritualised ways of entry into the singing tradition. Singing also in the home and at community gatherings outside the pub has been a focus of familial and societal involvement and consolidation; in its dynamics are reflected the dynamics of the society at large.

Further research is probably always suggested as a piece of work by necessity comes to a close, and as I drew towards the end of my field-work, new hypotheses and ideas started to present themselves which were, unfortunately, outside the scope of my time. It seems that the nature of the singing traditions in Snape and Blaxhall and what is said about them there are a reflection of the sexual balance of power in the villages, but further field-work on precisely this matter would be a sensitive exercise and one difficult to present for publication. Aligned with this is the hypothesis that suicide and singing in the older men are sometimes solutions to a common malaise or problem – extensive field-work as well as statistical research could be carried out on these matters, but unfortunately much evidence will be lost now as people die and emotional wounds heal and are forgotten. In any case, it is always doubtful how far a field-worker may expect to enter into the lives of his informants, and certainly how far confidences, evaluations and speculations that are given can be made public.

It is no longer the texts of songs that are of interest, or even the complete musical transcriptions of performance: now, man as a singing creature is studied as man who sings with his fellows, in a local environment that controls and extols his musical behaviour, and who reflects in his handling of tradition the varying mores and values of his living context. Thus, this work has attempted to present not only the singer and his songs, but also his life, his values, his forcefulness, his oral literary criticism and most of all his involvement through song in the multi-stranded society in which he lives and from which his tradition is succoured.

APPENDIX I: BIOGRAPHIES OF THE SINGERS AND OTHER MAJOR INFORMANTS

Basil Bennett. Born 1899. Father a shepherd at Chillesford Lodge; eleven children in the family. Basil took farm jobs as a young lad, volunteered for army in First World War and went overseas. Returned and worked as forester away from Suffolk. Biked to London and took work as a house porter. Married a girl he had met in Yorkshire, stayed London ten years as flat caretakers. Moved to Snape as landlord of the Plough and Sail Inn, owned by Maltings. After 28 years, lost pub when Maltings changed hands. Casual jobs since then. Died August 1976. Survived by wife, Hilda, and daughter, Margaret.

George (Seedy) Bennett. Born *c*. 1900. Brother to Basil. Bachelor, lives in caravan near Blaxhall, keeps ducks, pigs and poultry, and grows vegetables. Casual farm labourer.

Stanley Day. Born 1913 in Harwich. Father a master mariner, mother Sarah Elizabeth Ling from Blaxhall. An only child. Spent holidays in Blaxhall, cousin to Geoff Ling, Cyril Poacher, Wickets Richardson. Went to sea and retired to Blaxhall in 1955. A widower.

Arthur Drewery. Born 1925 in Blaxhall. Left school at fourteen, worked on farms, joined marines and came out in 1947. Has worked for a haulage contractor at Melton ever since. Took care of his invalid mother until her death two years ago.

Lil Durrant. Born *c*. 1914, Blaxhall. Frank Reeve's sister. Went into service after leaving school at fourteen. Worked in Women's Land Army during Second World War, and did other general farm work throughout her life. She is now a home help. Her second husband, Eli Durrant, died 1958. Has four children. Remembers her mother singing but does not sing herself.

Jake Foreman. Born *c*. 1935 in Snape. Lives with invalid mother in council house, does odd labouring jobs, likes to sing in the pubs.

Bessie Hammond. *Née* Howell. Born *c*. 1896 near Pontefract, Yorkshire, daughter of a miner. Went to Blackpool in service, worked there as a nurse during First World War. Nursed a Blaxhall man, Henry Hammond, married him 1920, moved to Blaxhall. He was a horseman at the Old Barn, died of tuberculosis after nine years. She did housework and nursing, raised two daughters alone, moved 1976 from Blaxhall to a pensioner's cottage in Woodbridge.

Bob Hart. Born 1892 at Sotherton, moved to Reydon near Southwold. Farming family. Mother died 1902 and Bob lived much of the time then with his grandparents. Worked on farm from age thirteen, then ran away to sea. 1914 joined army, went to France, had jaw blown away 1916, spent rest of war in hospital. Stayed with brother in Snape, married a Snape girl, took odd jobs, then worked at the Maltings for forty years. Retired, then lost wife and two sons in three years, and lived with his daughter-in-law until his death in January 1978.

Margaret Howell. Née Morley. Born 1888, Knodishall. Lived much of early life with grandparents in Snape. Left school at ten. Went into service, married, had a child. Husband cruel and she ran away. Avoided workhouse by taking work at Aldeburgh laundry. Eventually divorced and remarried a Snape man for whom she had been housekeeper. Lost two sons and second husband, lived alone in Snape until her death two years ago.

Reg Jay. Born 1915. Mother Celia Bailey from Tunstall, father Tom Jay from Blaxhall. Eleven children. Tom built a squatter's cottage in Blaxhall. Reg became a shepherd at fourteen, then worked for Catchment Board, and joined army. Married in Blaxhall after his return from Africa in 1945. Six children, some singers. Reg a drainage contractor and does odd jobs.

Reuben Kerridge. Born *c*. 1912, Wickham Market. Father a cobbler and Reuben apprenticed to the trade. Then on coastal defence, at the Maltings, as a sewage worker. Moved to Snape 1939 when he married a Snape woman. Plays banjo.

James Knights. Born 1880 near Woodbridge. Varied work history. Married when he was fifty, had seven children, six of whom survived. None of sons is a pub singer, although one has played in a band as organist.

Abraham (Abie) Ling. Born 1914, Blaxhall. Father Abraham, brother to Priscilla Savage, singer. Abie left school at fourteen, worked on cart selling paraffin around villages, worked on land, in army six years, then worked as tree feller and as labourer for nineteen years on Glemham Estate. Unmarried, lived with parents until their deaths. Used to sing but now has throat trouble.

Ben Ling. Born 1891 to Laura Ling, who had been in service in London. Brought up by grandparents and uncle in Blaxhall. Attended school and evening classes. Emigrated to Canada and farmed there. Returned and fought in First World War. Varied work. Married to Eva, with two sons. Lives in Blaxhall.

Bessie Ling. Born *c*. 1900, London. Worked in a cigarette factory there, met Blaxhall man who worked in hotel opposite factory, married him and moved to Blaxhall. Worked in fields most of her life and went to Ship Inn regularly. Liked companionship of father-in-law and other women. No children. Became blind after having influenza in early 1950s. A widow.

Geoff Ling. Born 1916. Oscar Ling was his father, Priscilla Savage's brother, a horseman at Stone Farm, Blaxhall; his mother was Susan Poacher (Cyril's father's sister). Seven children. Geoff took farm work with horses, called up for service in Second World War, Japanese prisoner of war, returned to Blaxhall and married a Smith – she is reported to sing at family gatherings. Geoff now works at Bentwaters Aerodrome.

John Ling. Born *c*. 1939, Snape. His father was a maltster. Nephew to Percy Ling. Joined army when he was seventeen. Married, three children, does odd jobs.

Percy Ling. Born 1906, Blaxhall. Farm labouring family, nine children. Percy left school at thirteen, began farm work. Army during Second World War as cook. Returned to Suffolk, married and had ten children; his wife was a singer as well. Now a widower, does odd labouring jobs having recently finished full-time work at Bentwaters.

Ruby Ling. Née Clark. Born 1905, Sibton. Father a horseman on the Wentworth Estate. Ruby went into service in Aldeburgh at thirteen, went to London at fifteen and worked for several different families.

Returned to Aldeburgh after four years, worked, married at 28. Husband at Maltings all of his working life. She did odd jobs and housework. Two daughters, both musical, but they do not sing.

Alice Messenger. Née Ling. Born 1905, Blaxhall. Father Esau, mother from Cambridge. Three children. In service until her marriage in 1934. Worked hard all her life – housework etc. Husband, Christopher, a maltster and labourer.

Ethel Pearce. Née Smith. Born 1899, Blaxhall. Worked in service at Aldeburgh at the age of thirteen. Married twice, first to Geoff Ling's stepbrother who died in middle age; then to Fred Pearce. Works as cleaner in the Ship and is also a home help. Five children. Does not sing but knows songs.

Fred Pearce. Born 1912, Rendlesham. Father a thatcher. Fred took odd farm jobs after working as a thatcher for several years. Moved to Blaxhall early 1930s. Was gamekeeper, rabbit-catcher, labourer. In army. Melodeon player. Married Ethel, died 1976.

Cyril Poacher. Born 1910 to Lewis and Alice (*née* Ling) of Blaxhall. Began farm work 1924. Married, joined army and was stationed at Catterick Camp during Second World War. Moved to Grove Farm, Blaxhall, as cowman in 1946, and worked there until he retired two years ago. Two daughters married to American servicemen in the United States. Now lives in Snape with his wife.

Frank Reeve. Born 1910, Blaxhall. Family of six children. Father a mole-catcher, then horseman, killed falling off a haystack. Sang in church choir. Wanted to be a schoolmaster but no opportunity. Worked as farm labourer, waiter, valet, and was in Royal Army Service Corps during Second World War. Owns general store in Blaxhall, married, no children.

Wickets (Alfred) Richardson. Born 1899, Blaxhall. His mother a Ling. Eight children. Father killed 1908 and life difficult. Began work as newspaper boy, joined army and was in France and Ireland. On returning to Blaxhall there was little work but he eventually joined the county council. Retired after 35 years. Wife died, he suffered a stroke, lived by himself for ten years, and then moved to an old people's home in Aldeburgh. Had two daughters. Died 1979.

Lenny Savage. Born 1913, son of Priscilla and Robert. Farm work, then in the county council and still is. Army during Second World War, moved from Blaxhall to Snape afterwards. Married with two daughters (wife, Violet, is sister to Basil and George Bennett). Suffers from asthma.

Priscilla Savage. Née Ling. Born 1881, Blaxhall. Her father crippled in a mining accident near Durham, mother took any work she could. Four children. Prissy spent some of her childhood with an aunt in Little Glemham. Went into service, returned home to nurse mother, married Robert Savage in 1902, a shepherd. Twelve children, eight of whom survived childhood. Died January 1975, soon after the death of her deaf and dumb son, Willy, with whom she lived. Some of her children sing or know songs.

James Smith. Born 1904, Snape. Father a maltster, James also worked there. Married, four children. Family sing songs, but none of his children sing solo. Died a year ago and is survived by his wife.

Percy Webb. Born 1897, Hemingstone, moved to Hasketon 1900. Father a shepherd until he died at the age of 73. Seven children. Percy started farm work at Tunstall, and wanted to work with horses. Joined army and was gassed in First World War. Went to India, returned to England and eventually got back his horseman's job. Married 1923, one son who is a harmonica player. Moved to tractor work with farming changes in 1940s, then worked at Bentwaters and in a chemist's shop in Woodbridge. Sang regularly until his death in May 1976.

Clive Woolnough. Born 1947, Blaxhall, a twin son of Frank. Grew up in Blaxhall, left school at fifteen, works as a bricklayer, is married and now lives in Chillesford.

Dick Woolnough. Born 1897. Second of four illegitimate sons to a Blaxhall woman. He began farm work at the age of thirteen, went to Maltings, and then went to sea. In army during First World War, court-martialled for insubordination. Lived in Snape after war and worked at Maltings for forty years. Married 1920, had only one child, a daughter, who survived babyhood. Wife an invalid for many years. He died 1976.

Frank Woolnough. Born 1900, Dick's brother. Worked as a drainage contractor for most of his life, and then took casual farm work. Has lived in Blaxhall most of his life. Four children, one son is a singer.

APPENDIX II: LIST OF SINGERS' RECORDED REPERTOIRES

Basil Bennett

Australian Homestead
Farmer's Boy
Group of Young Squatties
Sailor Boy
Three Old Ladies Locked in the Lavatory
Travelling on a Lone Train
Volunteer Organist

George Bennett

Bring Back my Bonny
Charlie Cribbin
Charlie Takeaway
Dab a Bit of Powder on it, Father
Forever and Forever
Glory for Me
Here we are Again
I have a Saviour
Jeremiah Jones
Keep Right on to the End of the Road
Laughing Policeman
Little Jimmy Tiddler
Lo, He Comes with Clouds Descending
Mid Shot and Shell
Old Grey Coat
Roaming in the Gloaming
Take me Back to Dear Old Blighty
Village Pump
When I Survey the Wondrous Cross

Arthur Drewery

Blackboard of my Heart
Boy with No Shoes (incomplete)
Don't Step on Mother's Roses
Father Christmas
Old Shep
Sailor and his True Love (The Larks They Sang Melodious) (incomplete)
You Never Know What Times May Bring You To

Jake Foreman

Missing in Action
Old Shep
Wild Colonial Boy

Bessie Hammond

Broken Doll
Don't Go Down in the Mine, Dad
If I Had My Way
If You Ever Go Across the Sea to Ireland
If Those Lips Could Only Speak
In the Heart of Lancashire
My Souvenirs
Springtime in the Rockies
Yours till the Stars Lose Their Glory

Bob Hart

After the Ball
All Getting Older Together
All Jolly Fellows that Follow

the Plough
All Through the Night
As I Strolled Out to Aylesbury
Australia
Banks of Sweet Primroses
Barbara Allen 1
Barbara Allen 2
Black-Eyed Susan
Bold General Wolfe
Bold Princess Royal
Bold William Taylor
Bonnie Mary of Argyle
Broadside
City of Laughter
Codbanging
Comrades
Dark Eyed Sailor
Death of Nelson
Drums Went Bang (Flanagan's Band)
Eat More Fruit
End of a Perfect Day
Farmer's Boy
Female Cabin Boy
Fireman
Foggy Dew
Funny Little Place to Have One
God Send You Back to Me
Granny's Song at Twilight
Great Red Dawn
Gypsy's Warning
Hearts of Oak
His Day's Work is Done
Hymns Mother Sang
If I were a Blackbird
If Those Lips Could Only Speak
If Those Lips Could Only Speak (parody)
I'm Sorry I Made You Cry
In the Shade of the Old Apple Tree
I will Take You Home Again, Kathleen
John Barleycorn
Jolly Jack the Sailor Lad
Just an Old Fashioned Lady
Just Before the Battle, Mother
Just Break the News to Mother
Keep the Home Fires Burning
Lincolnshire Poacher
Little Grey Home in the West (When the Golden Sun Sinks in the West)
Long, Long, Trail Awinding
Maria, my Girl
Memories
Mermaid Song
Miner's Song of Home
My Grandfather's Clock
My Old Kentucky Home
My Souvenirs
No Man's Land
No Rose in all the World
Old Farmer's Servant
Old Rustic Bridge
Old Shep
On a Summer's Night
One of the Best
One Touch of Nature
Pack Up Your Troubles
Paradise Street (Blow the Man Down)
Put me Among the Girls
Red Sails in the Sunset
Ring for the Girl I Love
Roast Beef of Old England
Rose of Tralee
Rule Britannia
Scarlet and the Blue
Seventeen Come Sunday
Ship that Never Returned
Silver Threads Among the Gold

Smile Awhile
Song of the Thrush
Spaniard that Blighted My Life
Take Me Back to Dear Old Blighty
Tanks in Picardy
Two Little Boys
Underneath the Apron
Varmer Giles
Village Pump
Watch Over You when You were a Baby
What a Time
When the Fields are White with Daisies
When the Sunset Turns the Ocean Blue to Gold
When You and I were Seventeen
When You Come to the End of a Perfect Day
White Wings
With Someone Like You
Won't You Buy my Pretty Flowers?
Why Have I No Daddy, Mummy?
Why Shouldn't We Sing?
You Taught Me How to Love You
Young Sailor Cut Down in his Prime

Margaret Howell

If I were a Blackbird
Over the Burning Plains of Egypt
Sailor Boy

Reg Jay

Farmer's Boy
Just an Old Fashioned Lady

James Knights

Be Kind to Your Parents
Charlie Dusn't Do It (incomplete)
I Love My Jean
I Went to Your Wedding
The Best of her, she's Irish (incomplete)
You Taught Me How to Love You (incomplete)
N.B. He claims to know over one hundred songs but cannot be coerced into singing them now except for payment.

Ben Ling

In the Shade of the Old Apple Tree
Song of the Thrush

Geoff Ling

Ball of Yarn
Green Bushes
Grief, O Grief
Group of Young Squatties
In the Shade of the Old Apple Tree
Little Brown Road Winding Over the Hill (Smiling Through)
Maggy May
My Souvenirs (parody)
My Sweet Irish Girl
Over the Burning Plains of Egypt
Suvla Bay
You Taught Me How to Love You

John Ling

I'm Nobody's Child
Old Shep
Queen of My Heart (incomplete)

Percy Ling

Boy with No Shoes
Cobbler
Don't Do It Tonight
Flanagan's Band
Flash Company
Group of Young Squatties
If I were a Blackbird
In the Spring
Just Like Darby and Joan
Lobster
Queen of my Heart
Two Convicts They were Seated
Underneath the Apron

Ruby Ling

All Alone by the Telephone
All Day I am Dreaming
All the Best Looking Girls
Always
Am I Wasting my Time?
Baby's Prayer (and) Paradise
Bouquet of Roses
Buttercup Joe
By the Waterfall
Cabin with Roses round the Door
Call on Mammy
Carolina Moon
City of Laughter
Clouds will Soon Roll by
Delaney
Duck Foot Sue
Eat More Fruit
Fairheaded Boy
Farmer's Boy
Flash Company
Forty Shades of Green
God Send You Back to Me
Granny's Song at Twilight
Happiness
Home
How Can You Buy Killarney?
Hymns my Mother Sang
I Don't Care What You used to be
I Haven't Said Thanks
I Married a Wife
I Never Interfere
I Want to be Happy
I was Born in Tipperary
I Wonder What's Become of Sally
If I were a Blackbird
If You Ever Go Across the Sea to Ireland
If You were the Only Girl in the World (and) My Love in Tennessee
I'm the Man You Don't Meet Every Day
In a Little Garden Subub [sic]
Isle of Capri
It Happened in Monterey
Just an Old Fashioned Lady
Just a Rose in a Garden of Weeds
Let the Great Big World Keep Turning
Little Grey Home in the West
Little Old Church in the Valley
Little Old Mill
Man who Broke the Bank at Monte Carlo
Melody that Made You Mine
Mother Kelly's Doorstep
Mother of Mine
Mrs Moore
My Blue Heaven
My Grandfather's Clock
Nelly Grey
No, No, a Thousand Times No
Now, Once, I Went to Margate
O How I've Waited for You
Old Grey Coat

Pasadena
Peggy O'Neal
Photo of the Girl I Left Behind
Polly Oliver
Railway Train
Ring Your Mother Wore
Romany Rose
Sailor Boy
San Francisco
Save Your Sorrow
She's Proud and She's Beautiful
Shut that Door
Sleepy Valley
Spanish Cavalier
Straight Banana
Sweethearts Will Never Grow Old
Swim Sam
There's a Laughter of Spring
Tie a String around Your Finger
Vagabond Lover
Varmer Giles
Volunteer Organist
Wheel Your P'rambulator
When the Fields are White with Daisies
When they Sound the Last All Clear
When You and I were Seventeen
When You Played the Organ
When You're Feeling Blue
When Your Hair has Turned to Silver
White Cliffs of Dover
Wireless on the Brain
Yes, I Wonder
Yes, We Have No Bananas
You Forget to Remember

Alice Messenger

Are We to Part Like This?
Beautiful Dreamer
Cockles and Mussels
Count Your Blessings
English Rose
For Old Time's Sake
Gypsy's Warning
I Passed by Your Window
I Will Take You Home Again, Kathleen
If I Could Plant a Seed of Love
If Those Lips Could Only Speak
In the Shade of the Old Apple Tree
It's a Great Big Shame
Just an Old Fashioned Lady
Just Like Ivy
Lassie from Lancashire
London is the Largest City in the World
Meet Me Tonight in Dreamland
My Grandfather's Clock
Nelly Dean
Old Rustic Bridge
Poor Old Joe
Smiling Through
Sweet Rosie O'Grady
Two Little Girls in Blue
Volunteer Organist
When the Fields are White with Daisies
Where the Praeties Grow
White Wings
Won't You Buy My Pretty Flowers?

Cyril Poacher

Australia
Black Velvet Band
Bonny Bunch of Roses
Broadside
Burden of the Spray (incomplete)
Dark Eyed Sailor

Farmer's Boy
Flash Company
Great Big Wheel
Green Broom (Broomfield Wager)
If I were a Blackbird
I'll be Your Sweetheart
Irish Jolting Cart
Joe Moggins (Young Man from the Country)
Just a Rose in a Garden of Weeds
Lamplighting Time in the Valley
Maid and the Magpie
Nancy from Yarmouth
Nutting Girl
Running Up and Down the Stairs
Sailor and His True Love (The Larks They Sang Melodious)
Sailor Boy
Sprig of Thyme (Once I had Plenty of Time, The Seeds of Love)
Strolling Round the Town
Two Little Girls in Blue
Whitewash (Slap Dab)

Frank Reeve

Bless this House

Lenny Savage

Dark Eyed Sailor
Foggy Dew
Nancy from Yarmouth
Rose of Tralee
Volunteer Organist

Priscilla Savage

Grief, O Grief
If I were a Blackbird
Johnson (Two Jolly Sportsmen)
William, Dearest William

James Smith

Cobbler
Last Night at my Sister's
Meggy
Mucking about the Garden
Old Dun Cow
Old Farmer's Servant
Peggy O'Neal
Straight Bananas
What Did the Little Moth Do Then?
Yes, We Have No Bananas

Percy Webb

After the Ball
After the Ball (parody)
All Jolly Fellows that Follow the Plough
As I Strolled out to Aylesbury
Ball of Yarn
Because I Love You
Black Velvet Band
Broken Doll
Bungay Roger
Can I Sleep in Your Barn Tonight, Mister?
Dark Eyed Sailor
Dressed Up in my Oilskin and Jumper (Fiddler's Green)
Farmer's Boy
Flanagan's Band
Flash Company
Gypsy Girl
Give Me Your Smile
Go and Leave Me if You Wish it
Green Bushes
Green Grow the Laurels
Group of Young Squatties
Have You Got a Light, Boy?
I Came Home Late Last Night
I Took my Wife to Burnhams

(All Over Me)
If I were a Blackbird
If those Lips Could Only Speak
If You Ever Go Across the Sea to Ireland
I'm an Old Country Carrier
Just an Old Fashioned Lady
MacCaffery
Memories
Mother McGee
Nutting Girl
Oak and the Ash
O, It's a Lovely War
O Where is the Boy Who Truly Regrets?
Old Farmer's Servant
Old Shep
On the Banks of the Clyde
One Day at the Docks
Sailor Boy
Seagull
She's Proud and She's Beautiful
Three Weeks Ago No Longer
Two Convicts they were Seated
Underneath the Apron
Wheel Your P'rambulator
Who is Kissing Her Now?
Wild Colonial Boy

Dick Woolnough

Flash Company
Little Irish Shamrock
London Apprentice Boy
Sailor Boy

Frank Woolnough

Bold Princess Royal
I'll be Your Sweetheart
London Apprentice Boy
My Lad was a Miner
My Son
Old Farmer's Servant
The Letter

APPENDIX III: TWO GENEALOGIES COMPILED FROM PARISH RECORDS, BLAXHALL

Genealogical Chart Showing Ling Family Interconnections(1)

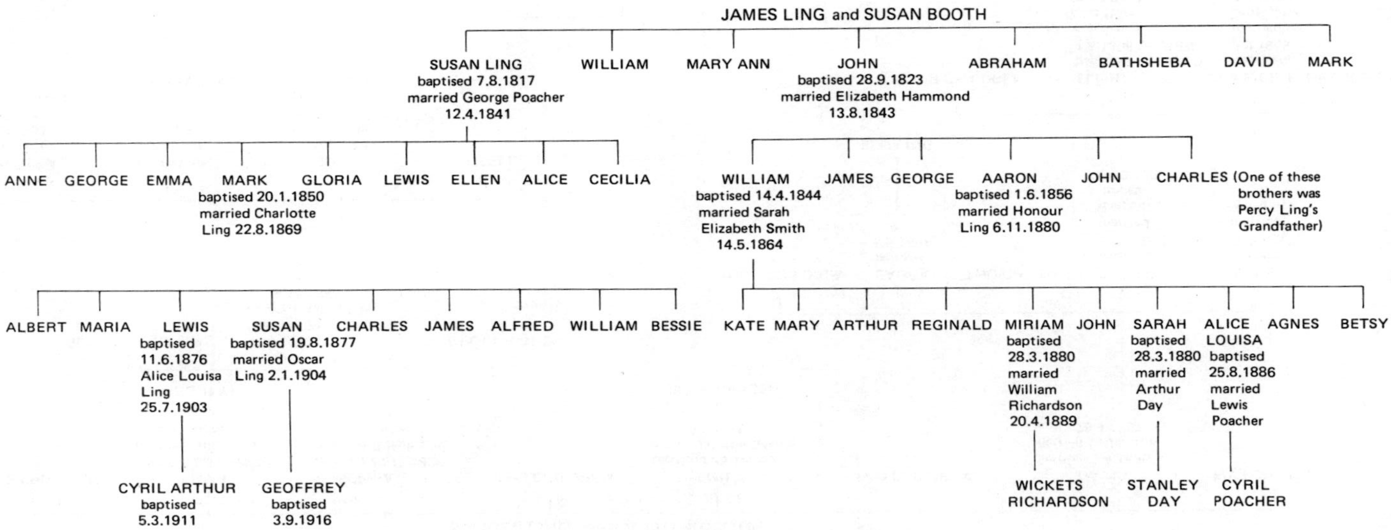

Genealogical Chart Showing Ling Family Interconnections (2)

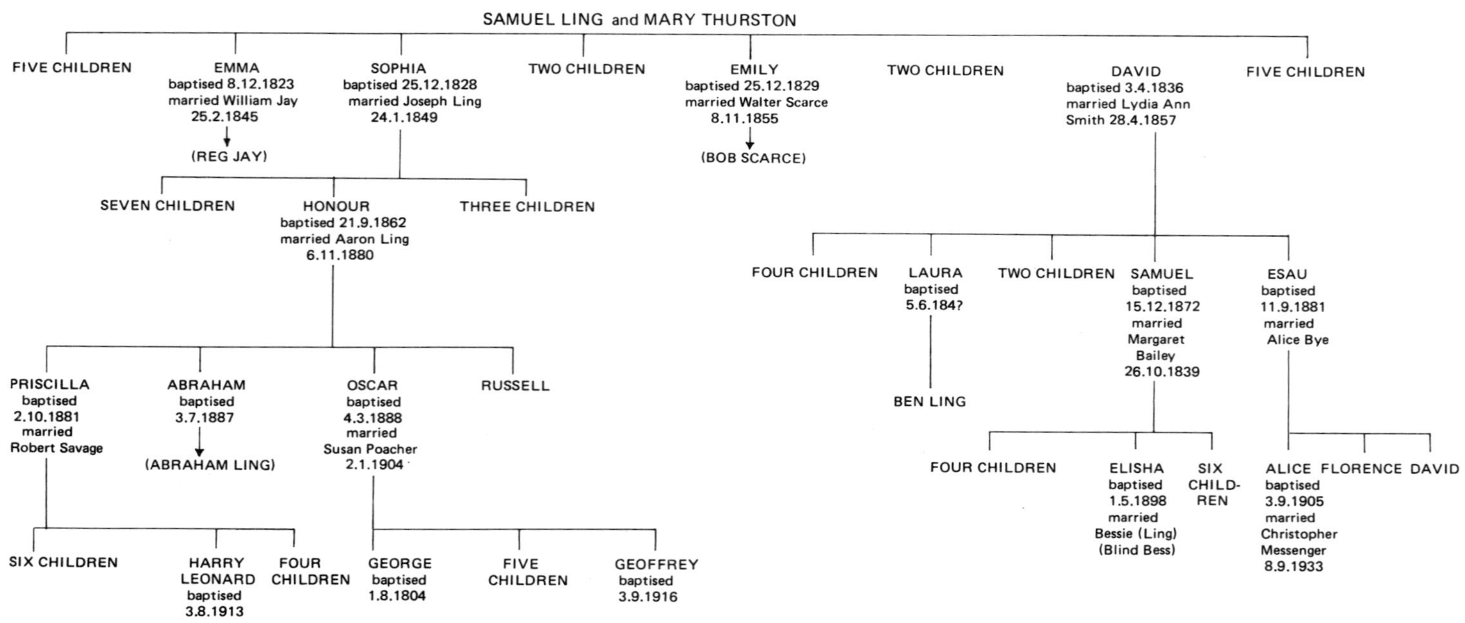

SELECT BIBLIOGRAPHY

Abrahams, Roger. 'Creativity, Individuality, and the Traditional Singer', *Studies in the Literary Imagination*, vol. 3 (1970), pp. 5-34

Abrahams, Roger. *Deep Down in the Jungle. Negro Narrative Folklore from the Streets of Philadelphia* (Aldine Publishers, Chicago, 1970)

Abrahams, Roger. *A Singer and Her Songs, Almeda Riddle's Book of Ballad* (Louisiana State University Press, Baton Rouge, Louisiana, 1970)

Beales, H.L. 'Victorian Ideas of Sex' in H. Grisewood (ed.), *Ideas and Beliefs of the Victorians* (Dutton Paperbacks, New York, 1966)

Blacking, John. *How Musical is Man?* (Faber and Faber, London, 1976)

—— *The Ethnography of Musical Performance* (forthcoming)

Bowley, Arthur L. *Wages in the United Kingdom in the Nineteenth Century* (Cambridge University Press, Cambridge, 1900)

Brown, E.H. Phelps, with Browne, Margaret H. *A Century of Pay. The Course of Pay and Production in France, Germany, Sweden, the United Kingdom, and the United States of America, 1860-1960* (Macmillan, London, 1968)

Buchan, David. *The Ballad and the Folk* (Routledge and Kegan Paul, London, 1972)

Caunce, Stephen. 'East Riding Hiring Fairs', *Oral History*, vol. 3, no. ii (1975), pp. 45-52.

Census of Great Britain. East Suffolk County Report (Her Majesty's Stationery Office, London, 1971)

Child, Francis James. *The English and Scottish Popular Ballads*, edited by Helen Child Sargent and George Lyman Kitteredge (5 vols., Dover, New York, 1965) (first published George Nutt, London and New York, 1905)

Corr, Gerard. 'Private MacCaffery's Revenge', *Lancashire Evening Post*, 17 December 1973

Dundes, Alan. 'From Etic to Emic Units in the Structural Study of Folklore', *Journal of American Folklore*, no. 75 (1962), pp. 95-105

Dundes, Alan. 'Metafolklore and Oral Literary Criticism', *Monist*, no. 50 (1966), pp. 505-16

Dunn, Ginette. 'Popular Singing Traditions in and around Snape and Blaxhall', unpublished PhD thesis, Institute of Dialect and Folk Life Studies, University of Leeds, 1977

Dunn, Ginette, 'The Aesthetics of a Singing Tradition' in John Blacking (ed.), *The Ethnography of Musical Performance* (Queen's University Papers in Social Anthropology, Vol. 5, forthcoming)

Evans, George Ewart. *The Horse in the Furrow* (Faber and Faber, London, 1960)

—— *Ask the Fellows who Cut the Hay* (Faber and Faber, London, 1966) (first published 1956)

—— *The Pattern Under the Plough* (Faber and Faber, London, 1966)

—— *The Farm and the Village* (Faber and Faber, London, 1969)

—— *Where Beards Wag All* (Faber and Faber, London, 1970)

Glassie, Henry, Ives, Edward D., and Szwed, John F. *Folksongs and their Makers* (Bowling Green University Popular Press, Bowling Green, Ohio, 1971)

Goldstein, Kenneth S. 'On the Application of the Concepts of Active and Inactive Traditions to the Study of Repertory', *Journal of American Folklore*, no. 84 (1971), pp. 62-7

Green, A.E. and Wales, Tony (ed.). Introduction to *Reminiscences of Horsham. The Recollections of Henry Burstow*, recorded and edited by William Albery (Norwood Editions, Pennsylvania, 1975)

Haggard, H. Rider. *Rural England. Being an Account of Agricultural and Social Researches Carried Out in the Years 1901 and 1902*, 2 vols. (Longmans, London, 1906)

Halpert, Herbert. 'Truth in Folk-Songs' in John Harrington Cox (ed.), *Traditional Ballads, Mainly from West Virginia* (National Service Bureau Publication No. 75-5, New York, 1939)

Hobsbawm, E.J. and Rudé, George. *Captain Swing* (Lawrence and Wishart, London, 1969)

Ives, Edward, D. *Larry Gorman. The Man Who Made the Songs* (University of Indiana Press, Bloomington, Indiana, 1964)

Klein, Josephine. *Samples from English Cultures* (Routledge and Kegan Paul, London, 1965)

Laslett, Peter. *The World we Have Lost* (Methuen, London, 1973) (first published 1965)

Lichman, Simon. 'The Marshfield Paperboys' (forthcoming PhD dissertation, University of Philadelphia, Pennsylvania)

Lomax, Alan. 'Musical Style and Social Context', *American Anthropologist*, no. 61 (1959), pp. 927-54

Lomax, Alan. 'Song Structure and Social Structure', *Ethnology*, vol. I (1962), pp. 425-51

Longmate, Norman. *The Waterdrinkers* (Hamish Hamilton, London, 1968)

Lord, Albert B. *The Singer of Tales* (Harvard University Press, Cambridge, Mass., 1960)

McKay, D. 'The Tradition of Pub-Singing in the Villages of East Suffolk' (unpubished BA dissertation, Institute of Dialect and Folk Life Studies, University of Leeds, 1971)

MacKenzie, W. Roy. *The Quest for the Ballad* (Princeton University Press, Princeton, 1919)

McLean, Mervyn. 'Song Loss and Social Context among the New Zealand Maori', *Ethnomusicology*, vol. 9, no. iii (1965), pp. 296-304

Orwin, Christabel S. and Whetham, Edith H. *History of British Agriculture 1846-1914* (Longmans, London, 1964)

Parry, Adam (ed.). *The Making of Homeric Verse. The Collected Papers of Milman Parry* (Oxford University Press, Oxford, 1971)

Parry, Milman, with Lord, Albert B. *Serbocroatian Heroic Song* (2 vols., Harvard University Press and the Serbian Academy of Arts, Cambridge, Mass., and Belgrade, 1954)

Pearsall, Ronald. *The Worm in the Bud. The World of Victorian Sexuality* (Allen Lane, London, 1971) (first published Weidenfeld and Nicolson, London, 1969)

Percy, Thomas (Bishop). *Reliques of Ancient English Poetry; consisting of Old Heroic Ballads, Songs, and Other Pieces of our Earlier Poets, Together with Some Few of Later Date*, with memoir and critical dissertation by George Gilfillan (3 vols., James Nichol, Edinburgh, 1858; new impression, Dover, New York, n.d.)

Ritson, Joseph. *Ancient Songs and Ballads from the Reign of Henry the Second to the Revolution* (2 vols., Payne and Foss, London, 1829)

Schofield, R.S. 'The Measure of Literacy in Pre-Industrial England' in Jack Goody (ed.), *Literacy in Traditional Societies* (Cambridge University Press, Cambridge, 1968), pp. 311-25.

Scott, Walter. *Minstrelsy of the Scottish Border: Consisting of Historical and Romantic Ballads, Collected in the Southern Counties of Scotland; with a few of modern date, founded upon local tradition*, 4th edn (3 vols., Longman, Hurst, Rees and Orme, Edinburgh, 1810)

Sharp, Cecil. *English Folksong: Some Conclusions* (EP Publishers, Wakefield, 1972) (first published 1907)

Sullivan, Keith F. 'Popular Singing Traditions and Cultural Change in the Old North Riding of Yorkshire' (unpublished PhD thesis, Institute of Dialect and Folk Life Studies, University of Leeds, 1978)

Trist, P.J.O. *A Survey of the Agriculture of Suffolk* (Royal Agricultural Society of England, London, County Agricultural Surveys No. 7, 1971)

Wilgus, D.K. *Anglo-American Folksong Scholarship since 1898* (Rutgers University Press, New Jersey, 1959)

INDEX